WEAPONS & WAR MACHINES

CRESCENT BOOKS

New York

In association with Phoebus

Illustrated by John Batchelor
Compiled by Andrew Kershaw and Ian Close
We are indebted to Ian Hogg as both weapons
consultant and major contributor

Ian V. Hogg enlisted in the Royal Artillery during World
War II, and served in Europe and the Far East – including
Korea – before becoming an Assistant Instructor-in-
Gunnery at the Royal School of Artillery. He subsequently
qualified in electronics and spent some years testing
military electronic equipment. In 1966 he joined the staff
of the Royal Military College of Science, from which he
retired in 1972 with the rank of Master Gunner. He then
became a professional writer, and his publications
include The Guns: 1939–45, Barrage, German Secret
Weapons, and Artillery with John Batchelor.

John Batchelor, after serving in the RAF, worked in the
technical publications departments of several British
aircraft firms, and went on to contribute on a freelance
basis to many technical magazines. Since then his work
for Purnell's Histories of the World Wars, and subsequently the Purnell's World Wars Specials, has established him as one of the most outstanding artists in his
field. A total enthusiast, he takes every opportunity to fly,
sail, drive or shoot any military equipment he can find.

ABOUT THIS BOOK

World War II, more than any other, was a war of machines and firepower. Although many early battles were won by the application of superior strategy and tactics, before long the land fighting on all fronts came to be governed to a large extent by the quality and numbers of tanks and guns. In this respect the war resolved itself into a struggle between the technological and industrial capacities of the opposing powers.

The fruits of this struggle were plain to see on the battlefield. With tanks in particular, one year's revolutionary design became the next year's obsolete cast-off. Anti-tank guns, too, developed rapidly in response to their more sophisticated quarry. But many basic weapons remained unchanged, and industry was geared up to churn them out in ever-increasing numbers. Rifles, machine guns and artillery, for example, were such vital items of equipment that it would have been unthinkable to change them in the middle of a raging conflict. There were some innovations of course, the German assault rifle – the world's first – being the most notable.

This book tells the story of the weapons and war machines of World War II. From the smallest pistol to the largest railway gun, each weapon is described with a wealth of fascinating technical and historical information and placed firmly in the context of its use in battle. In addition, the text is superbly complemented with John Batchelor's excellent technical illustrations, which combine with the many action photographs to give the full flavour of the greatest conflict of all time.

CONTENTS

US Marine at Okinawa, 1945

THE MEN WHO MEET THE ENEMY FACE TO FACE

There is an old joke which claims that the role of cavalry is to add tone to what might otherwise be merely an unseemly brawl; from this it might be inferred that the infantry's role in the battle is to promote the brawling. But there is a good deal more to it than that. Infantry is the basic element of the battlefield; tanks can roar back and forth like visiting Martians, guns can fire barrages for hours on end, aircraft can scream across the battlefield bombing and strafing, but when all this is done it requires a man with a rifle in his hand to walk across the ground on his two feet, occupy it, rule it, deny it to the enemy, and, in the words of an American General,"winkle the other bastard out of his foxhole and make him sign the peace treaty". There have been attempts to replace manpower with firepower, but the experiment has never succeeded. As long as there are wars, there will be infantry.

Another common misconception is that the infantry are no more than cannon-fodder, somewhat dense individuals unfitted for anything better or more mentally demanding than walking about with a rifle. This too is highly erroneous; the modern infantryman is a highly trained specialist, competent to handle several weapons and skilled in many arts. He is expected to master two or three types of rifle, machine-guns, submachine-guns, mortars, light artillery, radio, radar, infra-red devices and drive a variety of vehicles; he must have a good knowledge of first aid, he must be able to cook and look after himself in conditions verging on the appalling, find his way in featureless country, survive an atomic bomb, find direction by the stars, have a knowledge of water purification and sanitation, be able to use his enemy's weapons as well as his own, have a knowledge of minor tactics, be self-reliant in emergency . . . the list can go on and on.

The infantryman is the army's jack-of-all-trades, but with it he is master of one – the trade of fighting the enemy. He is a member of the world's most exclusive club – the men who actually meet the enemy face to face, eyeball to eyeball, and decide the issue on the spot. Artillery, tanks and aircraft can break an enemy's spirit, demoralise him, inflict casualties; but unless this is followed up by determined men on foot the advantage is lost and the effort wasted. Infantry are the army's backbone.

Organisation

The organisation of infantry units is much the same in all countries, since the tasks to be performed are the same. Starting at the bottom, the individual soldier forms part of a **section**, ten or a dozen men including one or two junior NCOs, the basic tactical unit. The section will contain one machine-gun and possibly one or two submachine-guns, the rest of the men carrying rifles.

In British practice the section split into two groups, the rifle group and the machine-gun group, the latter consisting of just three men with the light machine-gun. Thus it could move in 'bounds' when confronted with an enemy, the machine-gun taking up position to give covering fire while the rifle group moved forward. They in turn would take up position and give covering fire to allow the machine-gun group to move up and leapfrog them, taking up a fresh position to cover another move of the rifle group. This alternate movement would go on until the rifle group were close enough to come to grips with the enemy when, after a bombardment of grenades, the riflemen leapt up and charged at the enemy, firing as they went, assisted by the machine-gun's fire until they closed with the enemy, when the machine-gun would stop and move up to consolidate the position which had been taken.

This basic movement was called 'Battle Drill', and it was actually taught as a drill, on the parade ground, before it was practised on the ground. As a result it became ingrained in the individual soldier so that he understood the basic tactical move and, in emergency, could take command and continue the attack in the knowledge that he was doing the right thing. Moreover, the same basic premise governed the application of larger forces: one unit covering while the other unit moved forward – or as one contemporary instruction termed it, "one leg on the ground and one in the air". With minor variations it was the basic move of the infantry of any army.

The section formed part of the **platoon**; this usually contained three or four sections, plus a small headquarter element consisting of radio operator, officer in command, sergeant and one or two men. Thus the platoon could split up into sections or work as a whole, one section covering while the others moved, an enlarged version of the same Battle Drill.

The platoon, in its turn, formed part of the **company**; three or four platoons, plus a headquarter element, plus, perhaps, an anti-tank platoon or mortar platoon to provide specialist weapon support for the whole. Again, the company could act in its component parts or it could act as a complete entity, one platoon covering the movement of the others.

Three or four companies went to make up the **battalion**. Once more this would have a headquarter company, which might include further heavy weapons, radio, pioneer elements, transport elements and all the service troops needed to make the battalion a completely self-sufficient military unit. It could move itself, feed itself, had medical facilities and was really the lowest sub-unit capable of going into battle independently. The average soldier identified with his battalion; ask a private what unit he belonged to and the answer would rarely take account of the section, platoon or company – he was in the "Second Battalion of the so-and-so's"

The battalions formed part of the **regiment** – normally three to a regiment. The regimental structure was similar to that of the battalion in that it carried all the administrative services necessary to be

BRIGADE
(3,000-4,000)

DIVISION (12,000-14,000)

This chart gives an approxi-
mate break-down of the basic
components of a British army,
including supporting arms
and headquarter formations.

Obviously, the numbers were
not constant, and from
brigade level up strengths
varied enormously, depending
on the forces available and

CORPS (30,000-50,000)

SERGEANT

CORPORAL

LANCE-CORPORAL

ARMY (60,000-100,000)

HOW THEY FALL IN

BATTALION (700-800)

COMPANY (120)

PLATOON (32)

SECTION (8)

FIELD-MARSHAL

GENERAL

BRIGADIER

COLONEL

the tasks to be carried out.
The illustrations show officers and men of the British Army wearing uniforms of 1940

Drawings: Faulkner/Marks

MAJOR

CAPTAIN

LIEUTENANT

self-sufficient, plus more heavy weapons and communications, transport and supply echelons. But at this level there were many differences between different nations, depending on how they felt their role could best be accomplished.

The German Infantry Regiment, for example, had a very mixed composition: headquarters; signal section; motor-cycle despatch rider section; a mounted infantry platoon (though this was rarely implemented during war); a pioneer platoon to attend to such details as minefields, bridge-building and so on; an infantry gun company armed with 75-mm and 150-mm guns and howitzers; an anti-tank gun company armed with 37-mm or 50-mm anti-tank artillery; a transport column; an anti-aircraft gun section armed with 20-mm automatic guns; and three battalions each containing a headquarters, signal section, three infantry companies and a machine-gun company. This totalled 95 officers and 2,993 soldiers, with a firepower of 112 machine-guns, 144 submachine-guns, 36 heavy machine-guns, 27 anti-tank rifles, 45 mortars, 8 field guns, 12 anti-tank guns, 4 anti-aircraft guns and about 1,500 rifles.

But the regiment rarely operated on its own; it formed part of a **division** and, keeping to our German example, this became a very potent fighting force. The division

Bedford Truck
The Bedford was the absolute mainstay of the British Army as far as transport was concerned, especially for the infantry. It could carry loads of up to 3 tons, and was used for transporting men, weapons, ammunition, petrol and supplies

US Army Harley-Davidson Motorcycle
Known officially as the 'Chain Drive Solo Motorcycle', this was the civilian Harley–Davidson Model WLA with combat tyres and a bracket for mounting a Thompson submachine-gun. Widely used by messengers, reconnaissance scouts and Military Police

consisted of a headquarters; a divisional reconnaissance unit of armoured cars and cyclists; a signals regiment; three infantry regiments; an artillery regiment; an anti-aircraft battalion; an anti-tank battalion; an engineer battalion; a medical company; a veterinary company (for the German Army still relied very heavily on animal transport) and a service company which provided cooks, armourers and other specialists.

It must be said that this was the theoretical line-up: the actual composition of an infantry division varied depending on what was available, where the unit was going to operate, what sort of battle was envisaged, what sort of weapons were considered necessary and so forth. None of the world's armies produced infantry divisions in the field which exactly matched the paper composition. But the theoretical composition of the German infantry division given above produced a strength of 497 officers, 14,953 men, with 432 submachine-guns, 430 light machine-guns, 116 heavy machine-guns, 81 anti-tank rifles, 84 anti-aircraft guns, 75 anti-tank guns, 141 mortars, and 74 pieces of artillery.

There are, however, different kinds of infantry in some armies. The British Army distinguishes between infantry and light infantry, though the difference today is largely one of tradition. The light infantry in days of old were expected to be just that – light, and quick to move, ready to take advantage of the enemy while the slower-moving 'heavy' infantry followed up behind to consolidate. Their role was principally scouting and skirmishing, but the different nature of war in the present century has diminished their special role; they operate on the same lines as other infantry today.

Nevertheless, they still have their own idiosyncracies which stem from their old role; for example, they march at a faster pace than the rest of the army – 160 paces a minute against the normal 120 – which leads to confusion when they form part of a cere-monial parade with other troops; their arms drill is different, since they always carry their rifles at the 'trail' in one hand, instead of on their shoulders; they never refer to bayonets but always to 'swords' in some regiments; and during the Second World War they always asserted their individual-ity by wearing their field-service caps perfectly vertical instead of tipped over one ear like the rest of the army.

Different types
Other types of infantry which have appeared from time to time in different armies include 'mounted infantry' – moun-ted on horses to allow them rapidity of movement, but expected to dismount and fight in the usual infantry manner after contact with the enemy; 'lorried infantry', the same sort of thing but using petrol instead of horseflesh; 'motorised infantry', like lorried infantry but usually provided with armoured transport and backed up by attached armoured car units; and 'air-borne infantry', which could be either another name for parachute troops or could be ordinary infantry ferried into battle by aircraft or glider. There are also 'mountain regiments' of infantry which differ in that they operate more in the vertical plane than the horizontal, and usually include such esoteric specialists as ski troops and expert rock-climbers, backed up by mule-pack artillery. And there have even been such things as 'cyclist regiments' of infantry mounted on bicycles – used in the Second World War by the Japanese and Germans – and even 'motor-cyclist batta-lions' of the German Army which roared into action on BMW sidecar combinations.

It must not be thought that only infantry divisions contained infantry; armoured di-visions also carried their quota although, of course, the predominant arm was the armour. The German Panzer Division, for example, carried with it a lorried infantry regiment of 24 officers and 637 men, plus a motor-cycle battalion of 18 officers and 288 men. Not very much, considering the over-all strength of a Panzer division, but the tanks were there to do the fighting; the infantry were taken along to consolidate and hold the ground which had been taken. Which brings us back to the point where we came in.

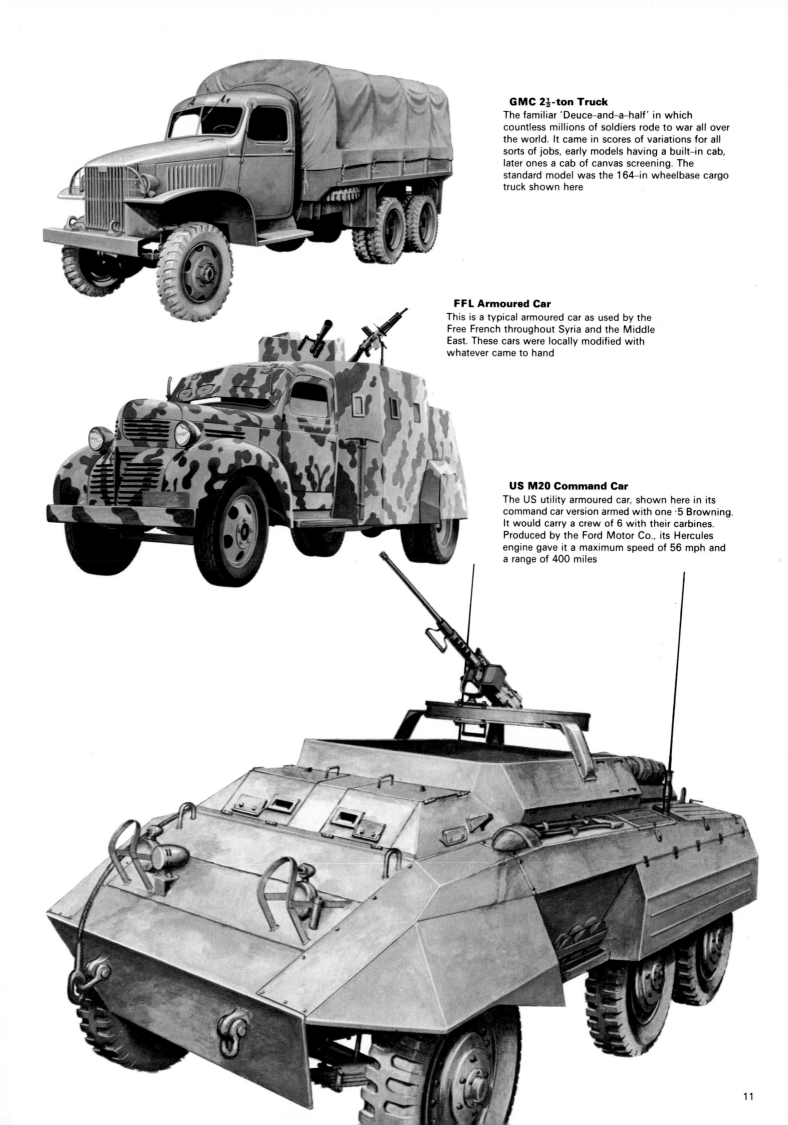

GMC 2½-ton Truck
The familiar 'Deuce-and-a-half' in which countless millions of soldiers rode to war all over the world. It came in scores of variations for all sorts of jobs, early models having a built-in cab, later ones a cab of canvas screening. The standard model was the 164-in wheelbase cargo truck shown here

FFL Armoured Car
This is a typical armoured car as used by the Free French throughout Syria and the Middle East. These cars were locally modified with whatever came to hand

US M20 Command Car
The US utility armoured car, shown here in its command car version armed with one ·5 Browning. It would carry a crew of 6 with their carbines. Produced by the Ford Motor Co., its Hercules engine gave it a maximum speed of 56 mph and a range of 400 miles

THE INFANTRY

READY FOR ACTION

A British soldier equipped for anti-tank work, with trenching tools, PIAT, and carrying his Sten submachine-gun. The PIAT was an alarming weapon to use, but effective enough

An American soldier carrying his rifle — the famous Garand ·30 M1, described, with good reason, by General Patton as the 'best battle implement ever devised'

BRITISH

AMERICAN

A German soldier armed with MP40 machine-pistol and with a stick grenade in his belt. Often, the Germans stuck their grenades in the tops of their jackboots

GERMAN

A Japanese soldier with his 6·5–mm Arisaka rifle, fitted with its sword bayonet. Japanese soldiers were not particularly well equipped: the first Arisaka was produced in 1897

JAPANESE

Arthur Gaye

13

A SOLDIER'S BEST FRIEND

Japanese 38th Year Rifle
Known also as the Arisaka, from the Colonel who was responsible for the design, this 6·5–mm weapon is largely based on Mauser features. It was used in the British Army during the First World War as a training rifle, and known as the ·256–in Pattern 1907; these were later sent to Russia

The basic weapon of the infantryman is, of course, his rifle; so much so that one normally speaks of 'rifle battalions' or 'rifle companies', though not, in British parlance, of 'Rifle Regiments' since this means something else again – a regiment of the Kings Royal Rifle Corps. Another common expression when speaking of the strength of an infantry unit is to refer to it as having "so many bayonets", reflecting the other standard infantry weapon. The rifle is generally represented to the recruit as potentially his best friend, though in the early days of training he rarely sees it in this light, thinking of it more as a somewhat demanding mistress, always in need of cleaning and polishing, and containing all sorts of pitfalls for the unwary in the way of unnoticed corners in which dust can accumulate, only to be detected, with dire results, by the eagle eye of the inspecting sergeant-major. But once on campaign, the truth becomes blindingly obvious, and from then on the rifle's care and protection is always foremost in the soldier's mind.

With the exception of the American Army, the standard rifle with which all combatants began the Second World War was an elderly bolt-action dating from the last years of the previous century. In those days rifles were built to last, constructed by traditional gunsmithing techniques of the finest materials, assembled carefully, and in the hands of a trained soldier deadly at a mile range. It is customary for target-shooters to look down their noses at military rifles as being inaccurate, but any military rifle, when properly zeroed and handled by a soldier who knows what he is doing, can put five shots out of five into a man-sized target at a thousand yards without much trouble.

Unfortunately, this is a technique which rarely needs to be exercised on the battle-field, and it took a long time for this fact to sink in, as will be seen. As a result, all standard bolt-action rifles used powerful ammunition, were heavy, recoiled somewhat forcefully, and reached out to over 2,000 yards. But withal, they were robust and reliable, simple to use, and deadly.

The oldest design was that in service with the Soviet Army, the Moisin-Nagant of 1891, known originally as the 'Three-Line Rifle'. This came from the calibre, three of the old Russian measurement known as 'lines', approximately one-tenth of an inch; hence three lines meant a calibre of 0·30-in. It was long (51·25 in) and heavy (9¾ lb) and mounted a socket bayonet around the muzzle. This was intended to be fitted all the time, and the rifle sights were graduated to take the weight and balance of the bayonet into account. Certainly, one rarely sees pictures of the Tsar's soldiers with this rifle without the bayonet being fitted.

Vast numbers

Although this was a sound enough rifle, it was too cumbersome, and in 1930 it was re-designed to a more compact length (40 in) and less weight (just under 9 lb). The sights were improved and it took the place of the 1891 model as the standard infantry rifle. However, there were such vast stocks of the 1891 that it remained in use as a training weapon and in the hands of reserve troops throughout the war. A number of them were also fitted with telescopic sights and used for sniping.

Next in order of age came the Japanese Arisaka, which first saw the light of day in 1897. This was chambered for a 6·5-mm cartridge and was more or less a copy of a

Mauser design but with some refinements of dubious value added by the Japanese. In 1905 the design was overhauled to do away with some of the less useful ideas and bring it more or less into line with an ordinary Mauser, and this stayed the standard rifle throughout the Second World War. However, experience during the Manchurian and Chinese wars in the 1930s led the Japanese to the conclusion that a 6·5-mm bullet was not sufficiently powerful, and after some experimenting they adopted a 7·7-mm cartridge, more or less copied from the British ·303 model except that the cartridge case was rimless.

The next step was to produce a rifle to fire the new round, and this was the Type 99, issued in 1939. Except for its different calibre and a reduction in length, it was simply the 1905 model over again, but the changing times were reflected in the fitting of a complicated anti-aircraft sight to allow the troops to shoot at attacking planes. It is open to question whether this was worth much in practice. In any case the production of this rifle never reached great numbers, and the majority of the Japanese Army continued to use the 6·5-mm model throughout the war.

An interesting development of the Type 99 rifle was a collapsible model for parachute troops, in which the barrel could be separated from the rest of the weapon by unlocking an interrupted thread joint, so that the two sections could be conveniently carried by a parachutist. Another arm specially developed for parachute troops was a short carbine version of the 6·5-mm rifle in which the stock was hinged behind the trigger and thus the butt could be folded alongside the action, again for convenience in carriage. Since the Japanese

French MAS36CR39 Rifle
This weapon was the last bolt-acton rifle ever to be adopted by any nation, the French taking it into use in 1936, the same year that the Americans were adopting the Garand. It is notorious for not having a safety catch

Italian M1891 Rifle
A Mannlicher–Carcano design, though the only Mannlicher feature was the clip-loaded magazine, the rest of it being more or less copied from Mauser. In 6·5-mm calibre, it was a reliable enough design, representative of its times

Italian Carbine Model 38
A design with some unfortunate features; this weapon has a sight which cannot be adjusted for range and some had folding bayonets underneath. Their war record was not particularly impressive, but the weapon goes down in history as the gun that killed President Kennedy in 1963

Practising for the real thing, these British
infantrymen go through a wartime rehearsal
for forthcoming amphibious landings

German Gewehr 98
The Mauser rifle which, in one form or another, armed many of the world's armies during the 20th century. The Gewehr 98 was the German Army's standard model, but similar versions under other names could be found all over the world. A cross-section of the mechanism is shown above

used their airborne forces very little, these weapons were not produced in large numbers.

Next in order of age comes the famous Mauser, standard rifle of the German Army since 1898, and always known by its year of introduction as the 'Gewehr 98'. The Mauser is, of course, the standard to which all other rifles are referred, and there is no doubt that more countries have been armed with Mauser rifles, or copies of Mauser rifles, or adaptations of Mauser rifles, than any other design. There is some room for the belief, however, that this was as much due to Mauser's salesmanship as to the intrinsic virtues of the rifle. While it was certainly accurate and robust, the bolt action was awkward to operate and difficult to clean, two features which argue against it as a combat rifle.

The original rifle version was, in common with most other designs of the 1890s, long and fairly heavy, and in the early years of the twentieth century it was supplanted by a short version, called the Karabiner 98, or Kar 98. Until 1903 it had generally been the custom throughout the world to produce two versions of the standard bolt action rifle, one long one for use by infantry and a short one for use by cavalry, the shorter version being called a 'carbine' or 'dragoon rifle' or some similarly descriptive term.

In 1903 the British Army decided that this

was unnecessary and produced a 'short rifle', shorter than the usual rifle and longer than the usual carbine, so that one weapon could be used to arm all troops. This example was soon followed by others; the Kar 98 was the German version and it soon became their standard rifle. The basic design was never altered from that day forward, the only changes being in the sights, to cater for improved ammunition, and in minor details which permitted the weapon to be mass-produced more easily. Other nations, after the First World War, took the Kar 98 as their model and produced their own versions, such as the Czechoslovakian Model of 1924, and the Belgian Model 1922, but a soldier trained on any one of them could easily find his way around any of the others.

Ten rounds in ten seconds
The British Army had introduced their first Lee-Enfield rifle in 1895, a long rifle in the same style as its contemporaries, and, as already related, in 1903 they produced a short rifle, known as the 'Short, Magazine, Lee-Enfield' and always abbreviated to SMLE by the troops. The Lee bolt action was, in theory, less efficient than the Mauser since the lugs which locked the bolt were at the rear of the bolt and not at the head; this meant that the body of the weapon had to be stronger and also that

when the rifle was fired the bolt was slightly compressed backwards. This, it was averred, led to inaccuracy. It may have done, if the firer was trying to take the pip out of the ace of hearts at a thousand yards, but for all practical battlefield purposes it made no difference.

Where the Lee-Enfield scored was in the ease of operation of the bolt, due to those same rear-end locking lugs. This came to the fore in a technique developed and taught during the Second World War for house-to-house fighting, in which the rifle was held at the hip with the thumb and forefinger of the right hand grasping the bolt and the middle finger inside the trigger guard; a quick flip of the wrist and the bolt was operated, and as the hand came to rest the middle finger fell onto the trigger and fired the rifle. It was possible to get off ten rounds in ten seconds very easily by this method; it may not have been accurate, but it kept the other man's head down until you could get close enough to throw a grenade at him.

At about the same time as the British Army were adopting the Lee-Enfield, the United States Army were looking for something to replace their Krag-Jorgensen rifle. After examining a wide range of alternatives, they came to the conclusion that the best answer was a Mauser. For $200,000 they obtained a licence from Mauser to

British Lee-Enfield Rifle
The British Lee–Enfield was criticised when it was first produced, but millions of soldiers proved the critics wrong. Probably the best combat bolt–action rifle ever invented, no less than 27 different versions were produced. It is still in service today, rebarrelled for the 7·62–mm NATO cartridge, as a sniping rifle

Russian Simonov Model 1936 AVS
Although not the first Russian automatic rifle, this was the first successful one. Produced in 1936 in 7·62–mm calibre, in automatic and semi–automatic versions, it was widely used by the Soviet army

cover certain of Mauser's patents and set about developing what came to be known as the 'Springfield' rifle. It was designated the Model 1903 although the first versions did not appear until 1905.

In a similar manner to the British, they moved away from the long rifle and carbine combination to produce a short rifle which could be used by any service. By the time of the Second World War it was obsolescent, being in the process of replacement by an automatic rifle, but since the supply of the automatic model took some time to get organised, the Springfield stayed in service throughout the war for training and in the hands of reserve and home defence troops. Indeed, it was still in service as a sniper's rifle in the Korean War in 1952. It saw a few modifications during its life, principally in order to make it easier to produce in quantity, but the design was basically unchanged after 1903.

MacArthur's decision
The automatic rifle which was to supplant the Springfield was, of course, the US Rifle M1, or, more familiarly, the Garand. John C. Garand had begun work on an automatic rifle in 1920, and in 1929 his design was the only one to survive some searching tests at Aberdeen Proving Ground. Development and perfection continued, and in 1936 it was officially adopted

as the standard service rifle. Responsibility for this far-reaching decision rested with General MacArthur, then Chief of Staff, and whatever MacArthur did or did not do in later years, this single decision ought to earn him the everlasting thanks of his country. The Garand wasn't perfect (the perfect automatic rifle isn't with us yet) but it showed that a reliable automatic rifle was possible, that troops armed with automatic rifles were not liable to blast all their ammunition off in the first two minutes of battle – a possibility which had haunted staff officers ever since the first inventor called on them with an automatic rifle design – and that the mechanics of an automatic rifle were not beyond the mental powers of the soldier – another belief of the traditional officers. General Patton said once that the Garand was "the best battle implement ever devised" and he wasn't far wrong.

The operation of the Garand was deceptively simple; on looking at it one wonders why it took so long to develop and why it wasn't in production fifty years earlier. But like all simple designs, it took time to get it simple and reliable. The bolt is a rotating bolt, much the same as that on an ordinary bolt-action rifle, but is operated by a rod which hooks over a lug on the bolt and then disappears beneath the woodwork of the rifle. The rod passes to a gas cylinder

beneath the barrel and also carries the bolt return spring. This spring also performs the task of placing pressure on the rounds in the magazine, to keep them feeding up to the bolt as it moves.

When a shot was fired, the gas, pushing the bullet through the barrel, was tapped off through a tiny hole near the muzzle and led into the gas cylinder. Here it pushed on the head end of the operating rod, which was driven back and, by its connection to the bolt lug and by suitably shaped cam surfaces, rotated the bolt and drove it back to extract and eject the fired cartridge case. At the end of the bolt's stroke, the return spring, which had been compressed by the movement of the operating arm, expanded again and pulled the bolt forward, stripping the top round from the magazine and chambering it. As the operating rod made its final movement it turned and locked the bolt once more, ready for the next shot. As the bolt moved to the rear, it also cocked the hammer, so that all the firer had to do was take aim and press the trigger.

The magazine was loaded by a clip of eight cartridges, and this, in the eyes of some authorities, was the only drawback to the Garand rifle. The clip was inserted complete – the rounds were not stripped out of it as were the charger-loaded rounds of bolt action rifles – and a follower arm in the magazine pushed the cartridges up as

A US paratrooper, armed with a Garand M1 rifle, takes a prisoner at bayonet point during the Allied advance in Normandy, 1944

Associated Press

US Rifle M1

John Garand's greatest effort, and the weapon which allowed the US Army to be the only one to enter the Second World War with an automatic rifle as standard. Five and a half million were made, and the design lives on in the present–day US Rifle M14 and Italian Beretta BM59 models

they were used. As the last round was fired and the bolt moved back, the empty clip was automatically ejected and the bolt held to the rear ready for another clip to be dropped in. But it had to be a whole clip or nothing; unlike most other designs, it could not be 'topped-up' by inserting one or two loose rounds.

The other defect was the ejection of the clip; it sailed through the air for several feet and when it fell on hard, particularly frozen, ground it gave out a distinctive ring. An alert enemy often heard this and then knew that the owner of the rifle was busy pushing a new clip in as hard as he could go; which gave the alert enemy a chance to stand up and get a shot in without much fear of being shot at himself.

Once production got into its swing, the Garand was turned out rapidly, and over four million were made by the end of the war. After the war another 600,000 were made and it was also built under licence by the Beretta Company in Italy, who subsequently re-designed it and used it as the foundation for a full line of automatic rifles. One of the impressive things about the Garand is that it saw practically no modification throughout its life; the design had been so thoroughly worked out before it went into production that it was not necessary to make any changes.

However, a number of experimental variations were tried out at one time and another: changes in, for example, the angle of the bolt-opening cam, changes in the gas piston design in order to try and reduce recoil, and so on. But the only variations on the standard pattern which ever got into production were the T-26, a shortened version intended for jungle warfare in the Pacific, and the various sniping rifles.

The T-26 was requested in July 1945 and a contract for 15,000 rifles was let out; but the war was over before they could be delivered and the contract was cancelled after a small number had been made. They were evaluated by the Army but turned down as being too violent in action (like all shortened standard rifles) and were eventually sold on the surplus market, usually being advertised as the 'Short Tanker's Model' for some unknown reason. The sniper rifles were known as the M1C and M1D, the differences being in the model of telescope fitted; except for being selected for their shooting capabilities and fitted with a flash hider on the muzzle, they were exactly the same as any other M1 rifle.

The cooks' rifle

The success of the M1 led to a request in pre-war days from the Infantry School for a lightweight semi-automatic rifle to arm such specialists as mortar crews, machine-gun crews, radiomen, cooks, bakers, and all the other members of a battalion who were normally engaged in other duties and found the carriage of a full sized rifle inconvenient. Most of them were provided with pistols, but with experience of the First World War behind them, the infantry knew quite well that there were never enough pistols to go round, and that moreover a pistol is not the easiest weapon to shoot without a good deal of practice. Their request was turned down, but when the war loomed closer they repeated it, and this time it reached more sympathetic ears.

The first step was to produce a suitable cartridge, since a lightweight rifle firing the normal ·30 rifle round would be too violent to handle. A ·30 calibre cartridge of smaller dimensions, using a straight-sided cartridge case and a round-nosed bullet was developed, and with this before them numerous manufacturers were invited to design a suitable weapon. As it happened, the Winchester Company had developed a full sized rifle in 1940 and this had been offered to the US and British Armies but had been turned down; not on account of any deficiency but because both armies were committed to their existing designs and could not afford to try changing horses in mid-stream. Indeed, the British report on the trial of the rifle said "with slight modifications this rifle is suitable for adoption into the British service".

The Winchester design used a unique form of gas operation in which the gas tapped from the barrel entered a small chamber beneath and drove a captive piston back for about one-tenth of an inch – enough to drive an operating rod to the rear and open and close the bolt. This gas piston design was now combined with an operating slide and bolt similar to that used on the Garand rifle to make a short carbine, and after testing alongside numerous others which had been submitted, the Winchester design was selected as being the best. It was put into production as the US Carbine M1 in October 1941. Shortly afterwards an M1A1 variation was produced in which the stock was a folding steel framework and a pistol grip was fitted, this version being for use by airborne troops.

Both these weapons were highly successful and popular, and after some experience with them in action, the infantry asked whether it would not be possible to arrange matters so that the carbine could be fired as an automatic – that is, keep firing as long as the trigger was pressed. In this way it would double as a submachine-gun. The request was considered reasonable, and a small modification was fitted, turning the design into the carbine M2.

Since this modification meant more rapid expenditure of ammunition, a 30-round magazine was developed to replace the earlier 15-round model. Firing at 750 rounds per minute, the M2 soon became the standard model, the M1 and M1A1 being relegated as 'limited standard'; over seven million carbines of all models were manufactured during the course of the war.

Russia's trial run

The only other army to have any automatic rifles at the outbreak of war was Russia's. They had been experimenting with various types from the early 1930s and in 1940 they had two Tokarev models in service in small numbers, largely as a trial run to see whether it was a good idea or not. The first was the Model 1938, the second the Model 1940, and as far as operation went they were almost identical. A gas cylinder lay above the barrel and carried a piston rod which protruded above the rifle chamber where it made contact with a 'bolt carrier', a heavy steel unit which surrounded the bolt. On firing, the gas pressure drove this piston rod back so that it struck the bolt carrier and drove it backwards; movement of the bolt carrier, through cams, lifted the bolt and unlocked it from the gun body, then drew it back to eject the fired case. At the same time, a return spring was compressed by the carrier and the hammer was cocked. When the carrier came to rest, the spring returned it and the bolt was taken forward, picking up a fresh round from the 10-round magazine and placing it in the chamber. The final movement of the bolt carrier as it reached the end of its travel drove the rear end of the bolt down to lock it securely.

Several thousands of the Tokarev were made, and they were used extensively in the Russo-Finnish war of 1939–40, but they were never entirely successful. The weight had been kept low by excessive paring of metal, leading to a degree of fragility, and the old rimmed 7·62-mm round was not well suited to use in an automatic weapon. One

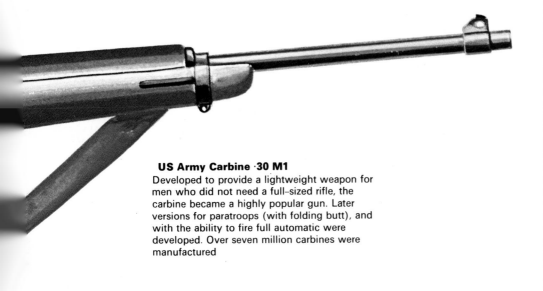

US Army Carbine ·30 M1
Developed to provide a lightweight weapon for men who did not need a full-sized rifle, the carbine became a highly popular gun. Later versions for paratroops (with folding butt), and with the ability to fire full automatic were developed. Over seven million carbines were manufactured

problem was extraction of the fired case, and the designers went as far as making the chamber with flutes milled in it so that gas could wash around the outside of the cartridge case and thus make it less liable to stick – which rather suggests that the design was basically unsound. The rifle apparently remained in production until 1944, but it never completely replaced the bolt-action Moisin-Nagant and appears to have been largely used as a sniping rifle. There was also a selective-fire version, ie. one capable of either single shots or automatic fire, but this was uncommon and was probably made simply to see if the idea was any good.

Not their best work

The British Army was alive to the advantages of a self-loading rifle, but although they had tested several specimens they had never found one which came up to their specification. Indeed, the specification was so stiff that it is doubtful if any automatic rifle of the present day could meet it in its entirety, and it was not until political pressure forced the modification of their demands that they were able to find a rifle with which to re-equip the army. But once the war was on, although various models were tested, there was no chance to re-equip, since the production capacity necessary to turn out the required millions of rifles would never be available. Moreover, one drawback to a successful rifle was the rimmed ·303 cartridge. The Army were well aware of this and had been considering a change to rimless ammunition for many years, but again the production problem involved, the immense logistic problem of changing over ammunition in the middle of a war, and – not least – the question of what was to be done with the millions of rifles and billions of cartridges already in existence, were enough to deter anybody but a lunatic from changing.

In Germany however, most of these same conditions applied except the ammunition problem, and numerous attempts at producing an automatic rifle were made before some successful designs appeared. The rimless 7·92-mm Mauser cartridge was well suited to an automatic weapon and after seeing the success of the Garand and the apparent success of the Tokarev, the Germans decided that they had to do something to equalise matters. In 1940 the hunt for an automatic rifle began; the following year saw two designs on trial, the Gewehr 41 (Walther) and the Gewehr 41 (Mauser).

Quite frankly, to anyone accustomed to the clever and ingenious designs emanating

from German gunsmiths, these two weapons come as a horrible shock, and one has the feeling that the designers were clutching at straws and not really feeling at their best just then. The system of operation in both designs relied on a cup-shaped muzzle attachment trapping some of the emerging gas behind the bullet, turning it back on itself and using it to operate a piston which encircled the muzzle of the rifle. It was a variation of an idea, evolved by a Dane called Soren H. Bang in the early years of the century, which had never been made to work satisfactorily. The Mauser rifle used the gas piston to operate a rotating bolt; the Walther design used a bolt which moved in a straight line and did not turn but had two flaps let into its side. These flaps were moved out to lock into recesses in the gun body and moved in to unlock the bolt by the action of the gas piston.

The Mauser design was dropped in favour of the Walther model and many thousand were made and issued to units on the Eastern Front in 1942–3, but it was never a very successful weapon. It was ill-balanced, difficult to make, easily jammed and difficult to clean and maintain. As soon as something better came along, production was stopped, but the weapons in the hands of the troops continued in use until the end of the war.

In view of what has already been said about the difficulty of changing ammunition during a war, what happened next is incredible; in fact it turned out to be the smartest thing the Germans did. During the pre-war years a number of senior German officers had applied themselves to a careful analysis of the infantry's use of the rifle, and they had come to the conclusion that the normal pattern of weapon, firing a powerful cartridge to 2,000 yards or so, was no longer needed. Except for specialists such as snipers, it was rare for an infantryman to have to fire at ranges greater than about 400 yards, and for this a much less powerful cartridge would be suitable.

They therefore set about laying down specifications for a short cartridge and a selective fire rifle to fire it. If the cartridge were shorter, then the mechanism of the rifle would have less distance to move, and so the rifle itself could be shorter and lighter. Also, if the round were less powerful, then the recoil shock would be less and again the rifle could be lighter and shorter. If the ammunition were smaller, then it would weigh less, and the soldier could carry more of it.

All these factors and many others were taken into account, and the more they

thought about it the more attractive it sounded. But by the time the whole thing had been hammered out and an experimental cartridge designed, war had broken out, and the arguments outlined previously were applied here – change of weapon, change of ammunition, what to do with the millions of rounds in stock, and so forth.

But the demands of the war showed that it was feasible after all, because new rifles were going to have to be made and fresh stocks of ammunition too, and they might just as well be in a more practical form. In order to make things a little simpler, the original cartridge design was scrapped and a new one drawn up which used a bullet of standard 7·92-mm calibre and a cartridge case based on a shortened version of the standard one, so that much of the work could be done on existing machinery. With this clear, the Haenel and Walther companies were asked to produce prototypes of an 'assault rifle', one of the most important features being that the design had to be suited to rapid mass-production.

The designs were ready in 1942 and became known as the Maschinen Karabiner 42(H) and 42(W). The Walther design used the same barrel-encircling piston as their G41 but drove it by a more conventional gas port in the barrel. The bolt was locked by tipping it upwards at the rear to lock into a recess in the gun body. The Haenel design used almost the same bolt mechanism but drove it by a more conventional gas piston moving in a cylinder mounted above the barrel. About five thousand of each were made for trials on the Russian front, as a result of which it was decided to drop the Walther design and put the Haenel model into volume production.

Outwitting the Führer

But now trouble arose. Weapon production had to be approved by Hitler, and when the project was put before him he refused to allow it to continue. As far as he was concerned, what an infantry rifle needed was range and a powerful cartridge – this, he said, he had realised from his own experience in the First World War – and all the explanations of the advantages of the new weapon were lost on him. Nothing doing.

The designers and promoters of the new weapon were somewhat put out by this, but being experienced in the politics of the time they knew what to do. They re-christened it the 'Machine Pistol 43' and put it into production; henceforth when anything appeared on paper about the project, Hitler

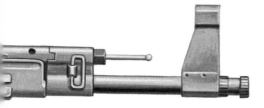

German MP43
Although called a Machine Pistol, this was a bit of political camouflage to get the weapon into production behind Hitler's back. It was actually the first 'Assault Rifle', firing a shortened cartridge and capable of single shot or automatic fire

NAME	CALIBRE	WEIGHT (lb)	MAGAZINE CAPACITY	ACTION	VELOCITY (F.P.S.)
Germany					
Kar 98K	7.92 mm	8.6	5	Bolt	2,450
G41(W)	7.92 mm	11.0	10	Gas	2,550
FG 42	7.92 mm	9.9	20	Gas	2,500
MP 43	7.92 mm	11.25	30	Gas	2,125
Great Britain					
Lee-Enfield No. 1 Mk III	.303	8.4	10	Bolt	2,400
United States					
Garand M1	.30	9.5	8	Gas	2,800
Springfield M1903A1	.30	8.0	5	Bolt	2,800
Italy					
Mannlicher-Carcano	6.5 mm	7.6	6	Bolt	2,300
Mannlicher-Carcano	7.35 mm	7.5	6	Bolt	2,500
Japan					
Ariska Type 38	6.5 mm	9.5	5	Bolt	2,400
Type 99	7.7 mm	9.1	5	Bolt	2,400
Soviet Russia					
Mosin Nagant 1930	7.62 mm	8.7	5	Bolt	2,660
Tokarev 1940	7.62 mm	8.6	10	Gas	2,725
Simonov M 1936	7.62 mm	8.9	15	Gas	2,519
France					
MAS 1936	7.5 mm	8.3	5	Bolt	2,700

assumed it to be a replacement for the existing submachine-guns, and as he was all in favour of these weapons, it all went past him unquestioned.

The weapons were being turned out from three factories and issued to the Russian Front, where every German unit was clamouring for the new gun when, at a conference at Hitler's headquarters, the whole affair was 'blown' by some divisional commanders from Russia asking Hitler point-blank when they were going to get the new weapons.

Hitler was furious and instituted an enquiry, but fortunately for the officers who had defied his ruling the report of the enquiry was so encouraging that Hitler changed his mind, gave the weapon his blessing, and announced that henceforth it would be called the *Sturmgewehr* or Assault Rifle. It is doubtful if any of the officers concerned felt like pointing out to him that they had already invented the name in the specification they issued three years earlier; there was no sense in asking for more trouble.

Official string-pulling
The German Parachute troops were part of the *Luftwaffe*, and when the first moves towards an assault rifle were reaching some sort of result, the promoters tried to enlist the *Luftwaffe's* aid by offering them the new assault rifle as a likely weapon for the paratroops. Unfortunately for this plan, the paratroopers had been the victims of some unfortunate experiences in the invasion of Crete, when they were brought under long range rifle fire from British troops. This convinced them that nothing but a full-power cartridge was of any use to them and they were quite firm in their refusal of the new weapon. They asked the Army if they would not reconsider their decision and develop a similar weapon using the standard cartridge, but the Army refused.

The parachutists, being soldiers attached to the Air Force, were able to use both channels when they wanted anything. Whatever the Army refused them the *Luftwaffe* would provide, and vice versa, and when things got too difficult they could always enlist the aid of Goering, Marshal of the *Luftwaffe*, who regarded the paratroops as his private army, for whom nothing was too good. So through *Luftwaffe* channels they now drafted a specification for a new rifle and gave it to Rheinmettal-Borsig who, by coincidence, were part of the Hermann Goering Werke combine.

The resulting weapon came into service in 1942 as the '*Fallschirmgewehr* 42' (Parachutist's Rifle Model 1942) but it was never

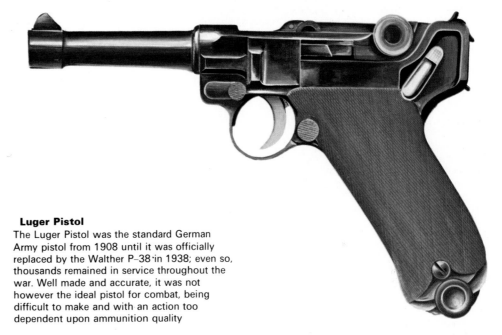

Luger Pistol
The Luger Pistol was the standard German Army pistol from 1908 until it was officially replaced by the Walther P–38 in 1938; even so, thousands remained in service throughout the war. Well made and accurate, it was not however the ideal pistol for combat, being difficult to make and with an action too dependent upon ammunition quality

perfectly right and modifications continued to be made throughout its life. Little more than 7,000 were made, one of the reasons being that the parachute troops in the German Army became less and less important as the war drew on.

The FG 42 was a remarkably good design. It was built in a 'straight-line' configuration, with the butt in prolongation of the barrel axis, which stopped the tendency to rise when fired at automatic; when fired at single shot it fired from a closed bolt – that is to say, the bolt closed and locked behind the cartridge without the weapon firing, and the firer then pressed the trigger to drop the hammer and fire the round. This gave greater accuracy because there was no movement going on at the moment of discharge. On the other hand, a machine-gun firing from a closed bolt is dangerous, since it means that when the finger is taken off the trigger the mechanism loads one last round but does not fire it, thus leaving it in what is probably a very hot chamber, in which it is liable to 'cook off' or explode from the heat, usually surprising the operator and catching one of his comrades unexpectedly.

When firing automatic, therefore, the FG 42 worked from an open bolt, so that

Webley Revolver
The British Army's revolver from 1887 to 1963 was the Webley. Hard–hitting, accurate and reliable, it was issued in ·455 calibre until the early 1930s when it was replaced by a ·38 model which was easier to shoot accurately

French Lebel Revolver
This is the Model 1892, standard French Army pistol until the Second World War. Although of old design and using a relatively small bullet (8–mm calibre) it was a reliable weapon

when the finger was taken from the trigger the action stopped with the bolt held back and an empty chamber; air could thus pass down the barrel and cool the weapon before the next burst. When the trigger was pressed again, the bolt went forward and chambered a round, firing it automatically as soon as the bolt was locked. All this, moreover, was accomplished in a weapon weighing less than 10 lb.

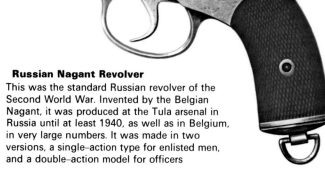

Russian Nagant Revolver

This was the standard Russian revolver of the Second World War. Invented by the Belgian Nagant, it was produced at the Tula arsenal in Russia until at least 1940, as well as in Belgium, in very large numbers. It was made in two versions, a single-action type for enlisted men, and a double-action model for officers

Polish Radom Pistol

The Radom was a Polish combination of the Browning Colt model 1911 and the 1935 high-powered FN Browning. Made at the Radom arsenal in Poland, it was used extensively by the German forces after 1939

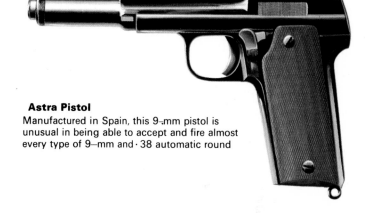

Astra Pistol

Manufactured in Spain, this 9-mm pistol is unusual in being able to accept and fire almost every type of 9-mm and ·38 automatic round

Nambu Automatic Pistol

The standard Japanese Army pistol, this 8-mm automatic, although resembling the German Luger, has a much simpler action

NAME	CALIBRE	WEIGHT (lb)	MAGAZINE CAPACITY	VELOCITY (F.P.S.)	Remarks
Germany					
Pistole '08 (Luger)	9 mm	1.9	8	1,150	Auto
Pistole '38 (Walther)	9 mm	2.1	8	1,150	Auto
Great Britain					
Pistol No 2 (S&W)	.38	1.5	6	650	Revolver
Pistol No 2 (Enfield)	.38	1.7	6	650	Revolver
Pistol Mk 4 (Webley)	.455	2.37	6	620	Revolver
Browning GP35	9 mm	2.2	13	1,100	Auto
United States					
Colt M1911A1	.45	2.5	7	860	Auto
Colt Army M1917	.45	2.5	6	860	Revolver
Smith & Wesson 1917	.45	2.25	6	860	Revolver
Italy					
Glisenti 1910	9 mm	1.8	7	1,050	Auto
Beretta 1934	9 mm	1.5	7	825	Auto
Japan					
Nambu 4	8 mm	1.9	8	1,100	Auto
Nambu 14	8 mm	2.0	8	1,100	Auto
Type 94	8 mm	1.75	6	1,000	Auto
Type 26	9 mm	1.9	6	750	Revolver
Soviet Russia					
Tokarev 33	7.62 mm	1.8	8	1,375	Auto
Nagant 1895	7.62 mm	1.75	7	1,000	Revolver
France					
Lebel	8 mm	1.9	6	625	Revolver
Spain					
Astra	9 mm	2.2	8	1,100	Auto

PISTOLS

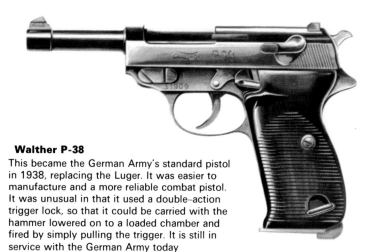

Walther P-38

This became the German Army's standard pistol in 1938, replacing the Luger. It was easier to manufacture and a more reliable combat pistol. It was unusual in that it used a double-action trigger lock, so that it could be carried with the hammer lowered on to a loaded chamber and fired by simply pulling the trigger. It is still in service with the German Army today

THE BOLT ACTION RIFLE

From the comparatively crude Dreyse Needle Gun of the Austro-Prussian War the modern rifle took shape, and became one of the major infantry weapons during both World Wars I and II.

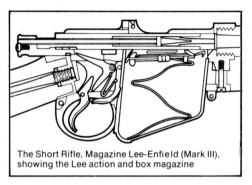

The Short Rifle, Magazine Lee-Enfield (Mark III), showing the Lee action and box magazine

The Russian M1891 Moisin-Nagant rifle with Moisin action and the Belgian Nagant magazine

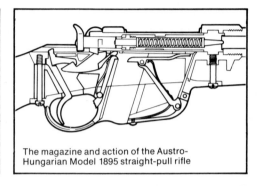

The magazine and action of the Austro-Hungarian Model 1895 straight-pull rifle

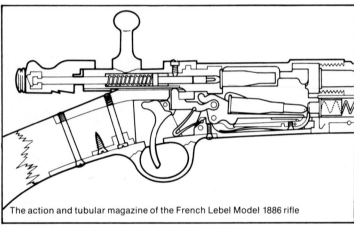

The action and tubular magazine of the French Lebel Model 1886 rifle

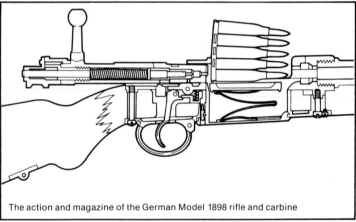

The action and magazine of the German Model 1898 rifle and carbine

The principle of the bolt action is relatively simple.

The bolt, in outline resembling an ordinary door bolt, contains a long, spring-loaded, firing pin. On sliding the bolt towards the breech, the bullet is inserted into the breech, the spring, making contact with the trigger mechanism via the cocking piece, is compressed, thus withdrawing the firing pin, and the bolt is locked into the breech mechanism. The most effective of the locking systems is by dual lugs which revolve into recesses in the breech; these can be either vertical or horizontal. Other locking systems are of a wedge type in the breech or by a rear lug. This last system, which is employed in the British Short Magazine Lee-Enfield, has been subjected to criticism because it allows too much 'play' in the bolt and, in general, is not as strong as the front locking system. Various methods of triggering the mechanism to release the firing pin have been developed. Essentially, however, the process is the same—by squeezing the trigger the resistance to the cocking piece is released and the firing pin makes contact with the percussion cap. With a turn-bolt, the locking mechanism is engaged by turning the bolt handle down when the bolt has been fully pushed home. The straight-pull bolt has an internal spiral system which automatically revolves the lugs into place as the bolt slides forward.

The box magazine, variations of which were employed by the majority of rifles of the period, is an extremely simple mechanism; it consists of a metal box incorporating a spring-loaded platform. The magazine is situated, forward of the trigger guard, below the mechanism. The capacity of the various designs varied from 3 to 10 rounds. For the most part, the magazines were an integral part of the rifle but there were several removable designs. In some instances, the cartridges were staggered within the box, in others they were in-line. Cartridges were injected into the magazine by means of a clip. Clips assumed a variety of different shapes, but the principle was the same in all. They consisted of open-ended slides or cases within which a number of cartridges, 3, 5, or 6, were gripped whether by the spring metal of the case or a spring incorporated in the base. When the bolt was withdrawn, the clip was positioned between the bolt-head and the breech, and the cartridges were usually pressed down into the magazine by the thumb. The subsequent forward movement of the bolt ejected the clip and pushed the first round into the breech. The major deviation from this method was that adopted by Mannlicher for most of his designs. The Mannlicher system involved placing the clip with the cartridges into the magazine, a spring then pushing the cartridges up *within* the clip. When the last round was in the breech, the clip would fall through an aperture in the bottom of the magazine.

Without doubt the German contribution to small arms design has been the greatest. In particular the rifles of Peter Paul Mauser demonstrated a remarkable ingenuity and have influenced rifle design throughout the world. The Mauser Gewehr 98 was probably the most successful rifle of its kind ever designed.

Second only to Mauser was Mannlicher. A frequently under-estimated inventor, he was often badly used. It is significant, however, that his designs and elements of his designs have been

British troops tackle typical cultivated terrain in Burma

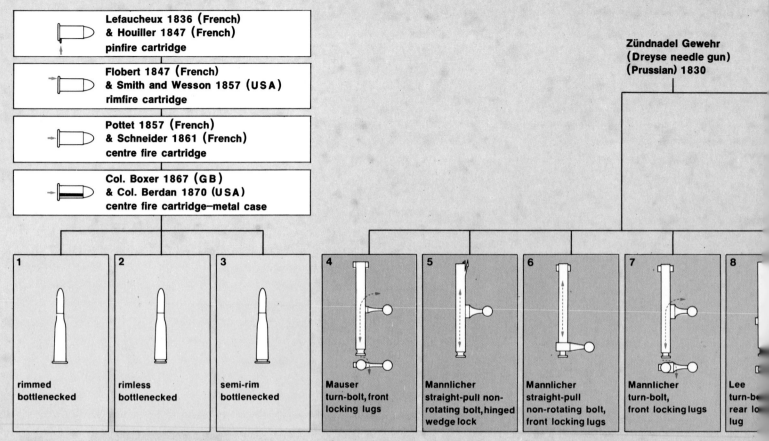

Lefaucheux 1836 (French)
& Houiller 1847 (French)
pinfire cartridge

Flobert 1847 (French)
& Smith and Wesson 1857 (USA)
rimfire cartridge

Pottet 1857 (French)
& Schneider 1861 (French)
centre fire cartridge

Col. Boxer 1867 (GB)
& Col. Berdan 1870 (USA)
centre fire cartridge—metal case

Zündnadel Gewehr
(Dreyse needle gun)
(Prussian) 1830

1
rimmed
bottlenecked

2
rimless
bottlenecked

3
semi-rim
bottlenecked

4
Mauser
turn-bolt, front
locking lugs

5
Mannlicher
straight-pull non-
rotating bolt, hinged
wedge lock

6
Mannlicher
straight-pull
non-rotating bolt,
front locking lugs

7
Mannlicher
turn-bolt,
front locking lugs

8
Lee
turn-b
rear lo
lug

CARTRIDGES   SYSTEMS

incorporated in the weapons of many different countries.

The United States claims much credit for advances in small arms design. Most of these advances, however, applied to weapons of eras before and after those which concern us here. The biggest single contribution from America was that of the Lee box magazine and Lee, although he worked in America, was born in Scotland.

Britain's contribution was in the field of rifling. Before the introduction of the smokeless 'cordite' propellant, the Metford system of rifling was general; the new propellant, however, necessitated a different system and the Enfield system was almost universally adopted and is still used. Illustrated are the genealogies of the major design features of some of these rifles and carbines, with the colour coding showing the provenance of each weapon's cartridge, bolt system and magazine.

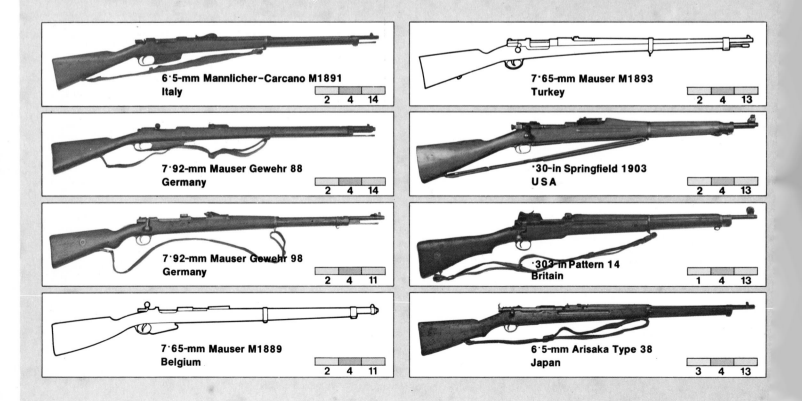

6·5-mm Mannlicher–Carcano M1891
Italy
2 4 14

7·65-mm Mauser M1893
Turkey
2 4 13

7·92-mm Mauser Gewehr 88
Germany
2 4 14

·30-in Springfield 1903
USA
2 4 13

7·92-mm Mauser Gewehr 98
Germany
2 4 11

·303-in Pattern 14
Britain
1 4 13

7·65-mm Mauser M1889
Belgium
2 4 11

6·5-mm Arisaka Type 38
Japan
3 4 13

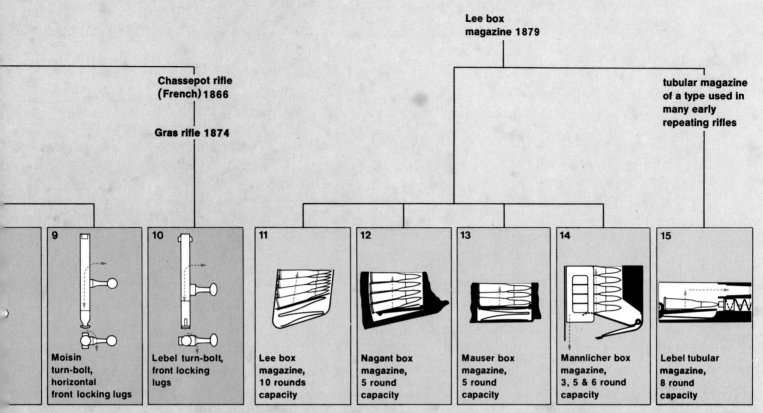

Lee box
magazine 1879

Chassepot rifle
(French) 1866

Gras rifle 1874

tubular magazine
of a type used in
many early
repeating rifles

9	10	11	12	13	14	15
Moisin turn-bolt, horizontal front locking lugs	Lebel turn-bolt, front locking lugs	Lee box magazine, 10 rounds capacity	Nagant box magazine, 5 round capacity	Mauser box magazine, 5 round capacity	Mannlicher box magazine, 3, 5 & 6 round capacity	Lebel tubular magazine, 8 round capacity

FEED DEVICES

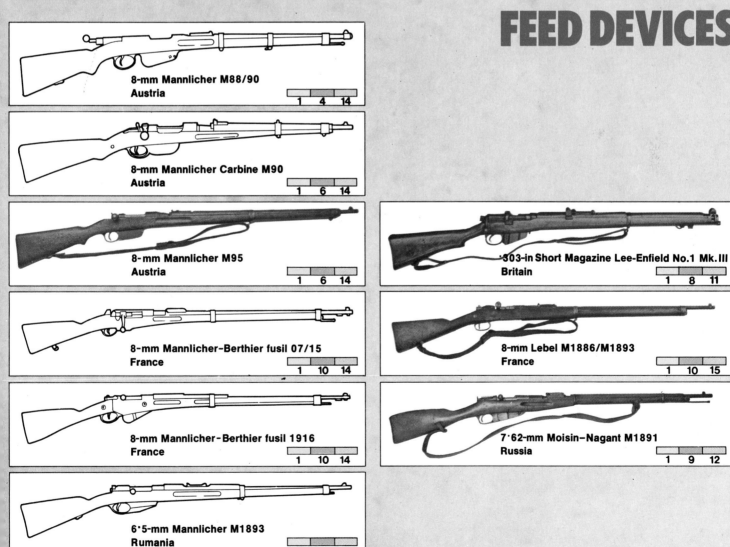

8-mm Mannlicher M88/90
Austria
1 4 14

8-mm Mannlicher Carbine M90
Austria
1 6 14

8-mm Mannlicher M95
Austria
1 6 14

·303-in Short Magazine Lee-Enfield No.1 Mk.III
Britain
1 8 11

8-mm Mannlicher-Berthier fusil 07/15
France
1 10 14

8-mm Lebel M1886/M1893
France
1 10 15

8-mm Mannlicher-Berthier fusil 1916
France
1 10 14

7·62-mm Moisin-Nagant M1891
Russia
1 9 12

6·5-mm Mannlicher M1893
Rumania
1 7 14

Chris Barker

PERSONAL WEAPONS OF THE EASTERN FRONT

1. KAR-98K 7·9-mm rifle (5 rounds in magazine)
2. MP-40 machine-pistol (32 rounds in magazine)
3. Walther P-38 9-mm automatic (8 rounds in magazine)
4. Standard hand-grenade

For a nation as advanced in weapon technology as Germany, one which had been rearming for six years prior to 1939, it is surprising to discover that the *Wehrmacht* was, at the opening of hostilities, still equipped with the Mauser bolt action rifle. Automatic rifles had been tried and discarded, and it was not until the arrival of the 'Machine Pistol 43' in 1943 that the German soldier's personal weapon was modernised. But along with the introduction of the 'Assault Rifle' as we know it today, the German soldier also received machine guns which were among the best in the world. Doubling as the squad automatic, the German Army's 'General Purpose Machine Gun' was — on a tripod — also usable as a heavy machine gun. A triumph of organisation indeed . . .

Soviet personal weapons were both rugged and cheap. Moreover, every weapon — pistol, rifle, machine gun and submachine gun — used the same calibre and the same rifling, so that barrels for any weapon could be rifled on the same machinery . . . a remarkable example of production planning. Ruling supreme, though, was the submachine gun, of which something like 8,000,000 were made during the war, and with which whole divisions were armed. Besides this, the standard weapon was still the bolt action rifle, and the élitist pistol was rarely seen in the front line.

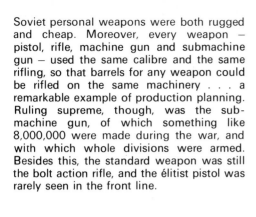

Even with the three firearms shown here, the impressive standardisation of the Red Army's equipment is strikingly obvious in their use of 7·62-mm calibre weapons

1. M-1930 7·62-mm rifle (5 rounds in magazine)
2. PPSH 7·62-mm submachine-gun (71 rounds in magazine)
3. Tokarev TT 7·62-mm automatic (8 rounds in magazine)
4. Standard hand-grenade

Deirdre Amsden

The US Army was the only one to go to war with an automatic rifle as its standard infantry weapon, a piece of far-sightedness due to General MacArthur, who had approved the Garand rifle during his term as Chief-of-Staff. This, though, was counterbalanced by the absence of a respectable light machine gun, for which the Browning Automatic Rifle — used as the squad automatic — was a poor substitute. While the M1 Carbine was introduced to replace the Colt automatic pistol in the hands of such men as machine-gunners, mortarmen and messengers, the .45 Revolver was still to be found in rear echelons. Their standard hand grenade was, like the LMG, a World War One design, but despite potential replacements the GI had just to soldier on and make the best of it.

LEND-LEASE FROM AMERICA

1. A P-14 ·300-calibre rifle (P-17 in USA)
2. A ·45-calibre Thompson sub-machine-gun (M-1)
3. A Colt ·45 automatic pistol (1911 model)
4. A Colt ·45 revolver (1917 model)

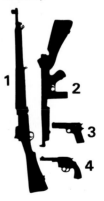

AMERICA'S PERSONAL ARMOURY

1. *M-1941 Johnson Rifle:* a semi-automatic infantry rifle like the Garand, but with a novel magazine design. This was of rotary action and had two more rounds than the Garand, but was only used for a limited period. *Calibre:* ·30-inch. *Magazine capacity:* ten rounds

2. *M-1 Carbine:* introduced as a semi-automatic weapon to weigh little and hit hard. Assessment reports said that troops were 'very enthusiastic . . . impressed by its high rate of automatic fire'. *Calibre:* ·30-inch. *Magazine capacity:* 15 rounds. *Effective range:* 300 yards

3. *M-1 Garand Rifle:* Patton called it 'the greatest battle implement ever devised'. Its high rate of fire earned it the same reputation as the British Lee-Enfield. *Calibre:* ·30-inch. *Magazine capacity:* eight rounds

4. *M-3 Submachine-gun:* replaced the famous Thompson submachine-gun in Marine and army service. It was produced in great quantities—with an extra barrel for captured German ammunition. *Calibre:* ·45-inch. *Magazine capacity:* 30 rounds. *Rate of fire:* 400 rounds per minute

5. *·45-inch Automatic:* this veteran of the First World War was eclipsed as an important infantry weapon by the carbine. But it retained its role as a personal defence weapon. *Magazine capacity:* seven rounds

6. *Smith and Wesson ·38-inch Revolver:* another well-trusted 'hand gun' used as a side-arm by officers, but whose importance ended with the general introduction of the machine-pistol

Deirdre Amsden

JAPANESE SIDEARMS

The Japanese army which invaded China was well-provided with modern equipment. It compared well with that used by other armies.
(1) Model 11 (1922) 6·5-mm Light Machine-Gun: a modification of the French Hotchkiss. *Weight:* 22½ lb. *Rate of Fire:* 500 rpm.

Ammunition: hopper holding 30 rounds.
(2) Model 38 (1905) 6·5-mm Rifle: produced in three standard lengths for issue to different types of unit. *Weight:* 9·4 lb. *Magazine:* Five rounds.
(3) Officer's Sword

(4) Model 94 (1934) 8-mm Pistol. *Magazine:* Six rounds.
(5) Model 14 (1925) 8-mm Pistol: ammunition interchangeable with the Type 94. *Magazine:* Eight rounds.
(6) Standard Hand-Grenade

BRITISH INFANTRY WEAPONS

British infantry weapons were noted for their toughness and reliability: **(1) Bren ·303 light machine-gun.** *Weight:* 22 lb. *Effective range:* 800 yards. *Magazine:* 30 rounds. *Rate of fire:* 500 rpm. **(2) Sten 9-mm submachine-gun.** *Weight:* 7·8 lb. *Effective range:* 200 yds. *Magazine:* 32 rounds. *Rate of fire:* 500-550 rpm. **(3) Lee Enfield ·303 rifle No. 4 Mk 1/2.** *Weight:* 8·8 lb. *Maximum range:* 2,000 yds. *Magazine:* 10 rounds. **(4) Lee Enfield ·303 rifle No. 5 Mk 1** (a jungle-warfare version of the standard rifle). *Weight:* 7·15 lb. **(5) Webley ·380 revolver.** *Weight:* 2 lb 6 oz. *Effective range:* 50 yds. *Magazine:* six rounds. **(6) Enfield ·380 No. 2 Mk 1* revolver.** *Weight:* 1·7 lb. *Effective range:* 50 yds. *Magazine:* six rounds. **(7) Browning FN 9-mm automatic pistol No. 2 Mk 1.** *Weight:* 2·06 lb. *Range:* 50 yds. *Magazine:* 13 rounds

British soldiers went to war with the Lee-Enfield bolt action rifle, undoubtedly the smoothest and fastest-acting bolt action ever built, and almost as good as a self-loader in the hands of a trained man. Similarly, British machine guns were also technologically less advanced than those of Germany but were nonetheless of the utmost reliability. Both the elderly Vickers, introduced as far back as 1912, and the Bren, derived from a 1924 Czech design, exhibited traditional gunsmith's standards; it was only with the Sten Gun, turned out by the million for less than £3 each, that the realities of modern war were first accepted. The British were also the last major army to retain the revolver, using the .38 Enfield and .38 Smith & Wesson models, though they too began to adopt the Browning High-Power automatic for airborne and Commando troops towards the end of the war. In British eyes *reliability* came before anything else, and the performance of British weapons in every theatre of operations more than proved the point.

Japanese soldiers, on the other hand, deserve credit for their successes in spite of the weapons they carried, not because of them. The standard infantry weapon, for instance, was the Arisaka bolt action rifle, which dated from the 1890s; the machine gun was usually a badly executed copy of a French Hotchkiss of 1914 which was prone to jamming; the hand grenades were erratic in their action, and a submachine gun was a rarity since the total Japanese production was less than 15,000. The above, though, is a case where an inferiority in personal weapons was counterbalanced by an aggressive spirit, and this is precisely how the Japanese soldier made his mark. To add to the confusion, in 1939 the Army began to change from 6.5 mm calibre to 7.7 mm calibre for its rifles and machine guns, and there was thus a constant ammunition supply problem to be faced – of getting the right cartridges to the right weapons at the right time in the heat of battle.

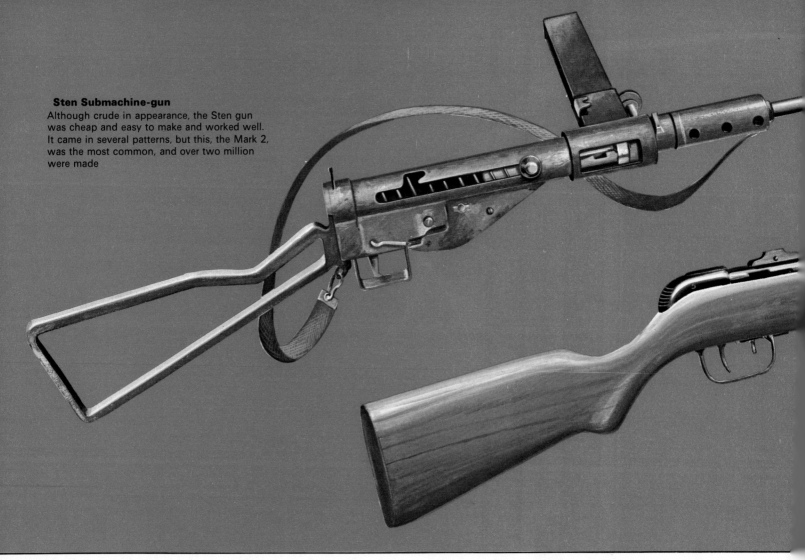

Sten Submachine-gun
Although crude in appearance, the Sten gun
was cheap and easy to make and worked well.
It came in several patterns, but this, the Mark 2,
was the most common, and over two million
were made

The next category of weapon we should consider is the submachine-gun, and in this class the Germans and Russians had a clear lead over the rest of the world since they had been able to do some field research during the Spanish Civil War. Both of these countries, and Italy, sent troops, thinly disguised as popular volunteers, and an assortment of weapons they wished to have tried out, and as a result the superiority of fire of the submachine-gun was noted and studied.

The Germans already had a variety of submachine-guns in service in small numbers, but the reports from Spain led them to think seriously about a standard model to be produced by the million. After looking at the current models, the German Army sent for the director of a company called the *Erfurter Maschinenfabrik B. Geipel GmbH*, who had produced a number of designs under the name 'Erma'. They handed him a specification and told him to produce a weapon to suit and be quick about it.

As it happened, the company had been working on a fresh design and with a little modification this was produced and offered for the Army's approval. Approval was given and in the middle of 1938 the Erma company began producing the submachine-gun which has almost become a German Army trademark – the Maschinenpistole 38.

The MP-38, for some unknown reason, attracted the name "Schmeisser" during the war, and it has generally stuck. Although Hugo Schmeisser did design many machine pistols and submachine-guns during his life, he had nothing whatever to do with this one; it was designed by one Heinrich Vollmer. The nearest Schmeisser ever got

to it was to manage a factory which was making them during the war.

The MP-38 was a leader in its field, and some of the ideas seen in it have been copied many times over in later designs. It was the first to adopt a folding stock which was successful, the first to utilise stamped steel and plastic in its construction and the first weapon to have no wood of any sort. Like almost every other submachine-gun, the MP-38 fires from an open bolt and operates on the system generally called 'blow-back' because the firing of the cartridge causes the case to be blown back against the bolt and thus force it to the rear to start off the cycle of operation. One might think this would lead to the case being blown out at dangerous speed, but since the weight of the bolt is enormous compared with the weight of the bullet, the bullet has left the barrel and the pressure in the barrel has dropped to safe limits before the inertia of the bolt has been overcome and it starts to move.

German grumbles
Though the simplicity of this system has a lot to commend it, it also has one or two drawbacks. For example, if the weapon has a magazine fitted and is dropped sharply on its butt, then the bolt will slam back against the spring and, going forward, will collect a round from the magazine and fire it – since the firing pin is part of the bolt and as soon as the bolt closes it fires the cartridge.

This was one of the defects of the MP-38, as it was of many other submachine-guns, and in 1940 this, plus the fact that the MP-38 was not easy to manufacture, led to it being re-designed as the MP-40. The difference

between the 38 and 40 is not easy to see, but the best clue is that the body of the 38 is made of corrugated steel with a plain magazine housing, while the 40 has a plain body and corrugated magazine housing. The other differences are largely concerned with easier mass production, but one important feature was the alteration of the cocking handle so that it could be moved inwards to lock the bolt securely in the forward position, removing any danger of bouncing the bolt and accidentally firing a round.

One of the complaints of the German soldiers on the Russian Front was that the Soviets were using submachine-guns which had 71-round drum magazines, while the Germans were using weapons with 30-round magazines. An interesting attempt to try and even things up was a modification of the MP-40 which changed the magazine housing into a sliding assembly. Two standard 30-round magazines could be clipped in and the assembly pulled over to one side so that one magazine was lined up with the bolt. After emptying this magazine, the firer simply pushed the sliding assembly across and brought the other magazine into line. It was not particularly good, because the all-up weight of the machine-gun now rose to over 12 lb, which is something of a handful. It seems that very few were made.

The Russians also learned from the Spanish Civil War. They had adopted a submachine-gun in 1934, the PPD designed by Degtyarev, a name which frequently crops up when discussing Russian firearms. This had been used with considerable effect by the various Communist 'volunteers' and as a result the Russians decided to put it

CRUDE BUT EFFECTIVE

Soviet PPSh Submachine-gun
One of the simplest and crudest submachine-guns ever made, the PPSh Model of 1941 was none the less effective. Firing 900 rounds per minute, most models were built so that they only fired automatic; over five million were made before the end of the war

into volume production. The first model was known as the PPD34/38 and after a few thousand had been made it was improved into the PPD40 model, which used a rather better design of magazine. This was the 71-round drum which the Germans found such a nuisance in later years. Its mechanism was a simple blowback, and it was recognisable by its wooden stock and fore-end, and the slotted cooling jacket round the barrel. The PPD40 however was not simple to make, being machined from solid steel, and when the German Army invaded, the cry was for a weapon which could be rapidly produced by semi-skilled labour. Fortunately the Red Army had been testing a gun which fitted this demand, and in 1941 it was approved for production, the PPD40 being dropped.

The new weapon was the PPSh41, designed by Georgi Shpagin, another well-known Russian arms designer, and it was, compared to any other submachine-gun previously known, crude beyond belief. The entire body and jacket were welded up from steel stampings, the parts of the firing mechanism were stamped out, and the only pieces made with any sort of precision were the bolt and barrel. The jacket extended beyond the muzzle and folded over to form a primitive muzzle deflector which helped to keep the muzzle down when fired, since – like most of its type – the recoil tended to force it up.

In 1942 the German Army beseiged Leningrad, and the occupants of the city were desperate for weapons. Supply from the rest of the Soviet Union being almost impossible, a local engineer, A. I. Sudarev, designed a submachine-gun which was

built in local factories and sent straight out to the nearby Front. This became standardised as the PPS-42. He later improved it into the PPS-43, though the changes are largely concerned with even simpler production and make little difference to the operation or appearance.

All or nothing
The PPS-42 and -43 models were probably the most crude devices ever put into the hands of troops. They were entirely put together from stamped steel components, welded and riveted together; the bolt is as simple as can be, and only that and the barrel demand any sort of precision in manufacture. The stock folds over to the top of the gun, and as with the PPSh the barrel jacket runs round the front of the barrel to form a primitive muzzle brake or deflector. The magazine was a curved box holding 35 rounds and there was no provision for firing single shots; it was all or nothing with this weapon. Its manufacture continued until after the war was over, but it never reached the vast quantities of the PPD or PPSh models.

The vast number of submachine-guns produced by the Soviets is a reflection of the particular attraction this weapon had for them. In the first place it was simple to teach and simple to understand, a great factor when you are confronted with the problem of turning millions of peasants into soldiers overnight. There is also a good deal of logistic sense in arming whole battalions with the same weapon, from the commanding officer down; it simplifies ammunition supply and weapon replacement immensely. The production of such crude

and simple weapons by the use of semi-skilled labour is much easier. And the submachine-gun lends itself to the Soviet way of fighting. It is no good sitting in a hole with a submachine-gun and hoping to snipe at somebody three hundred yards away. The only way to use it is to get out of the hole and go looking for the enemy.

The best employment of these weapons is shown by the peculiar Soviet innovation of Tank Rider Battalions. These were 500-strong units, armed solely with PPSh submachine-guns and carrying as many spare magazines as they could. They rode into battle on the back of tanks, and when the tank found some enemy they leapt off and went for him, covered by the tank. If the tank was hit, those who were still capable leapt off and grabbed the next tank along. Their training was very simple, since the only thing they knew was the assault; they never retreated and they left the consolidation to others. From all accounts their life expectancy was short.

The British Army, along with the US Army, had long resisted the submachine-gun, referring to it in disparaging terms, but when the war began in 1939 the British soon realised that these despised weapons were a necessity in modern war. They had, it is true, tested almost every type ever made over the years and thus were in a position to be able to say what they wanted, but by that time it was more a question of what they could get. The best, they considered, was the Finnish Suomi, but the Finns were taking all the weapons the factory could produce, so they turned to the next best, went to America and bought the Thompson submachine-gun.

Armed with an MP40 submachine-gun, this German paratrooper finds cover in a shell-hole during the fight for Monte Cassino in January and February, 1944

Thompson Submachine-gun
The original Thompson model was the 1928 which could be fitted with a drum magazine; this was not required for military work, since it was too heavy and too noisy, so when the weapon was simplified into the M1, shown here, only a box magazine was used

The Thompson had certain drawbacks. It was heavy, it was difficult to make, and it was expensive. But it had one virtue which over-rode all that – it was reliable. And even when cheaper and newer submachine-guns came along, a lot of people refused to part with their Thompsons for just that reason, that they could rely on them in a tight corner. The first models were provided with the 50-round drum magazine so beloved of the G-Men and their opponents, but what goes down in a Chicago alley doesn't always work in war, and the British infantry patrols on the Saar front in 1940 reported that the rounds in the drum slapped back and forth, making a noise at night and drawing enemy fire. The drums were replaced with box magazines and no British submachine-gun ever again had a drum.

But the expense and difficulty of supply of the Thompson led the British to think about manufacturing a gun of their own, and the events of 1940 led them to speed up their deliberations. After much consideration of various designs it was decided that the best thing to do was to make a British copy of the German MP-28, one which was designed by Schmeisser during the First World War. It was a blowback gun with a wooden stock and box magazine at the side, and plans were drawn up to manufacture this under the name of Lanchester, the engineer responsible for modifying the design to suit British engineering standards.

Just as this was about to go into production, two designers from the Royal Small Arms Factory at Enfield came forward with a weapon they had put together – the Sten gun. In appearance it was almost as bad as some of the Russian weapons, all metal, with a tubular stock and made up of stamped and welded sheet metal. But it worked very well and it was cheap and easy to make, and without much more argument the Sten went into production.

The first model, the Mark 1, had a spoon-like flash hider-cum-deflector on the muzzle and a wooden foregrip, and about 100,000 were made. Then the Mark 2 – the most common version – was introduced. This did away with the foregrip and flash hider, had a simple perforated tube doubling as a barrel locking nut and hand grip, and a single-tube butt. Two million of these were

made, and untold numbers of them were dropped over Occupied Europe, where they still turn up from time to time. A silenced version was also made for clandestine operations. Then came the Mark 3, with a long welded jacket completely covering the barrel; this was made in vast numbers in Canada and Britain. The Mark 4 was an experimental model for paratroops which never saw service; finally came Mark 5.

Did it really work?
This was somewhat more elegant than the earlier models, in an attempt to produce a weapon which would inspire its owners with more confidence It had a pistol grip and a wooden butt and fitted a bayonet on the muzzle, but for all that it was still the same old Sten gun at heart. It was first issued to Airborne units but later replaced all the other marks as standard issue and remained in British service until the 1950s.

The US Army also took the Thompson in 1941 when the rapidly expanding army showed the need for such a weapon. Prior to this a small number had been bought for evaluation, and the US Marines had used them since 1928. The Thompson as adopted by the US Army was known as the M1928 or 1928A1, and was the original Thompson design; this was somewhat different to the other submachine-guns we have discussed

A US Marine sights in on a Japanese sniper on Okinawa with his Thompson submachine-gun

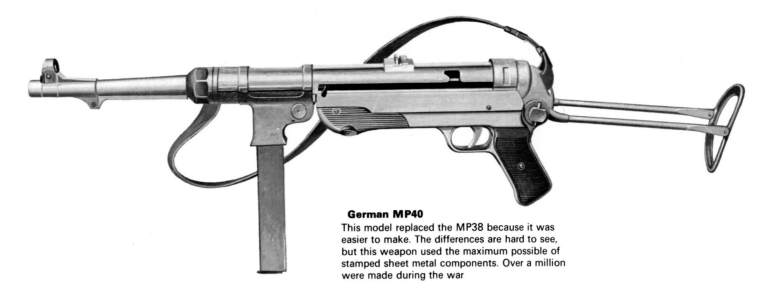

German MP40
This model replaced the MP38 because it was easier to make. The differences are hard to see, but this weapon used the maximum possible of stamped sheet metal components. Over a million were made during the war

because it was of a type of action known as the 'delayed blowback'. In an attempt to keep the breech closed until the pressure had dropped, the bolt of the Thompson had an inclined slot cut in it, in which rode a separate locking piece. This locked the bolt to the gun body at the moment of firing. The angle of this slot was carefully calculated so that under extremely high pressure, as when the round was fired, the slot and locking piece jammed securely together and into the body slot. Then, as the pressure dropped, so the friction lessened until the locking piece could ride up the slot and unlock the bolt from the gun body and allow it to move back to complete the unloading and loading cycle.

There has always been considerable argument as to whether this system did or did not achieve any locking at all, but one thing it did do was make the gun that much more difficult to manufacture. As a result, the US Army demanded a simpler version so that production could be speeded up, and the lock system was dispensed with, turning the weapon into a simple blowback with no ill-effects. Sundry other small changes were made and the new weapon was known as the M1, and was adopted in April 1942.

In spite of this the Thompson was still a manufacturing problem and tests were now done on a variety of other designs which were put forward for possible adoption. None was entirely successful and eventually the Army itself designed a cheap and simple weapon, more or less the American equivalent of the Sten gun, known as the M3 submachine-gun; due to its shape it was instantly called the 'grease gun' and the name stuck.

Weaknesses dealt with
The M3 was a simple blowback gun made entirely from steel stampings except, of course, for the bolt and barrel. Cocking was done by a lever on the side, the stock was a collapsible wire form, and – one unique feature – it could be adapted to either the US Army standard ·45 cartridge or the European standard 9-mm cartridge by simply changing the barrel and bolt; when used with the 9-mm cartridge, an adapter was slipped into the magazine housing and Sten gun magazines were used. But although this design was simple and cheap, it soon became apparent that it could be made even more simple and even cheaper.

After complaints from units in the field drew attention to weaknesses in the cocking device, the weapon was redesigned, doing away with the cocking handle and bringing the cocking procedure down to the simplest possible level. A large flap in the gun body was opened, a finger poked into a hole in the bolt, and the bolt hauled to the rear, and that was that. Closing the lid entered a steel pressing into the hole in the bolt and thus acted as a safety catch. One or two other small changes were made and the result entered service as the M3A1. All these guns were made by the Guide Lamp Division of the General Motors Corporation, and they produced no less than 646,000 of both types before the war ended.

We have not mentioned Italy so far in this narrative, since by and large their weapons were not particularly noteworthy, but in the submachine-gun field they deserve mention since, although little known, they possessed one of the best submachine-guns of all time – the Beretta. The Italians were, in fact, in the forefront of submachine-gun development, as they had a submachine-gun in the hands of their infantry as early as 1918, and in the intervening years the company of P. Beretta had worked on improving their design. The Model 1938 was a 9-mm weapon, wooden stocked, with a perforated barrel jacket, a 40-round box magazine and a bayonet. Large numbers of this excellent weapon were provided for the Italian infantry units and subsequent modifications were made in order to simplify production. It remained in production until the 1950s, many thousands being sold to other countries in the postwar years.

NAME	CALIBRE	WEIGHT (lb)	MAGAZINE CAPACITY	RATE OF FIRE (R.P.M.)	VELOCITY (F.P.S.)	REMARKS
Germany						
Bergmann MP 34	9 mm	8.9	24 or 32	650	1,250	Largely used by SS Troops
Erma	9 mm	9.1	25 or 32	500	1,250	
MP 38 or 40	9 mm	8.75	32	500	1,250	
MP 3008	9 mm	6.5	32	500	1,250	Copy of Sten-Gun
Great Britain						
Sten Mark 2	9 mm	7.75	32	450	1,000	Commonest model
United States						
Thompson M1	.45	10.6	20 or 30	700	900	M1928 similar; also 50-round drum
M3A1	.45	8.2	30	400	900	M3 similar data
Reising 50	.45	6.75	20	550	900	Used only by US Marines
Italy						
Beretta 1938A	9 mm	9.25	30 or 40	600	1,350	
Japan						
Model 100, 1941	8 mm	8.5	30	450	1,100	1944 model fired at 800 rpm; few made
Soviet Russia						
PPD 40	7.62 mm	8.1	71	800	1,600	Drum Magazine
PPSh 41	7.62 mm	8.0	35	900	1,600	71-round drum also available
PPS 43	7.62 mm	7.4	35	700	1,600	

SUBMACHINE GUNS

THOMPSON SUBMACHINE GUN

General John T. Thompson called it a 'broom to sweep trenches.' *Time* magazine was to call it, in 1939, 'the deadliest weapon, pound for pound, ever devised.' The Thompson gun had, in the 20 years between the end of the First World War and the beginning of the Second, made itself a reputation which went far beyond anything it might achieve on the battlefield. For the weapon which became the symbol of violence in prohibition America, the gun celebrated in the ballads of the Irish Republican Army, and part of the badge of the R.M. Commandos, was the right weapon at the wrong time. A gun which packed the firepower of a rifle platoon went looking for a war to fight.

As a reserve Brigadier-General in the U.S. Ordnance Department, Thompson had seen how the inventions of two Americans, Hiram Maxim and John Browning, had turned Europe's war of 1914 into a stalemate of machine-gun nests and wire. Heavy machine-guns worked on Maxim's recoil system or Browning's gas, necessarily complex and heavy. Thompson sought to develop a new kind of automatic rifle, light and reliable enough to be hand-held, and to restore offensive power to the advancing infantryman.

To find a simple, reliable, self-operating breech mechanism, the heart of any automatic weapon, two possibilities opened. The 'blowback' principle, using the force of gas pressure to hold the cartridge case against the bolt and re-cock the hammer, could only be used with pistol ammunition. The independently patented 'Blish' lock seemed to be a way of locking the breech for high-powered rifle ammunition, and, dependent on only two moving parts, it could unlock, open, eject the cartridge, close and lock again — the cycle for a simple and effective automatic weapon.

In a high stakes gamble Thompson undertook development in the face of the U.S. industrial-military establishment and the Auto-Ordnance Corpora-

Top: Thompson submachine-gun M1928 A1, with box magazine and Cutts compensator. Above: The Tommygun, badge of Combined Operations

tion was born. Nobody foresaw just how the gamble would pay off.

Chief engineer Theodore Eickhoff had to tell Thompson in September 1917 that his 'Autorifle' could only fire the short, fat .45-calibre Colt pistol round — what he had was a kind of super automatic pistol. Almost by accident the 'trench broom' was born.

The first true submachine-gun was there in outline, described as a handheld, fully automatic small-arm chambered for pistol ammunition. Working day and night, the Auto-Ordnance team produced a viable prototype, and the aptly named 'Annihilator' had its chance on the firing range. A squeeze on the trigger unleashed a jet of flame from the muzzle, a shower of cartridges, and the roar of 20 bullets being fired in under a second. The first prototype reached the New York docks,

bound for France, on November 11, 1918, the day World War I ended.

There were no more trenches to sweep. But the war had spawned an era of political tension and violent social change. While Auto-Ordnance marketed their weapon as the 'ideal weapon for the protection of the home,' the Thompson became the instrument of rebellion from the I.R.A. to the 'motorised bandits' of the prohibition era. While the U.S. military shunned the unconventional new weapon, the gun was making its reputation as the 'Chicago Piano,' the infamous 'Chopper' of Al Capone and 'Machinegun' Jack McGurn. To General Thompson's dismay the 'Tommygun' became the symbol of the underworld, and the violence of the strikebreakers and bonus marchers of the Depression.

It was in American cities that the Thompson was rattling and, meanwhile, the U.S. Marine Corps had to borrow guns from the Post Office for a series of intervention actions from Nicaragua to Shanghai.

Ironically, the 'Chopper' was proving its tactical potential for a coming war. Spraying fat, lazy bullets, the S.M.G. was ideal for the close combat, street and jungle warfare of World War II. Although obsolete by 1939, the model M1928 A1 was the only S.M.G. in production in any Allied country. The gun was simplified to a simple 'slam-fire' weapon, eliminating the Blish lock and peace-time frills such as the complex Lyman sight.

The days of the Thompson gun were numbered, however, as the cheap and simple Sten and German Schmeisser designs of stamped metal proved their equal merit. The two million Thompsons built before production ended in 1944 rehabilitated its tainted image in actions from Home Guard patrols to the Battle of Stalingrad.

The U.S.'s own Sten-type S.M.G., the M3, which could do all the Thompson could and more, never took on the mixture of respect, admiration and fear which the Thompson gun's chequered career had earned.

THE STEN

△ Barrel unit

▽ Main body with trigger mechanism

▽ Shoulder stock

Magazine (obverse) △

Magazine (reverse) △

Few firearms were more suited to the needs of total war than the Sten gun, seen in operation below. The simplicity of its breakdown meant that its parts could be carried in a large handbag; it was easy to operate; and its faults (shoddiness, tendency to jam, and short range) were more than compensated by its ease of manufacture and supply in high numbers. Magazine capacity: 32 rounds, 9-mm. Rate of fire: 500-550 rounds per min. Effective range: 200 yards

MACHINE-GUNS
COVERING FIRE FOR THE RIFLEMEN

So far we have only considered some of the personal weapons of the infantryman, those he actually carries and uses for both offence and personal defence. Let us now, for a moment, move to the weapons used for supporting the movement of the troops – the machine-guns. These, it will be remembered, formed in most cases the pivot of action; the machine-gun covered while the riflemen moved and vice versa. The only army in which this basic principle was less well defined was the US Army, since, with every man having an automatic rifle, an immense firepower could be brought to bear by rifle fire alone, and the squad machine-gun was less important. This was just as well, since the US Army never had anything which could have been charitably called a squad machine-gun.

What passed as the light machine-gun with the US Army was the Browning Automatic Rifle. This had been developed in 1917-18 as a weapon to be fired from the hip as the infantry advanced across No Man's Land to the German trenches, the idea being to keep the enemy's heads down until the troops were closed in. Since the war was over before many Brownings could be got across to France, the correctness or otherwise of this theory never had a chance to be proven, but with thousands of BARs coming off the production line, something had to be done. So they were fitted with a bipod and called the squad automatic.

They were not the best choice for the job. The design was such that they were violent in action, which led to inaccuracy. The magazine held only 20 rounds and was fitted beneath the weapon, making it difficult to change when laid on the ground; there was no provision for changing the barrel when it got too hot, so sustained fire was out of the question. But like it or not, that was all there was, and the US Army soldiered through the Second World War with it and even used it in Korea. Many ex-GIs swear that it was the greatest, but one feels that if they had ever had the chance to use a real light machine-gun in action they would have rapidly changed their opinion.

In an attempt to provide something better, the Infantry Board grafted a butt and bipod on to the venerable Browning air-cooled medium machine-gun and called it a light machine-gun, but they weren't fooling anybody. It was four-and-a-half feet long and weighed 32½ lb, and that isn't a light machine-gun by anybody's standards.

The British Army undoubtedly had the best light machine-gun of the war in their Bren gun. This was a Czechoslovakian

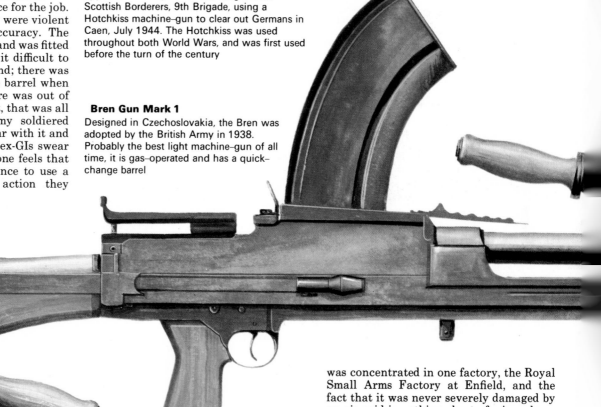

Opposite: Infantrymen of the King's Own Scottish Borderers, 9th Brigade, using a Hotchkiss machine-gun to clear out Germans in Caen, July 1944. The Hotchkiss was used throughout both World Wars, and was first used before the turn of the century

Bren Gun Mark 1
Designed in Czechoslovakia, the Bren was adopted by the British Army in 1938. Probably the best light machine-gun of all time, it is gas-operated and has a quick-change barrel

design which they had examined in 1935 and for which they had bought the manufacturing rights. Gas operated, air-cooled, with a quick-change barrel, fed by a 30-round box magazine on top, it was simple to use, accurate, extremely reliable and trouble-free; it formed the base of fire for the British infantry section from 1938 onwards and, re-worked to the NATO calibre, continues to do so today.

One of the odd features about the Bren gun was that the entire British production was concentrated in one factory, the Royal Small Arms Factory at Enfield, and the fact that it was never severely damaged by an air raid is nothing short of miraculous. But the War Office was well aware of the possibility and asked the famous Birmingham Small Arms Company to develop a simplified version of the gun which could have been built rapidly in any light engineering shop as an insurance against the disruption of Bren production. Harry Faulkner, BSA's Chief Designer, rapidly produced the Besal Gun which although simple in construction was nevertheless reliable. It was made in prototype and proved, then the drawings and jigs were put to one side to await the day they would be needed; they never were, and the Besal – or as it later became known, the Faulkner

machine-gun – never came into production.

Another insurance against enemy interference was to have the gun made in Canada, and eventually about 60 per cent of all Bren guns were made there both for the British Army and also in 7·92-mm calibre for the Chinese Nationalist Army. The Bren was probably the most widely used of all light machine-guns, seeing service with the British, Canadian, Australian and New Zealand Armies, as well as with the free forces of France, Czechoslovakia and Poland, the Indian Army, the Chinese Army and even, in its original Czechoslovakian form, with the German Army.

For heavier support the British relied, as

they had done for years, on the well-tried and faithful Vickers medium machine-gun. This was, in essence, the Maxim Gun of 1887 improved by Vickers in 1912, and it was a water-cooled and tripod mounted weapon which could fire at 450 rounds a minute for hours on end. It was normally issued to machine-gun companies to support attacks or deploy in defence, but each battalion had an allocation of them for organic use. Some regiments – the Manchester Regiment for example – became purely machine-gun regiments, supplying gun companies across the front when needed.

Maxim's original design also appeared in Russia, their standard heavy machine-gun being the Maxim 1910 model. For some unknown reason, probably connected with ensuring reliability in Arctic cold, the Russian version weighed far more than any other pattern of Maxim and, with its peculiar wheeled mounting, tipped the scales at over 160 lb, which was probably why it had wheels. It could also be fitted to a type of sledge for dragging across the snow, and was frequently towed into action by squads of ski-troopers hauling on lines. But a water-cooled gun was not the best answer for the conditions of warfare in Russia, though it took the Russians a long time to realise this. Eventually they introduced the Goryunov SG43, an air-cooled weapon with a heavy barrel, gas operated and also fitted to a wheeled carriage. Like that of many other Soviet weapons, the interior of the barrel was chromium-plated, giving much longer life and allowing sustained fire for long periods without excessive wear.

The standard light machine-gun of the Soviet Army was one of Degtyarev's designs

and known as the DP (for Degtyarev Infantry). This was a very successful design and remained in first-line service with the Soviets for many years. It used a 47-round flat drum mounted on top, was gas operated, and was the foundation of a series of guns for tank and ground use, all based on the same basic mechanism.

Doing the most damage

The German Army, after its experiences in the First World War, had some very definite ideas on machine-guns; they regarded the machine-gun as the prime tool of the infantry, with the riflemen there merely to back it up. The machine-gun was the killer, and all efforts were devoted to putting it into a position where it could do the most damage. After the Armistice in 1918 the Allied Disarmament Commissions made short work of the various gunmakers and placed severe restrictions on manufacture, so that when Hitler came to power in 1933 and began to re-equip the army, there was no problem of what to do with the huge stock of weapons still on hand from the war, as there was in other countries. Thus the Army were ready for a new machine-gun, and due to their views on the tactical use of the weapon and some clever designing, they were to be provided with some of the most effective machine-guns developed during the war, guns which considerably influenced both design and handling in the years which followed.

One of the problems for German gun designers in the post-First World War years was the problem of keeping busy; they were not allowed to produce some types of weapon, and only limited quantities of the permitted types. So rather than fire all their skilled designers they resorted to various subterfuges to keep them working. The famous Rheinmettal company secretly bought control of a small Swiss engineering firm and set them up in business as *Waffenfabrik Solothurn*. The rest of the world thought "What clever designers these Swiss are", but in fact every design which

THE HEAVY MACHINE GUNS

By the end of the First World War the massive firepower of the new machine-gun had brought a radical change to military thinking by giving defenders a great superiority over attacking forces. With the opening of the Second World War, new weapons restored mobility to the battlefield, but throughout the war the infantry of all the main combatants were supplied with automatic weapons which were now the focus around which they were organised. These weapons fell into two main categories: light machine-guns (such as the British Bren gun, the US Browning Automatic Rifle, and the Russian 'Degtyarev' LMG) which were the main armament of an infantry section (between six and ten men); and heavy machine-guns (some of which are illustrated here) which were issued to battalion support companies. These were used to supply heavier, more sustained, and more accurate fire, and usually had a larger, steadier mounting and a more sophisticated gun-sight

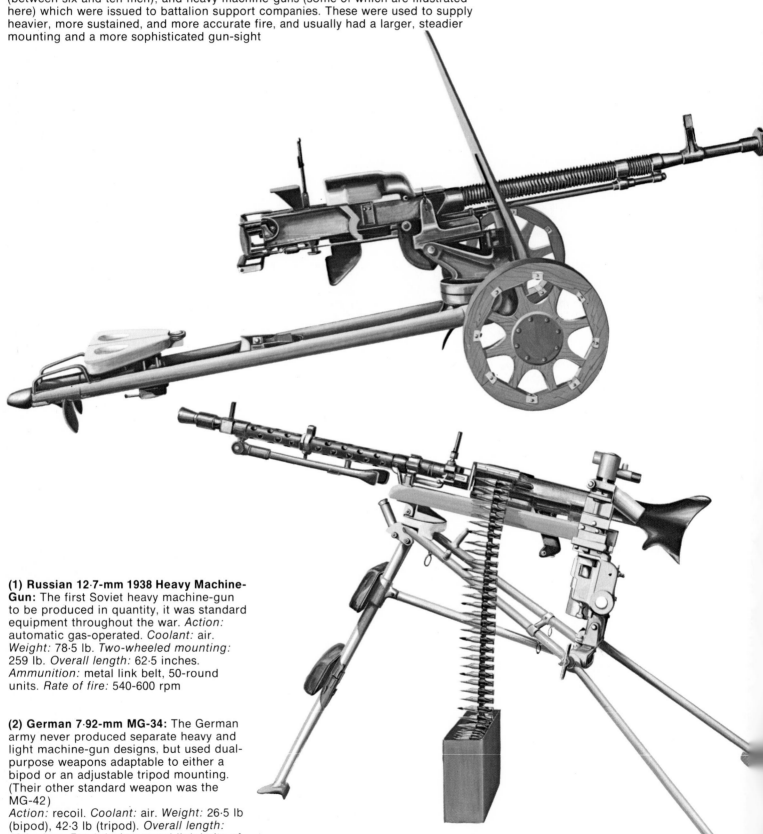

(1) Russian 12·7-mm 1938 Heavy Machine-Gun: The first Soviet heavy machine-gun to be produced in quantity, it was standard equipment throughout the war. *Action:* automatic gas-operated. *Coolant:* air. *Weight:* 78·5 lb. *Two-wheeled mounting:* 259 lb. *Overall length:* 62·5 inches. *Ammunition:* metal link belt, 50-round units. *Rate of fire:* 540-600 rpm

(2) German 7·92-mm MG-34: The German army never produced separate heavy and light machine-gun designs, but used dual-purpose weapons adaptable to either a bipod or an adjustable tripod mounting. (Their other standard weapon was the MG-42)
Action: recoil. *Coolant:* air. *Weight:* 26·5 lb (bipod), 42·3 lb (tripod). *Overall length:* 48 inches. *Feed device:* metal link belts of 250 rounds, made up of 50-round units. *Rate of fire:* 800-900 rpm

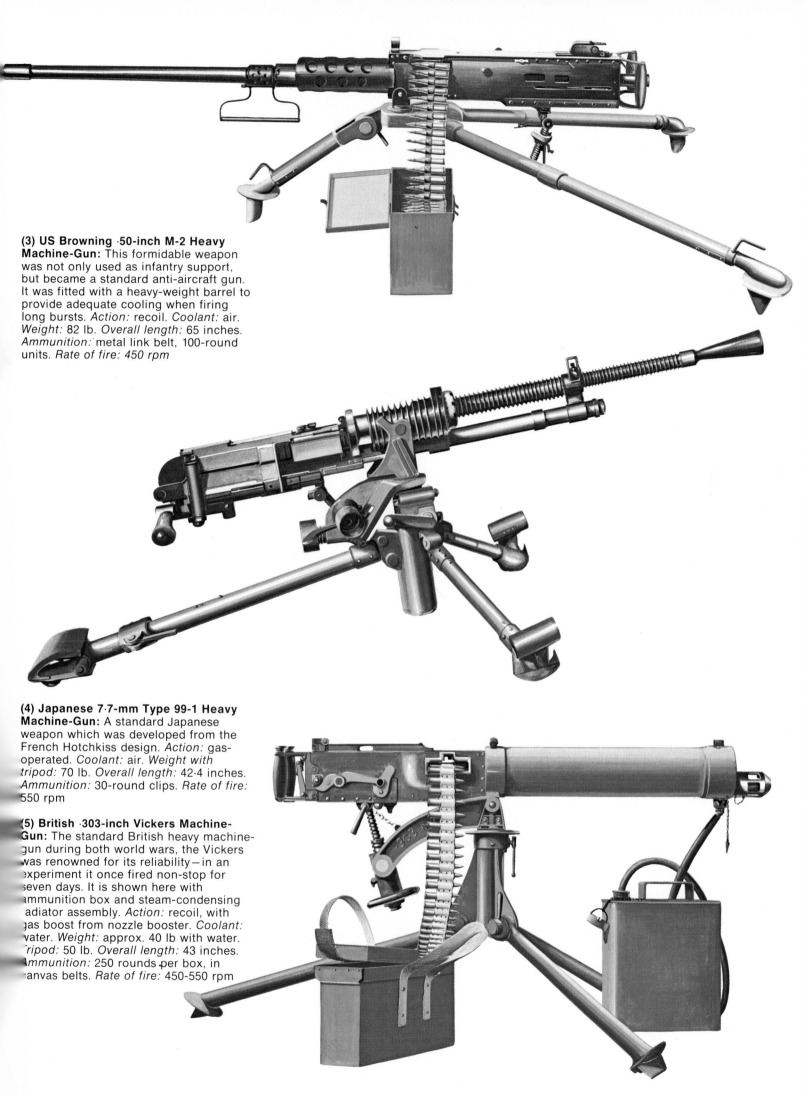

(3) US Browning ·50-inch M-2 Heavy Machine-Gun: This formidable weapon was not only used as infantry support, but became a standard anti-aircraft gun. It was fitted with a heavy-weight barrel to provide adequate cooling when firing long bursts. *Action:* recoil. *Coolant:* air. *Weight:* 82 lb. *Overall length:* 65 inches. *Ammunition:* metal link belt, 100-round units. *Rate of fire: 450 rpm*

(4) Japanese 7·7-mm Type 99-1 Heavy Machine-Gun: A standard Japanese weapon which was developed from the French Hotchkiss design. *Action:* gas-operated. *Coolant:* air. *Weight with tripod:* 70 lb. *Overall length:* 42·4 inches. *Ammunition:* 30-round clips. *Rate of fire: 550 rpm*

(5) British ·303-inch Vickers Machine-Gun: The standard British heavy machine-gun during both world wars, the Vickers was renowned for its reliability—in an experiment it once fired non-stop for seven days. It is shown here with ammunition box and steam-condensing radiator assembly. *Action:* recoil, with gas boost from nozzle booster. *Coolant:* water. *Weight:* approx. 40 lb with water. *Tripod:* 50 lb. *Overall length:* 43 inches. *Ammunition:* 250 rounds per box, in canvas belts. *Rate of fire: 450-550 rpm*

German Machine-gun 42
Designed by Mauser to replace the MG34, this
was intended for mass–production and introduced
a number of novel features. It survived the war,
and modernised versions of it are still in service
with the German Army

The Vickers Machine-gun
The medium machine–gun of the British Army
from 1912 to 1966 and, like all Maxim designs,
a model of reliability; 10,000 rounds an hour of
sustained fire has been recorded in tests with
this weapon

came from Solothurn originated in Dusseldorf. Through Solothurn they were also able to share in the control of an Austrian company, the *Waffenwerke Steyr*, so that weapons were designed in Germany, made in prototype and tested in Switzerland, and then put into production and sold commercially from Austria. One of the weapons which was put forward by the Solothurn Company was a new machine-gun called the MG30.

The MG30 was a highly ingenious design, deriving its operation from the recoil of the barrel. As the barrel went back, the bolt was unlocked by two rollers working in tracks in the gun body; the barrel then returned to the firing position while the bolt travelled back and forwards once more to extract and re-load. It was fed from a fifty-round belt and fired at 800 rounds per minute. Due to careful design it was very stable and accurate, but for some unknown reason the German Army did not take to it. After some improvements had been made it was re-submitted and accepted but then passed to the famous Mauser Company for some improvement. This they did, and the final result was issued as the MG34 and became the standard German machine-gun. As might be expected from such a company, the weapon was excellently made and finished, but this meant that it was not easy to produce, and before the war was over five factories were hard at work turning out more and more of them, trying to keep up with demand.

Great ingenuity

Because of the production problem, and because the fine tolerances of the MG34 led to trouble when firing in dust and dirt, a fresh design was begun which resulted in the MG42. Work started in 1941, and although the 42 looks very much like the 34 from a distance, both mechanism and construction are vastly different. The main point about the 42 was that it was designed for mass-production, utilising stamped metal components and paying less attention to high quality finish. The mechanism was changed so that the bolt, instead of rotating, unlocked in a straight line by rollers which moved in and out of recesses in the gun body. The belt feed mechanism was highly ingenious and built into the top cover of the gun, and has since been widely copied in other designs. The rate of fire was very high – over 1,200 rounds a minute – and this made the gun rather hard to control,

Italian Machine-gun Breda Model 30
An awkward–looking weapon, with a peculiar hinged magazine, fixed to the gun, which had to be filled from rifle clips. Notice that there is no carrying handle; the gunner had to sling it on his shoulder or carry it in his arms

French Machine-gun 24/29
Known also as the Châtellerault, from its place of origin, this was a gas–operated gun with a mechanism very similar to that of the Bren. Numbers were captured and used by the German Army after 1940, but it remained in French Army service until the 1950s

Overleaf: A defensively-sited German MG34 awaits the Red onslaught west of Smolensk in the summer of 1943

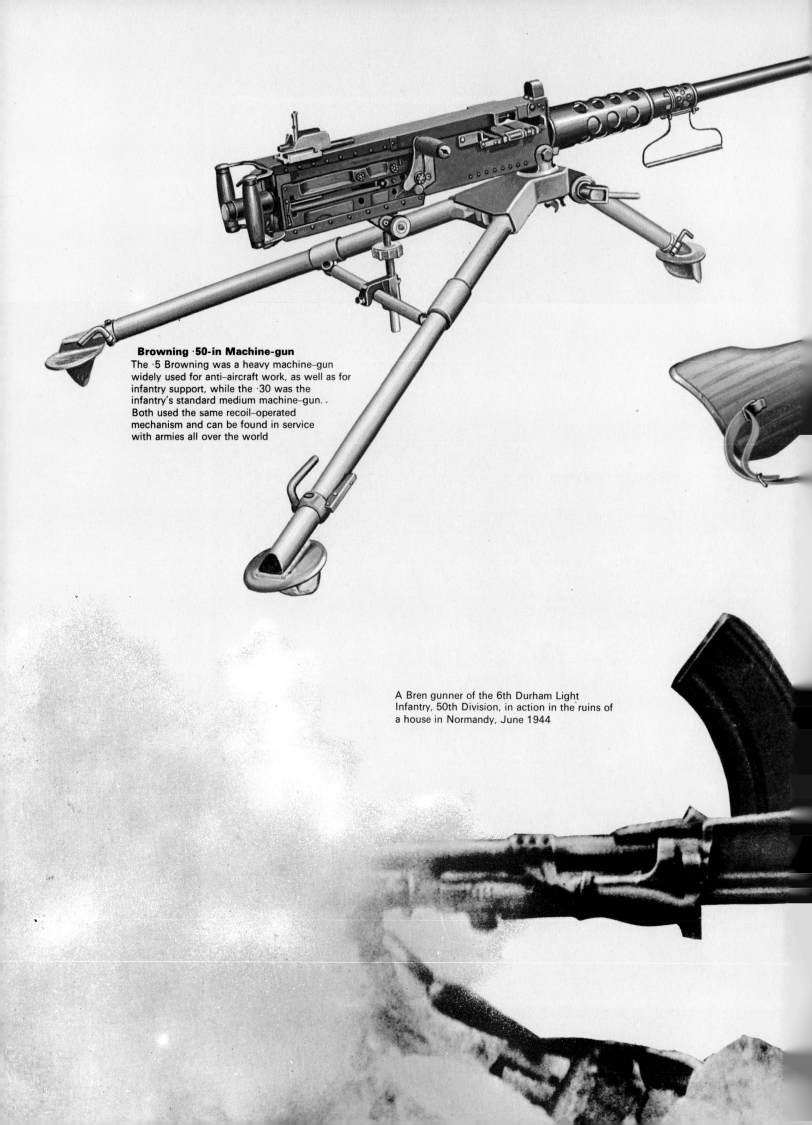

Browning ·50-in Machine-gun
The ·5 Browning was a heavy machine-gun widely used for anti-aircraft work, as well as for infantry support, while the ·30 was the infantry's standard medium machine-gun. Both used the same recoil-operated mechanism and can be found in service with armies all over the world

A Bren gunner of the 6th Durham Light Infantry, 50th Division, in action in the ruins of a house in Normandy, June 1944

Japanese Machine-gun Type 96
An improvement over an earlier model, this weapon used a normal box magazine instead of a cartridge hopper and a rear sight based on the Bren design. Notice the finned barrel, a common Japanese feature, designed to improve cooling

that it could and did fulfil both roles quite happily. A quick-change barrel allowed the guns to be fired for long periods, changing the barrels every 300 rounds or so.

This multiple-role idea took hold during the war; in the early days of the war there was still a distinction between light and medium machine-guns, the MG34 usually acting as the medium gun. To fill the role of light gun there were a number of different designs, most of which had been adopted in the late 1930s simply in order to have some machine-guns – any machine-guns. The MG15, for example was originally designed as an aircraft gun, but by the addition of a bipod and butt it became a light machine-gun; another was the Swedish-designed Knorr-Bremse, a cheap and nasty affair which had the distressing habit of falling to pieces while it was being fired. But these were only regarded as stop-gaps until there were sufficient MG34s to go round, and although many of the light weapons re-

as it only fired at full-automatic. In spite of this it was well liked by the Army. It was hoped that it would entirely replace the MG34 in service, but the demands of the war were so great that it never did, both guns remaining in use throughout the war.

One interesting thing about these two guns was their manner of use. The Germans issued each type with a bipod, so that it could be used as a light machine-gun, and with a tripod and optical sight so that if required it could work as a medium machine-gun; it was all things to all men. Although slightly heavy for a light gun, it was a good deal lighter than most medium guns, so

mained in service throughout the war, they were gradually relegated to reserve and occupation troops, with the better designs going to the combat units.

But when it comes to poor designs, the Italian and Japanese Armies were in the forefront; indeed, one wonders how they managed at all with some of their machine-guns. Take, for example, the Italian Model 30. This was an awkward-looking weapon, full of pieces sticking out and corners to catch the dust. It worked on the blowback system, which may be very well in a sub-machine-gun but which is stretched to its limits when used with a powerful rifle cartridge in a machine-gun. The problem is that the pressure inside the chamber causes the cartridge case mouth to expand and seat firmly in the chamber; but since it is a blow-back gun, at the same time the bolt is opening and trying to extract the case. This usu-ally tears the case in half and jams the gun.

To overcome this the Italian designers fitted an oil pump and tank inside the gun which squirted oil on to the cartridge as it was being inserted into the chamber, so that it would slip out without ripping to pieces. This sort of idea works well in a nice clean trials environment, but put the gun down in a sandy desert and it becomes a different story. The dust settles on the oily cartridge, and every round acts like a valve-grinder as it goes into the chamber, scoring and wearing the steel away to a rough surface

Japanese Machine-gun Type 92
Known widely as the 'Woodpecker' from its peculiar stuttering noise, this was the Japanese Army's medium machine–gun. It was little more than a remake of an earlier design, using a larger calibre

Hotchkiss FM 1922
A French 7·5–mm light machine–gun, developed in 1921, and widely issued to French infantry companies in the years leading up to the war

which eventually grips the cartridge worse than ever and promotes even more trouble.

Another masterpiece from the same designer was the Model 37, the standard medium machine-gun. An air-cooled and gas-operated weapon, it would have been an excellent gun had the design of the bolt allowed a less violent extraction. As it was, it meant that once again the rounds had to be oiled before they went in, with all the attendant troubles. But in addition to this the Model 37 had one of the most peculiar feed and ejection systems ever devised. The cartridges were clipped into a 20-round tray and inserted into the left side of the gun. The mechanism extracted one cartridge from the tray, loaded it, moved the tray across, fired the round, extracted the empty case . . . *and put it neatly back into the tray* before extracting the next round. The tray came out of the right side of the gun filled with empty cartridge cases, which the unfortunate gunner's mate had to strip out by hand before he could start re-loading.

The Japanese also had some odd ideas on feed systems. Their Model 11 light machine-gun had a large square hopper on the left side, into which six ordinary rifle clips were dropped, and the mechanism then stripped the rounds from the clips one at a time, throwing out the clip every fifth round. The original idea was that any rifleman could contribute ammunition to the gun in emergency, but this was ruined by the discovery that the gun did not work very well with the standard rifle ammunition and had to be supplied with special low-powered rounds. To add to the problems, this was another gun where the extraction was violent and the cartridges had to be oiled before they went in.

In 1936 the gun was redesigned to try and do away with these problems; an ordinary box magazine was fitted and the oiler removed, but the extraction trouble persisted and so the machine issued for filling magazines was fitted with an oiler. If anything this was worse, because it now meant that instead of an oily round being open to collect dust for the fraction of a second before it was loaded, the magazines full of oily cartridges were carried around by the gunners, sometimes for several days, collecting dirt and grit all the time.

Eventually the Japanese saw the light and developed a new gun using 7·7-mm ammunition and based very much on the Czechoslovakian ZB26 design which was the basis of the British Bren gun. It was no longer necessary to oil the rounds or provide special ammunition, but production of this gun never reached great numbers and the earlier models were still used throughout the war.

MACHINE GUNS

NAME	CALIBRE	WEIGHT (lb)	MAGAZINE CAPACITY	ACTION	RATE OF FIRE (R.P.M.)	VELOCITY (F.P.S.)	REMARKS
Germany							
MG 15	7.92 mm	28.0	75	Recoil	850	2,500	Ex-aircraft gun
MG 34	7.92 mm	26.7	75	Recoil	850	2,500	Also belt fed
MG 42	7.92 mm	25.5	Belt	Recoil	1,200	2,500	
Knorr-Bremse	7.92 mm	22.0	20	Gas	500	2,600	Principally used by SS units
Great Britain							
Bren Mk 1	.303	22.3	30	Gas	500	2,450	
Vickers Mk 1	.303	40.0	Belt	Recoil	450	2,450	Water-cooled medium
Vickers-Berthier	.303	22.0	30	Gas	600	2,450	Indian Army only
United States							
Browning Auto Rifle	.300	16.0	20	Gas	500	2,800	Squad automatic
Browning M1919A6	.300	32.5	Belt	Recoil	500	2,800	Squad automatic
Browning M1917A1	.300	32.6	Belt	Recoil	500	2,800	Water-cooled medium
Browning .50	.50	84	Belt	Recoil	550	2,930	
Italy							
Fiat-Revelli 1914	6.5 mm	37.5	50	Blowback	400	2,100	Water-cooled medium
Breda 1930	6.5 mm	22.5	20	Blowback	475	2,000	Squad automatic
Breda 1937	8 mm	43.0	20	Gas	450	2,600	Air-cooled medium
Japan							
Taisho 3	6.5 mm	62.0	30	Gas	400	2,400	Air-cooled medium
Taisho 11	6.5 mm	22.5	30	Gas	500	2,300	Squad automatic; hopper feed
Type 99	7.7 mm	23.0	30	Gas	850	2,350	Squad automatic
Type 92	7.7 mm	122	30	Gas	500	2,400	Weight includes tripod
Type 96	6.5 mm	20	30	Gas	550	2,400	
Soviet Russia							
Maxim 1910	7.62 mm	52.5	Belt	Recoil	550	2,800	Water-cooled medium
SG 43	7.62 mm	30.25	Belt	Gas	600	2,800	Air-cooled medium
DP	7.62 mm	20.5	47 drum	Gas	550	2,750	Squad automatic
DShK	12.7 mm	78.5	Belt	Gas	550	2,800	Heavy support and anti-aircraft
France							
MG 24/29	7.5 mm	24.5	25	Gas	600	2,590	
Hotchkiss FM 1922	7.5 mm	19.25	N.A.	Blowback	550	2,250	Approximate figures

10 000 ROUNDS AN HOUR

VICKERS ·303 MACHINE GUN

Hiram Maxim's recoil operated machine-gun was eagerly adopted by Europe's armies. The British went to war in 1914 armed with its finest development, the Vickers .303 Mk. 1, which is still in use today.

Below: Infantry officers are introduced to the new Vickers .303 machine-gun at the Hythe School of Musketry, 1914

I.W.M.

The first machine-gun to be employed in British service was the .45-in. Gardner, adopted in 1882. It was soon followed by the Gatling and the Nordenfelt. All these weapons were 'mechanical' machine-guns which relied on the gunner operating a crank or handle to provide the motive power to load, fire, and unload the gun.

In 1883 Hiram Maxim contemplated these weapons and saw the fundamental flaw in them: the power generated by the explosion of the cartridge was being largely wasted. Only about 25 per cent of the energy in the cartridge goes to propel the bullet, and Maxim realised that some of the untapped 75 per cent might well be used to replace the man on the handle and provide a completely automatic gun.

In February 1889 the 'Gun, Maxim, 0.45-in. Mark 1' was officially introduced into the British Army. In fact it was already in use by that time and had taken part in its first battle in The Gambia on November 21, 1888. A small punitive expedition under General Sir Francis de Winton had been sent out to deal with a tribe which had been making a nuisance of itself by raiding settlements, and among the

Above: Hiram Maxim (left of group) watches a demonstration of his 1884 model gun for the top-hatted gentlemen of the War Office. Over 600 rounds per minute impressed the government and by 1891 a scale of 2 guns per battalion was authorised for the Regular Army. Below: The King's Royal Rifles pose with their Maxim on the North-West Frontier during the Chitral campaign, 1897

armament was a newly-issued Maxim.

On arrival at the fortified village of Robari, the general himself set up the Maxim and opened fire with it. According to his despatch, 'the bullets rained in through the loopholes and between the planks, killing numbers of the enemy. The breastwork and other towers were treated in the same manner, and in a few minutes it was seen that the garrison were issuing from the fort and flying for their lives.' The machine-gun era had arrived.

The Maxim gun was a mechanical triumph but it was a heavy and expensive weapon. Many of the components were heavy bronze castings, carefully machined and fitted, and the whole gun was built with an eye to safety and absolute reliability, with the result that the gun—without tripod or cooling water or ammunition—weighed 60 lbs. Maxim set up a company to build the gun, using manufacturing facilities at the factory of Albert Vickers at Crayford, Kent.

In 1888 the Maxim Gun Company amalgamated with the Nordenfelt Company, moving operations to Erith, and then, in 1892, Vickers bought out the Maxim-Nordenfelt Company and

Above: Dressed as for a Victorian Derby Day, Vickers workers pose with their .45-in. Maxims on tripod and carriage mount in a photographer's studio of the late 1880s. The recoil cup became a standard feature of the Vickers Mk. 1. Below: Maxim action. The barrel recoiled on firing, carrying the toggle and breech block with it. The curved crank handle was forced against its stop and made to rotate the crank in a clockwise direction, making the toggle break downwards, allowing the breech to open as the barrel halted. The crank movement tensed the 'fusee spring' providing power to close the breech and reload

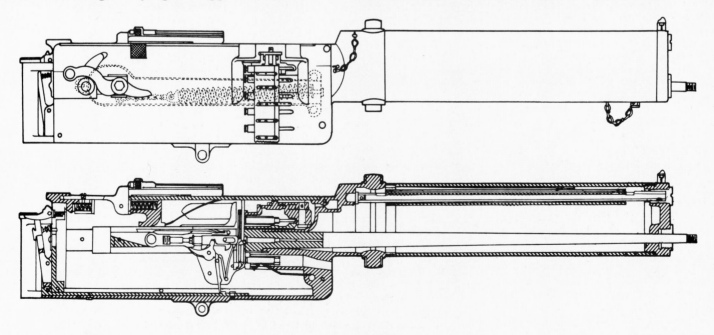

Maxim guns accompanied the BEF to France in 1914 and fought opposite the 7.92-mm. Maxims used by the German forces throughout the early battles. Left: Highland machine-gunners at Landrecies. Below left: Maxim section of the 2nd East Lancashires at Neuve Chapelle. Right: R. Wollen's painting of the Canadians at the second Ypres battle. Inset: 'With our forces in France,' a Maxim section features on a British postcard of 1914

with it the rights to the Maxim gun. Production of the Vickers Maxim continued for several years, but in the early 1900s the Vickers designers decided that there were some improvements which could usefully be made, and they set out to redesign the Maxim. On November 26, 1912 the 'Gun, Vickers, .303 Mark 1' was approved for service.

Human Leg Principle

To understand the redesign it is necessary first to see how the Maxim gun worked. The motive power was the recoil force, developed by the firing of the first cartridge. This cartridge was held firmly in place in the breech by a breech block, and this, in its turn, was securely locked by a toggle-joint unit attached to side plates forming an extension behind the barrel.

This toggle joint is best understood by comparing it with the human leg. The hip, knee and ankle joints are the joints of the toggle, the thigh and shin the struts. In the Maxim toggle the hip joint was anchored to the end of the barrel extension, while the cartridge was held in place by the sole of the foot, the leg being straight. Any pressure on the foot, from the cartridge explosion, passed up the rigid leg to the hip, and since this was firmly attached to the barrel extension there could be no relative movement between the barrel and the breech block. As a result the whole unit—barrel, barrel extension and toggle—recoiled inside the gun casing.

After a short recoil distance a trip lever rotated the 'hip' joint; this caused the 'knee' joint to drop, and suddenly the toggle was no longer a rigid strut but a collapsible collection of parts. The barrel and extension then stopped moving, but the breech block, driven by the momentum of recoil and no longer resisted by the toggle joint, could separate from the barrel, extracting the empty cartridge case. While this was going on the movement of the barrel in recoil had actuated a feed arm which moved the ammunition feed belt across the gun, so that when the breech block began to separate from the barrel it also pulled a fresh cartridge from the belt, holding it in a T-slot in the face of the breech block.

As the block came to the end of its stroke it forced the barrel and extension back into their forward position; then the block itself began to move forward under pressure of a spring. As it moved, so a feed arm forced the new cartridge down the T-slot until it was lined up with the breech, knocking the empty case out of the bottom of the slot and clear of the gun. Finally the block forced the new cartridge into the breech, the toggle slammed up to form a solid strut once again, and the cartridge was fired, starting the whole sequence over again.

This performance was repeated 600 times a minute—ten times a second—and it could be kept up as long as there was ammunition in the belt and somebody kept the trigger pressed. And since 30 per cent of the cartridge energy was expended in the form of heat, it followed that unless something was done about it the whole affair would be red hot in a matter of seconds. To counter this the barrel was enclosed inside a bronze water jacket into which a gallon of water was poured. The barrel heat now went into the water and the barrel remained relatively cool, though the water soon reached boiling point—whereupon it emitted a plume of steam which gave away the gun's position.

Interchangeable Parts

The principal change made by the Vickers engineers was to build the entire gun from steel or light alloy, doing away with the bronze and brass components which weighed so much. By doing this they reduced the weight by one-third. Next they carefully dimensioned the parts so that pieces from one gun were interchangeable with those of another gun, instead of each gun being individually hand-fitted. This, of course, meant that in an emergency a damaged or spare gun could be 'cannibalised' for spares, with the knowledge that the interchangeable parts would fit.

The mechanical arrangements were cleaned up, the biggest alteration being the inversion of the toggle so that the 'knee' moved up when broken instead of down. (By an odd coincidence

BRITISH MAXIM GUN IN ACTION.

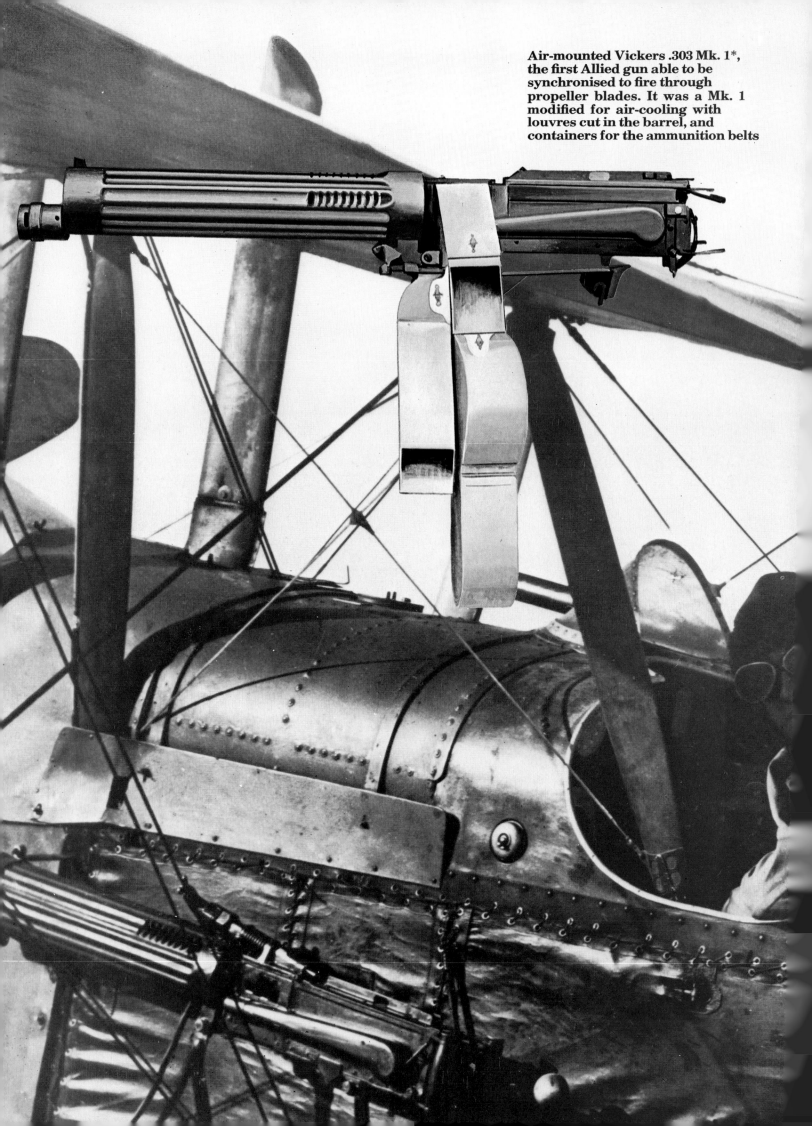

Air-mounted Vickers .303 Mk. 1*, the first Allied gun able to be synchronised to fire through propeller blades. It was a Mk. 1 modified for air-cooling with louvres cut in the barrel, and containers for the ammunition belts

a small German company had been given the task of improving the German army's Maxim gun at about the same time, and their solution was almost identical with Vickers; invert the toggle, cut down the weight, make everything interchangeable.)

Lastly, Vickers developed a water-condensing system to attach to the cooling jacket, so as to economise on water by condensing the steam, and added a recoil booster on the end of the barrel to make the recoil a little heavier and thus provide a reserve of power to cope with the occasional tight cartridge case resisting extraction.

In spite of the improved cooling, sustained fire could still wear out a barrel in 10,000 rounds. At the normal rate of fire of 200 rounds a minute in bursts, this was less than one hour's firing. Consequently the barrel had to be capable of being changed rapidly in action, and that without losing all the water in the jacket. A technique was evolved which, performed by a skilled gun crew, allowed the old barrel to be slipped out and a new one fitted inside two minutes and with the minimum waste of water during the change.

The gunner opened the gun body, removed the spade grips and trigger and elevated the gun. He then pulled the barrel assembly back until the muzzle entered the water jacket, whereupon his assistant pushed a cork into the hole in the jacket. Now the gunner depressed the gun and withdrew the barrel, then slid the new barrel into position. As it reached the front end of the jacket so it pushed out the cork and seated itself in place.

An RE8 prepares for take-off armed with a single Vickers Mk. I* and a flexible Lewis for the observer. Inset: SE5a cockpit with cocking lever for the twin synchronised Vickers, left

Both pics: I.W.M.

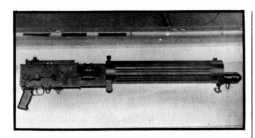

Vickers .303 Mk. 4 prototype

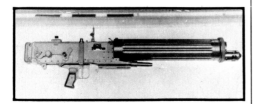

Vickers .303 Mk. 4b

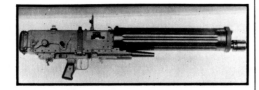

Vickers .303 Mk. 6 AFV gun

Vickers .303 Mk. 7 AFV gun

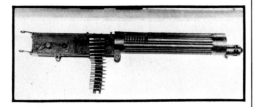

Vickers .303 Mk. 1*

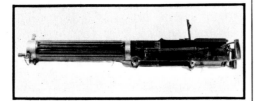

Vickers .5 Mk. 1 prototype

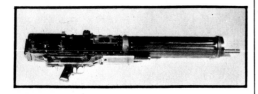

Ian V. Hogg **Vickers .5 Mk. 2**

While the water was draining out of the barrel the gunner put the rest of the gun back and fed a new belt into place, and the gun was ready for another 10,000 rounds. With a good crew the only water lost was that which got inside the barrel as it was being pushed into place.

Absolute Reliability

The Vickers gun accompanied the BEF to France in 1914, and in the years that followed proved itself to be the most reliable weapon on the battlefield, some of its feats of endurance entering military mythology. Perhaps the most incredible was the action by the 100th Company of the Machine Gun Corps at High Wood on August 24, 1916. This company had ten Vickers guns, and it was ordered to give sustained covering fire for 12 hours onto a selected area 2000 yards away in order to prevent German troops forming up there for a counter-attack while a British attack was in progress.

Two whole companies of infantrymen were allocated as carriers of ammunition, rations and water for the machine-gunners. Two men worked a belt-filling machine non-stop for 12 hours keeping up a supply of 250-round belts. One hundred new barrels were used up, and every drop of water in the neighbourhood, including the men's drinking water and contents of the latrine buckets, went up in steam to keep the guns cool. And in that 12-hour period the ten guns fired a million rounds between them. One team fired 120,000 from one gun to win a five-franc prize offered to the highest-scoring gun. And at the end of that 12 hours every gun was working perfectly and not one gun had broken down during the whole period.

It was this absolute foolproof reliability which endeared the Vickers to every British soldier who ever fired one. It never broke down; it just kept on firing and came back for more. And that was why the Mark 1 Vickers gun was to remain the standard medium machine-gun from 1912 to 1968.

With a reputation like that, the Vickers was an obvious choice when machine-guns were demanded for new tasks. When the aeroplane became a fighting machine and demanded armament, the Vickers was chosen as the fixed, forward-firing gun. Fitted with the Constantinesco synchronising gear, which ensured that the gun only fired when the propeller blades were out of the line of fire, the Vickers found employment in virtually every Allied fighter.

In the interests of lightness the water jackets were abandoned and replaced by a thin steel casing perforated with holes which allowed the airstream and propeller blast to blow across the barrel to cool it. Since aircraft combat was a matter of short bursts of fire and not the hours of sustained fire required of ground guns, air cooling was quite satisfactory.

The only other modification required was to produce guns in which the feed mechanism was changed to allow the belt to be fed in from the left-hand side instead of from the right. In this way two guns could be mounted on the aircraft cowling and both would feed their belt in from the outer side, simplifying maintenance and installation.

The next new departure in warfare was the tank, but during World War I the Hotchkiss gun was the standard tank machine-gun, largely because the Vickers was in urgent demand for infantry and aircraft and there were plenty of Hotchkiss guns around which nobody else wanted. It was not until 1930 that a special Vickers tank-gun was approved for service.

This was the standard water-cooled gun but with a pistol grip and trigger underneath the body instead of the familiar spade grips, and a shoulder pad at the rear end for the gunner to steady the weapon. This tank model appeared in a variety of marks, the last of which (the Mark 7) was unusual in having pipe connections on the water jackets which allowed them to be connected to a cooling system built into the tank. In emergency these connectors could be shut off and the gun removed from the vehicle and fired as a ground gun, using a small bipod.

One of the ideas which emerged from World War I was a conviction that a machine-gun firing a heavier bullet than normal might be a useful weapon, especially for dealing with tanks. Vickers simply scaled-up their existing design, scaled-up the .303 cartridge to .50-in. calibre, and by 1924 limited numbers of .50 Vickers machine-guns came into use.

Short-range AA Weapon

The Mark 1 was intended to be a tripod-mounted infantry gun, but it was a heavy beast and the infantry were not at all certain that they wanted it, so only a handful were ever made. The Mark 2 was a tank-gun and got a better reception, going into a number of tanks and armoured cars in the early 1930s. The Mark 3 gun went to the Royal Navy who were anxious to find a fast-firing, multiple-barrelled anti-aircraft gun. The Vickers .50, mounted in fours on special shipboard mountings, proved to be a devastating short-range AA weapon, pouring out 2800 rounds a minute from the four barrels. Finally came the '.50 Class B,' an aircraft gun for the last of the biplane fighters of the 1930s, fighters in which it was still necessary to have guns mounted in front of the pilot where he could get at them and where they needed synchronising to fire past the propeller.

But by 1938 the Vickers began to lose its place. The new monoplane 8-gun fighters carried their guns in the wings, outside the propeller arc, so that synchronisation was no longer needed,

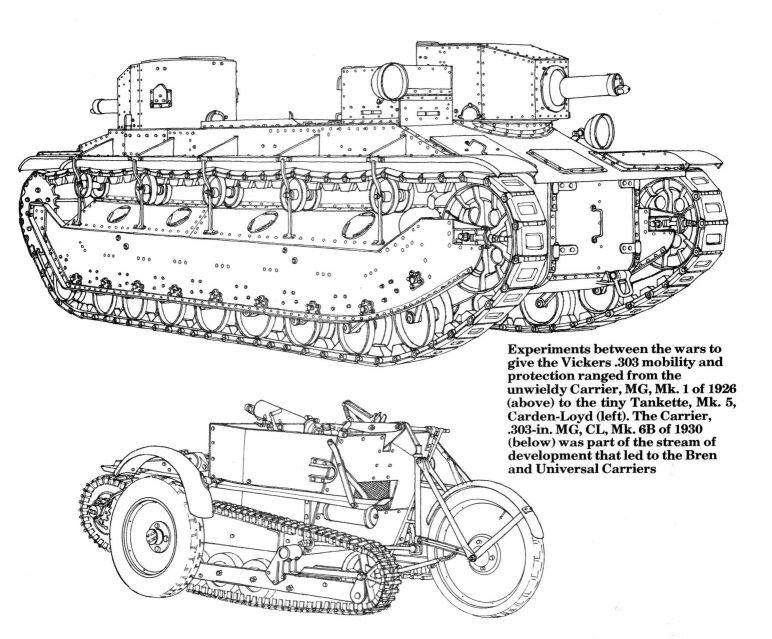

Experiments between the wars to give the Vickers .303 mobility and protection ranged from the unwieldy Carrier, MG, Mk. 1 of 1926 (above) to the tiny Tankette, Mk. 5, Carden-Loyd (left). The Carrier, .303-in. MG, CL, Mk. 6B of 1930 (below) was part of the stream of development that led to the Bren and Universal Carriers

The Vickers was employed in almost every action of the British armies during World War II. Above: A rearguard of BEF machine-gunners covers the retreat to Dunkirk, 1940. Right: Indian machine-gunners prepare for action

and they relied on quantity of fire rather than the effect of a heavy bullet. So the Vickers was taken out of service and replaced by the Browning gun.

In tanks, the water-jacket of the Vickers had long been recognised as a vulnerable spot. One splinter or bullet hole and the water was drained out in seconds, after which the gun soon siezed up due to overheating. In 1938 the Czech-designed Besa air-cooled gun came into service on tanks, and the only Vickers left in service was the old original infantry Mark 1.

During World War II the Vickers added to its reputation in hundreds of actions all over the world. In 1939 a new bullet, the .303 Mark 8, had been introduced for use in Vickers guns. This had a streamlined base which gave it better accuracy at long range, and using this ammunition it was quite possible to put down fire at ranges as great as 4500 yards—2½ miles—a feat which few modern machine-guns can duplicate.

Eventually the marvels of modern

science and technology caught up with the Vickers. New designs of gun came along which were easier and cheaper to make, and new types of steel made it possible to produce an air-cooled machine-gun capable of sustained fire. Moreover, new tactical ideas were against the policy of having 'light', 'medium' and 'heavy' machine-guns. A machine-gun was a machine-gun, and the German army had demonstrated that it was possible to use the same gun as either the squad light automatic or the company heavy support gun.

The day of the 'General Purpose Machine-Gun' had arrived, and there was no place in it for the water-cooled Vickers, in spite of its irreproachable record. In 1961 it was officially pensioned off from British Army service, but since replacement guns were slow to appear, it lingered until being finally declared obsolete in April 1968. That year, in fact, saw its last combat use in the hands of British troops when it was used by the Parachute Regiment in the Radfan.

But in spite of being abandoned in the land of its birth, the Vickers lives and soldiers on. The armies of India, Pakistan and Afghanistan still have numbers of them in their armouries, and the .303 ammunition for them is still made—in Czechoslovakia. The Venerable Vickers will be making itself felt for a few years yet.

GRENADES
THROW AND DIVE FOR COVER

German hand grenades in action during the second Kharkov offensive, 1942

Having taken time out to regard the variety and application of machine-guns, we now turn to another aspect of the infantry-man's personal weaponry: the grenade. Few infantrymen would dream of going into battle without a few grenades in their equipment, for nothing was so lethal at short range. How they were carried was a matter of personal preference; the drill books said one thing, but the soldiers did what they felt was most convenient and carried them in whatever fashion allowed them to be reached quickly. The German soldier was fond of carrying his stick grenade tucked into the top of his jackboot; the Russian had his tucked into his belt or in the pockets of his smock jacket; the conserva-tive Englishman kept them discreetly in his pouches, largely because the design did not lend itself to being carried any other way; the American usually hung them on his equipment by their handles, which was a trifle hazardous.

The range of grenades available was limited when the war began, but as more and more peculiar problems arose, more and more grenades were designed to deal with them, until by the end of the war the number of different grenades in use ran into hund-reds. We can only afford space to consider some of the better known and some of the more unusual models.

Broadly speaking the grenades with which the war began were the same ones which had seen the end of the First World War, largely because many authorities con-sidered they were only suitable for trench warfare. This was soon found to be wrong, but since the old designs were perfectly sound, they stayed in service throughout the war and in many cases are still in use with their respective armies. The British 'Mills Bomb' is a case in point; this was patented in 1915, went through a number of minor modifications during the following three years, and has remained the standard British hand grenade ever since, although from time to time there have been attempts to replace it with something modern.

Action stations

The Mills is the classic 'pineapple' shape, with the cast iron body deeply grooved to allow it to break into lethal fragments. A central striker is held up by the hand lever and locked by a safety pin. The thrower grasps the grenade so as to hold the hand lever firmly, pulls the pin and throws. As the grenade leaves his hand, the lever flies off due to the striker spring power, and the striker hits a cap, lighting a short length of fuse which burns through to a detonator which in turn explodes the grenade. A good thrower should be able to drop the grenade where he wants it up to a range of about thirty yards, but since the explosive was capable of scattering the fragments much further, once he had thrown it he had to be quick to get behind some cover.

In order to reach out further, it was pos-sible to screw a flat disc on to the bottom of the Mills Bomb and fire it from a special cup fitted on the end of the service rifle, using a blank cartridge to launch it. This gave a range of up to 200 yards but, since the flight over this distance took longer, it was necessary to have a fuse in the grenade which burned longer. The standard grenade fuse which catered for both hand and rifle launching burned for seven seconds and in peacetime everybody had been happy with that. But in 1939 when the British Army went to France and began patrolling against the Germans, they found that the seven second fuse had some disadvantages in a hand grenade – the Germans picked them up and threw them back before they had time to explode. Some urgent messages were sent back to England and a new four second fuse was developed for use when the grenade was hand thrown. There were some very surprised Germans on the French frontier soon afterwards.

Eggs and Potato Mashers

The Germans, for their part, were using their stick grenade, commonly known to millions of soldiers as the 'Potato Masher' from its shape. This too had first emerged in 1915 and had been somewhat improved over the years. Its mechanism was a system widely used by the Germans but rarely by other nations, a 'friction igniter'. The handle of the grenade was hollow, with the explosive-filled head screwed on to the end. Into the head went a detonator assembly, from which a string ran down the hollow handle, ending in a porcelain bead. The spare string and bead were tucked into the handle and held there by a screw cap. When the time came to use it, the screw cap was removed so that the bead fell out on the end of its string. Holding the handle in one hand, the thrower pulled the string with the other and threw the grenade. Pulling the string pulled a roughened steel pin through a sensitive chemical, causing it to ignite; this lit the five second fuse, which in turn fired the detonator and exploded the grenade.

An alternative issue to the German Army was the 'Egg Grenade', an oval light steel device about the size of an orange. Screwed into the top was a dark blue button; unscrewing this revealed a string, and the ignition was just the same as the stick grenade – pull the string and throw. But the Egg Grenade lent itself to some unpleasant modifications; the blue igniter could be removed and replaced with a red-capped version which had a delay of only one second, which was of little use as a hand grenade, but if left lying around a position after a retreat often gave unpleasant surprises to any new arrival who didn't know the colour code.

Even more devastating was an unofficial modification dreamed up on the Russian Front. The standard blue igniter set was removed and, using two pairs of pliers, dismantled and the safety fuse removed. The detonator was now screwed back directly into the friction igniter and the grenade was left lying around for a Russian soldier to pick up when the Germans left the position. Of course, since the blue cap looked normal, Ivan was likely to pick it up to throw at the retreating Hermann; he unscrewed the cap, pulled the string, and there was an instantaneous explosion which usually killed him.

Anti-tank warfare

One of the greatest problems of the war was the question of how the infantry soldier could deal with an enemy tank. As we shall see later he was given a number of missile weapons at various times, but there was always a demand for some sort of grenade which every soldier could use if the need arose. An ordinary hand grenade was useless – after all, this was the sort of thing

which tanks were intended to be proof against – so it had to be some special type. The answer to this problem had been discovered just before the war in the phenomenon called the 'Hollow Charge'.

It had been found, many years before, that if a charge of explosive were hollowed out, and the hollowed face placed against a piece of steel, the shape of the hollow was reproduced in the plate. After much experiment and research it was found that if the hollow were made into a regular cone or hemisphere and thinly lined with certain metals, the explosion of the charge would convert the liner into a stream of molten metal which was, in effect, focused by the shape of the hollow and directed at a point on the target armour at such speed and pressure that it blasted straight through. Once this was appreciated, numerous grenades were developed to utilise the principle, for now a small charge of explosive was capable of piercing four or five inches of hard armour. Once the armour was pierced, a jet of flame and hot gas went into the tank and, if it struck a fuel tank, ammunition or one of the crew, it did considerable damage.

The only problem was how to make sure that the hollow portion was in correct alignment with the tank armour, and to do this numerous tricks were tried. One of the most effective was the German Magnetic Anti-tank grenade. This was a cone charge with a handle similar to that of the stick grenade and with the same friction igniter.

Around the cone were three powerful magnets; the soldier could either run up to the tank, stick the grenade firmly in place and then pull the string and run for it; or he could pull the string and throw the grenade so that the magnets struck the armour and adhered. Either way the tank was as good as dead. An alternative, forced on them by the shortage of the special metals needed to make good quality magnets, was to coat the edge of the cone with a very sticky adhesive to hold the charge in place.

Finally they developed the *Panzerwerfmine* – literally translated as the 'thrown anti-tank charge'. This did away with the time action of the fuse and used a simple impact fuse which set off the charge as soon as it struck, so that it was no longer necessary to worry about magnets or sticky stuff. To make sure it landed with the hollow charge pointing in the right direction, a canvas tail was fitted.

But nevertheless, it sometimes happened that the German grenadier was confronted with a Russian tank when he had no special anti-tank grenades handy. He developed his own solution to this problem – the 'Bundle Charge'. He took eight or ten stick grenades and unscrewed the explosive heads, removing the fuses. Then, using a complete stick grenade as the foundation, he strapped the spare heads around it with insulation tape or cord. When a Russian tank appeared, he lay quiet until it went past him, then jumped up, pulled the string

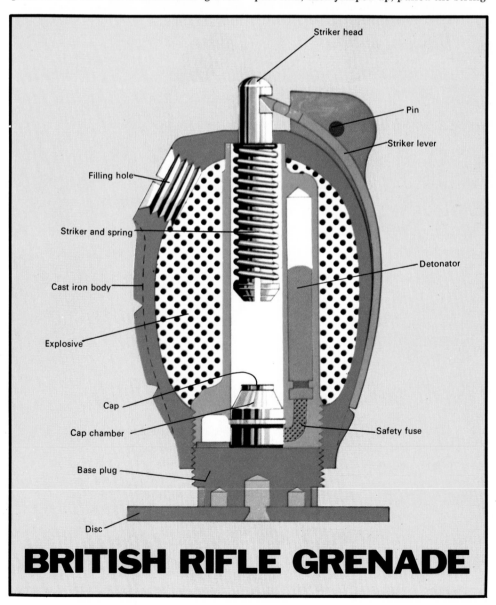

Striker head

Pin

Striker lever

Filling hole

Striker and spring

Cast iron body

Detonator

Explosive

Cap

Cap chamber

Safety fuse

Base plug

Disc

BRITISH RIFLE GRENADE

of the central stick grenade and threw the bundle on to the engine deck of the tank and ducked. The central grenade acted as a primer for the rest, and the explosion which followed was enough to wreck the engine of any tank and stop it dead.

The British Army also had a hollow charge anti-tank grenade, but this was to be rifle-launched from the same cup attachment as was used with the Mills Bomb. Called the 'Number 68' it had four small fins and an impact fuse and was quite effective against two or three inches of armour at ranges up to about 100 yards. But the most way-out British designs came about after Dunkirk, when everybody was trying to produce weapons to repel the forthcoming invasion. From this period came the 'Sticky Bomb', a glass flask filled with nitroglycerin and coated with cloth soaked in bird-lime. The handle carried a striker and lever very similar to that of the Mills Bomb. The thrower pulled the pin and flung the bomb at a tank; the sticky coating adhered to the armour and the nitroglycerin, though un-likely to blow a hole in armour, would severely damage tracks or engine compartments so that the tank would be stopped and then dealt with by some other weapon.

Another fearsome anti-tank weapon was the 'Self-Igniting Phosphorus Grenade' which was a high-sounding name for a lemonade bottle full of phosphorus and benzene. When thrown at a tank the bottle would break open and the phosphorus would ignite spontaneously on coming into contact with the air; this lit the benzene and the liquid fire would run into the various apertures in the tank.

As with Britain and Germany, the American standard hand grenade originated in the First World War, but not with the Americans. It had begun as a French grenade and was adopted by the US Army as being a quicker solution than trying to design and produce one of their own. The ignition system was a trifle erratic, so during the inter-war years the US designers improved it into the well-known 'mousetrap' system, so-called because the lever held down a small spring-loaded arm with a firing pin which, when the lever was released, snapped across like a mousetrap and fired the fuse.

Unlike the Mills design, the lever of the US grenade stood away from the grenade body, so that it was easy to hook it through loops on the clothing or equipment and carry several grenades festooned around the chest ready for instant use. If they were used fairly quickly this was harmless enough (though there was always the danger that some sniper might hit one with a bullet), but if they were carried for several days there was the danger that the handle would

be deformed and, when the pin was pulled, although the lever was still held down its other end could slip free and allow the striker to swing over and light the fuse. If the thrower didn't notice and get rid of it immediately, the results were drastic.

For anti-tank work the US Army had a hollow charge rifle grenade which was used rather differently to other people's designs. Instead of having a cup on the muzzle of the rifle, into which the grenade fitted, the American grenade launcher was an extension to the barrel. The grenade had a long hollow tail which slipped over the extension and the grenade was shot off the end by a blank cartridge. It was highly effective and was later adopted by the British Army.

The cast-iron pineapple grenade used by the US Army was thought to be old and inefficient – though in reality it was no worse than many others still in use – and

efforts were made to try and produce something better. One of the designs proposed was the 'Beano' grenade; the theory here was that, since all Americans could throw baseballs, then the grenade ought to be shaped like a baseball and weigh the same amount. Then there would be no need to train men to throw grenades, since they merely had to use the same technique they had been using since their schooldays.

Unfortunately, it took a long time to get the grenade working satisfactorily, since instead of a time fuse it was decided to use an impact fuse; and since there was no way of telling how the grenade would land, it had to be a fuse which would work no matter which way the grenade fell. By the time the design was perfected the war was over and the 'Beano' never got into service.

The Italians also developed grenades with 'all-ways' impact fuses, which had a

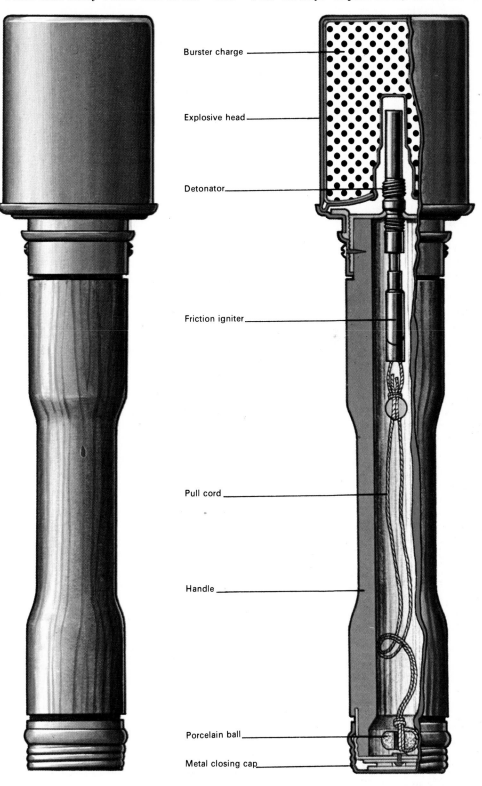

Burster charge

Explosive head

Detonator

Friction igniter

Pull cord

Handle

Porcelain ball

Metal closing cap

British Grenade No. 36M (left)
Last of the 'Mills Bomb' family, the 36M was developed in 1918 but has remained in service ever since. Extremely reliable, it could be fired from a rifle discharger cup by screwing a flat plate onto the base

German Stick Grenade
This was the German Army's favourite grenade from 1915 to 1945, and it changed very little in those years. The friction igniter is screwed into the base of the head and its operating string runs down the hollow handle. On pulling the string a roughened wire is drawn through a sensitive chemical to light the 5-second fuse

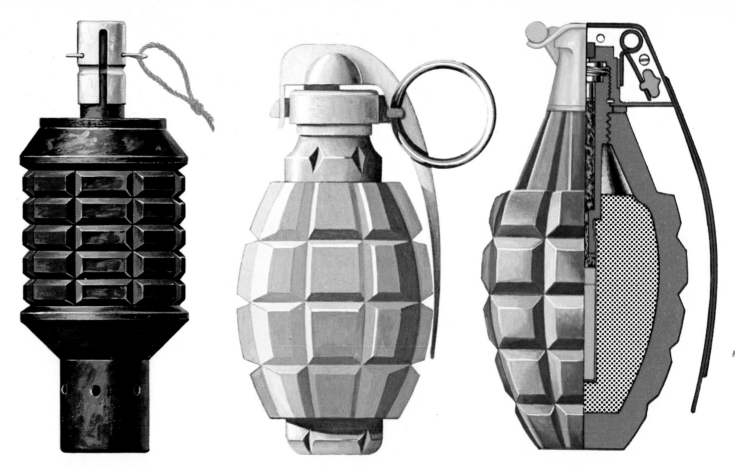

distressing habit of not always working when they landed, but working very effectively if anybody disturbed them afterwards. They were all painted a vivid red, and their violent habits led to them being nicknamed "Red Devils" by the British troops in the North African campaign.

Perhaps the most astonishing grenade was one developed in the latter days of the war by the Japanese. They had tried one or two anti-tank grenade designs without much success and finally, relying on the suicidal desperation of the Japanese soldier, they produced what the Allied troops called the 'Lunge Mine'. This was a powerful hollow charge unit mounted on the end of a bamboo pole and fitted with an instantaneous fuse operated by a string tied to the pole. On the approach of an Allied tank the Japanese volunteer would leap from hiding, holding the lunge mine in front of him, rush up, and jam the explosive charge against the tank. He then said a quick prayer and pulled the string. The resultant explosion pierced the tank with the hollow charge – and the soldier with the bamboo pole.

When it came to stretching the range of the grenade just that little bit further than

the soldier could throw, the rifle grenade was the usual technique, but the German Army came up with a new idea. Every infantry section was provided with a signal pistol; this was the usual one-inch bore single-shot weapon which was loaded with a cartridge containing coloured lights or an illuminating star on a parachute. But the Germans developed a number of small grenades which could be loaded into the signal pistol and launched as offensive weapons. Their size was not very great but they made a satisfying bang and were capable of being aimed fairly accurately.

The next step was to give it a longer rifled barrel, turning it into what they called the 'Battle Pistol'. This could still fire signal cartridges, but also had a range of rifled grenades, similar to the pattern fired from the rifle discharger cup. Some of these were anti-tank grenades, using the hollow charge principle, and in order to give a worthwhile effect at the target, the heads of the grenade were much larger than the bore of the pistol, so that they had to be muzzle loaded with a small-section stem entering the pistol barrel. It took a fairly determined and courageous man to attack a tank with this device, but the grenade was highly effective if it was directed at a part of the tank where the armour was thin.

Japanese Model 91 Grenade (top left)
A fragmentation grenade which could also be fired from a small mortar. In the grenade role the pin was removed and the striker smacked against the boot–heel to start the fuse burning before throwing it. For firing from a mortar a small propelling charge unit could be screwed on to the base

French 'Pineapple' Grenade (top centre)
The French Army's 'Defensive' grenade, which used a mechanism slightly different to that of the British Mills bomb but handled in the same way – hold the lever, pull the pin, and throw

US Army Grenade Mark 2 A1 (top right)
This was developed from the French model after the First World War. The firing mechanism was improved to the 'mousetrap' system, but the operation is the same. It was generally filled with smokeless powder instead of high explosive in order to give larger and more lethal fragments

South African troops in action in the Western Desert, January 1942

Imperial War Museum

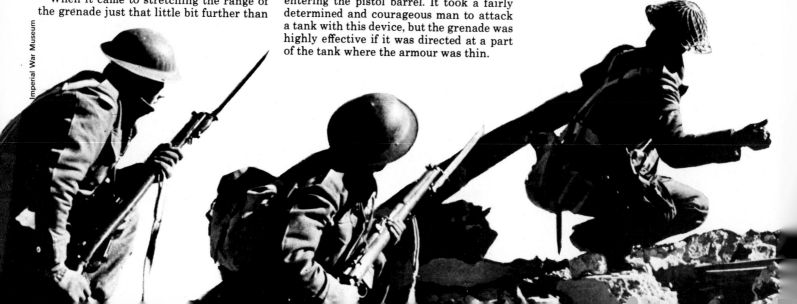

ANTI-TANK WEAPONS
FROM BULLETS TO BOMBS

After loading a Bazooka, an American soldier takes cover as the weapon is fired. The firer kept the Bazooka on his shoulder while it was being loaded, but the loader had to stay well clear of the rear of the weapon as it was fired, because of the flash from the projectile's rocket motor

When it came to the business of attacking tanks at a distance there were some radical changes in technique as the war progressed. At the outbreak, all the major nations with the exception of the United States provided their infantry with an anti-tank rifle. This was no more than a very powerful and heavy rifle firing a special hard slug which could penetrate about half an inch of armour plate. The propelling cartridges were large and the calibre usually about half an inch, so that the weapon had to be heavy to try and soak up some of the recoil. In spite of that, they still kicked like mules and they were far from popular with the men who had to carry and use them. Moreover, after the first few months of the war, the tanks became thicker and harder to stop and the anti-tank rifle soon fell so far behind in the race that most armies got rid of them. The only army to retain them throughout the war was the Soviet Army, though it is doubtful whether they saw a great deal of use after 1943, but since the Soviets never developed any other anti-tank weapon for the infantry to use, they had to keep the rifle for lack of anything better.

In the British Army the anti-tank rifle was replaced by a device called the Projector, Infantry, Anti-Tank, which was shortened to PIAT for convenience. This was a 'Spigot Discharger', the invention of a Lieutenant-Colonel Blacker, who was, in fact, an artillery officer. The PIAT had no barrel; the projectile was a hollow-charge bomb with a long tail and fins, and the tail section was a hollow tube with a cartridge inside it.

Enter the Bazooka

This bomb was laid on a tray at the front of the PIAT, and when the trigger was pressed, a steel rod was driven by a powerful spring into the tail tube of the bomb, where it struck and fired the cartridge. The resulting explosion blew the bomb off the spigot and out of the tray, to send it about 150 yards or so through the air and, hopefully, hit a tank. The explosion also blew the spigot back into the body of the weapon, re-cocking it ready for firing the next shot. It was unpleasant to fire, and it was a trifle alarming to look up after firing it to see the bomb sailing slowly through the air, but when it hit a tank it was highly effective.

The Americans had no anti-tank rifle to replace, but having seen the result of the *Blitzkrieg* in 1940 they realised that some sort of infantry anti-tank weapon was necessary and set about organising one. Back in 1918 a Doctor Goddard had offered them a rocket tube which could be fired by one man, but since the war was over before much could be done with it, and since there seemed to be very little use for it, the idea was turned down. Now it was revived, and the rocket bomb given a hollow charge head. The weapon was a simple smooth-bore tube which the soldier could lay on his shoulder, taking aim through an open sight at the side. His assistant loaded a finned rocket into the tube and connected an electric firing wire; the firer pressed the trigger which connected two torch batteries in the pistol grip and fired the rocket motor by electricity. The rocket launched itself from the tube, giving no recoil to the weapon since the blast simply shot straight through the end of the tube, and there was a very potent anti-tank weapon.

The question then arose of what to call it. Officially it was the 2·36-in Rocket Launcher,

but that was a bit of a mouthful. Some unknown bystander remembered a radio show he had just heard on which a comedian called Bob Burns produced a peculiar musical instrument of his own invention as a comic prop; he called this thing his "Bazooka". And from that moment on the 2·36-in Rocket Launcher was the Bazooka. It was first used in the North African campaign where, according to legend, a German tank commander surrendered after one of his tanks had been hit by a rocket, complaining that he saw no future in going on when he was being shot at by 155-mm guns.

And the Stovepipe

The German Army, in 1942, were beginning to find out a lot of things about Soviet tanks that they didn't know before, such as how hard they were to stop and what a lot of them there were. In desperation the infantry cried for something better than their anti-tank rifles; as it happened an American Bazooka had just been captured in North Africa and, with some rockets, flown back to Germany for examination. The Germans were so impressed with this weapon that they immediately designed a copy, increasing the calibre to 3·5 inches so as to get a more effective warhead. It was officially known as the *Raketenpanzerbuchse* or 'Rocket tank rifle', but the German soldiers, like the Americans and British, preferred to call things by their own names, and this device was christened "Stovepipe" from the flame and smoke which came from it when it was fired. It was also called *Panzerschreck*.

Although Stovepipe was good, the army wanted something easier to carry and more powerful in its effect, while the production people in Germany were concerned at the amount of propellant that a rocket device used. To try and solve all three problems at once sounded impossible, but an ingenious German scientist produced, as his solution, one of the most famous anti-tank weapons of the war. This was the *'Panzerfaust'*, a simple but deadly weapon which was produced in tens of thousands and could stop any tank in existence.

'Tuck it under your arm'

The weapon consisted of nothing more than a mild steel tube about three feet long and an inch and a half in diameter, carrying a primitive backsight and a trigger. Inside the tube was a small charge of gunpowder. Into the front of the tube went a hollow charge bomb; the head was six inches in diameter and carried a charge of three and a half pounds of explosive, powerful enough to pierce seven inches of armour. The tail stem of the bomb had four flexible fins which wrapped around the stem so that it could slip into the firing tube. The foresight was a pin on the edge of the bomb. All the firer had to do was tuck the tube under his arm, take aim, pull the trigger and throw the empty tube away. Pressure on the trigger fired a cap which lit the black-powder charge, this exploded, and a portion of its energy drove the bomb out of the front of the tube, while the remaining blast went backwards and out of the rear. The blast passing out of the rear balanced the recoil due to the bomb being launched, and thus the *Panzerfaust* was a recoilless gun and not, as has often been said, a rocket launcher. It was, moreover, the first 'expendable' weapon; fire once and throw away, a policy which has caught on in postwar years with a number of one-man anti-tank weapons.

Panzerfaust

One of the most remarkable anti-tank weapons developed during the war, the Panzerfaust was turned out in the hundreds of thousands in a variety of sizes. Basically it was a small recoilless gun firing a large over-size bomb. Its hollow-charge warhead could penetrate any tank in the world — and did

Projector, Infantry, Anti-tank
Better known as the PIAT, for obvious reasons, this was the British Army's lightweight anti-tank weapon. It was a spigot launcher, using a heavy steel rod to fire a hollow-charge bomb to about 100 yards. It took nerves of steel to wait until the tank was that close, but the bomb was certainly effective

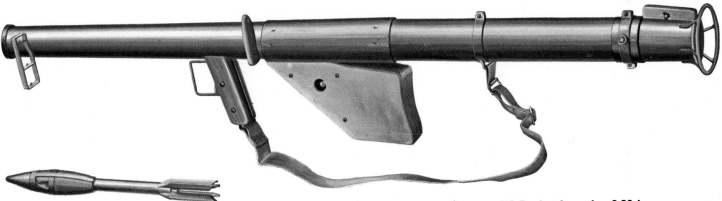

US Rocket Launcher 2·36-in
Better known as the Bazooka, this shoulder-fired hollow-charge rocket launcher could deal with tanks in a surprising fashion. There were various versions, the later models coming apart for easier carriage. A 3·5-in 'Super-Bazooka' was designed but was considered unnecessary, and it did not see service until the Korean War

Panzerschreck
Firing an 88-mm rocket, this launcher was copied from the first US Bazookas which the Germans captured in North Africa. It was an improvement on the Bazooka, and highly effective against the Russian tanks. The blast of flame and smoke from the rear caused it to be nick-named 'Stovepipe' by the German soldiers

PROJECTORS

NAME	CALIBRE	WEIGHT (lb)	LENGTH (in)	TYPE OF SHELL	WEIGHT OF SHELL (lb)	PENETRATION—ALL RANGES (in)	REMARKS
Germany							
Panzerfaust 30*	1.9 in	2.0	31.5	Ho Chg	7.0	7.0	Recoilless
Panzerschreck	88 mm	20.0	64.0	Ho Chg	7.25	4.0	Rocket launcher
Great Britain							
Piat	–	32.0	39.0	Ho Chg	3.0	4.0	Spigot discharger
United States							
Bazooka	2.36 in	13.25	54.0	Ho Chg	3.4	6.0	Rocket launcher

General note: Penetration figures refer to all ranges, since, as the hollow charge bomb operates by the explosive inside it and its special shape, it is independent of range and velocity.

***Note:** Panzerfaust came in other models–60 and 100–which differed only in the propelling charge and consequently in the maximum range. The number indicates the fighting range in metres.

Infantry anti-tank weapons. *Left, top to bottom:* Armed only with small arms and *Panzerfausts*, these last-ditch defenders of the Fatherland were expected to stem the tide of Allied armour in 1945. *Top right:* Polish insurgents take aim with a British PIAT gun during the Warsaw Uprising in 1944. *Bottom right:* A German soldier fires his *Panzerschreck* rocket launcher during fighting in Italy in 1944

MOBILE ARTILLERY

SiG 33s: 150-mm infantry assault guns on PzKpfw I Ausf B chassis

150-mm SiG 33 auf PzKpfw III
Length: 15·58 ft *Width:* 7·34 ft *Weight:* 26,455 lb *Speed:* 25 mph *Range:* 124 miles *Armour:* 20 mm max *Armament:* 150-mm SiG 33

150-mm SiG 33 auf PzKpfw II

Yet another conversion of a foreign tank, the 105-mm light field howitzer on the Lorraine Schlepper

105-mm Light Field Howitzer on Char B1 bis
A conversion of the captured French tank
provided a makeshift SP gun

THE ARMOURED WORKHORSE

Assaulting infantry need close support fire-power. The *Sturmgeschütz* III was the German Army's very own battering ram.

When the German armoured divisions broke into northern France in May 1940, it was not only the tanks that spread chaos and panic among troops and civilians alike. Thrusting into the corridors cut by the armour came the motorised units, the Panzer grenadiers that formed an essential part of the Panzer divisions.

In many cases the advance of these élite units was spearheaded by a weapon at that time exclusively German—the armoured assault gun, or *Sturmgeschütz*. Comparatively few were available for service in the West in 1940, but these weapons were later to be employed in increasing numbers. One particular type was to become familiar in almost every theatre of

StuG III Ausf B, armed with the short 75-mm. L/24 low-velocity gun, climbs a snow-covered bank in the Russian forests

war, and actually reached its peak of production in the last year before Germany's surrender in 1945. This was the Sturmgeschütz (StuG) III.

Mobile Warfare

Throughout World War II, tracked and armoured self-propelled guns were used on a far greater scale by the Germans than by any other of the warring nations. This was initially due to the fact that, even before the war started, Hitler's advisers foresaw the need for such a weapon in the new form

of mobile warfare for which they were preparing.

At a later stage, Germany's industrial limitations encouraged the production of these assault guns. Their manufacture was quicker and easier, and made less demands on scarce materials and manpower than tanks proper.

Another advantage was that, when a tank became obsolete, the model could be adapted for conversion into a self-propelled gun. In this way existing manufacturing resources could continue to be utilised. This process must ultimately have had an adverse effect on the output of tanks; but it was part of the improvisation to which the Germans had often to resort. They also found this an effective way of using captured armoured fighting vehicles. The chassis from tanks of various nationalities were adapted for use as gun-carriages.

There was nothing new in the idea of the self-propelled gun. Wheeled and tracked self-propelled artillery had been produced in World War I. But the concept had not been seriously developed in the inter-war period until the Germans realised its possibilities. In the role for which they intended it, they saw the importance of giving the gun-crew protection comparable to that given by a tank.

The assault gun, as conceived by the Germans, was much more than a piece of artillery moving under its own power instead of being drawn by horses or a tractor vehicle. It was to be designed for use in the most forward areas, in close support of attacking infantry—including the mobile infantry elements of Panzer formations.

Greater Calibre

It was in June 1936, at a time when Hitler's rearmament programme was moving into full gear, that plans were first approved for the production of an assault gun. The specification demanded a tracked and fully enclosed armoured vehicle, mounting a gun of substantially greater calibre and power than any then carried by tanks. At this stage two firms were involved in the design and development of the new weapon. Daimler-Benz were to be responsible for the chassis and superstructure, and Krupp for the gun.

It was not thought necessary to design a completely new chassis for the assault gun. Instead it was decided to adapt the chassis of the PzKpfw III tank (Panzerkampfwagen III)—hence the denomination StuG III.

The gun chosen for the first StuG IIIs was a 75-mm. low-velocity weapon. This, it was considered, would be effective enough for infantry support purposes without placing too great a strain on the mounting. Being mounted in the hull, the gun had a limited traverse.

Unlike the tank, the assault gun had no turret. This allowed a greater weight of armour to be carried on the hull. The frontal protection was 50 mm. thick, while at the sides and the rear, and overhead, the thickness varied from 10 to 30 mm. A further advan-

Süd-Verlag

Above: Assault-gun commander ranges his target with a binocular sight. Assault-gun troops wore the double-breasted jacket of the Panzer troops but cut in field-grey cloth with artillery piping and distinctions. Right: StuG III Ausf D. Experience in Russia made it essential that assault guns should have an anti-tank capability. The long 75-mm. StuK 40 L/43, as fitted to the Panzer IV, was fitted from February 1942. Further improvements included anti-hollow-charge side skirts and a turret-mounted MG 34 machine-gun

Alfredo Zennaro

StuG III Ausf B. Above: Cutaway shows clearly the PzKpfw III chassis and the low-profile fighting compartment. Right: Ausf B advancing at infantry pace

tage of dispensing with the turret was that the vehicle presented a low silhouette, and offered a less exposed target to enemy fire.

Like the Panzer III, the StuG III, which carried a crew of four, was powered by a Maybach 12-cylinder engine. The original engine, the HL 120 TR, developed 250 h.p., giving a speed of 20 m.p.h. on a good surface. In subsequent models it was replaced by the 300-h.p. HL 120 TRM, which increased the speed to 25 m.p.h.

In the earliest model, transmission was effected through a highly complex, preselective gearbox, giving 10 forward speeds. This was soon replaced by a simpler and more practical six-speed system. The chassis was readily recognisable by its six-a-side road wheels, with a drive sprocket at the forward end, through which power was transmitted to the track. The latter returned by way of an idler sprocket at the rear, and three return rollers above.

Tested in Russia

The StuG IIIs battle-tested in 1940 were part of a limited pilot production. Before the end of that campaign, production in quantity was already under way. When, a year later, Hitler embarked on his fateful gamble of invading the U.S.S.R., the *Sturmgeschütz* had plenty of opportunities to

show its worth and its capabilities.

As the German columns thrust into western Russia, the sturdy assault guns were widely employed in the role for which they were originally designed. Operating with infantry divisions, they could push forward where conventional field artillery could not venture, and their mobility and flexibility were invaluable.

As winter approached, the *Wehrmacht* discovered, in spite of their sweeping advances, a growing and unexpected power on the part of the Russians to resist and fight back. The armies which had threatened Moscow, reaching the very suburbs of the city,

were now themselves threatened, as were the German forces on the rest of the vast Eastern Front.

With many of their tanks destroyed or disabled, they came to rely more and more on their assault guns. But now it was a defensive role that the StuG III was called on to play. It did sterling work in this capacity—even against tanks; though for this purpose its short-barrelled, low-velocity gun had obvious limitations.

It was clear that, as an anti-tank weapon, the StuG III needed a more powerful armament. This was now provided in the form of a long-barrelled 75-mm. gun, designated *Sturmpanzer-*

kanone 40 (abbreviated to StuK 40 or PAK 40). This had a much higher muzzle velocity than the shorter gun. It could fire a 12½-lb. projectile up to a range of 8400 yards. It was designed for use with either high-explosive or anti-tank ammunition. For the latter, of course, its effective range would be much shorter.

Change of Armament

The StuK 40 was, in the first place, fitted with a muzzle-brake. This device, extensively used by both sides in the war, consisted of an attachment to the muzzle which trapped some of the discharged gases so as to reduce recoil effect. Later the muzzle-brake was apparently considered unnecessary, as it was omitted. In fact, modifications to the mounting and suspension necessitated by the added stress of the more powerful gun seem to have caused no serious problems.

Hitler, it was said, had insisted on the change of armament. He also demanded an increase in the thickness of armour. But for the time being it was not found possible to effect.

As Germany gathered her strength to renew her offensive in the east in 1942, she had urgent problems in the matter of tank production. The emergence of the Russian T-34 tank—then superior in armour, fire-power, and general performance to any other armoured fighting vehicle in service in the world—had taken the *Wehrmacht* by surprise. So had the general toughness of the Russian resistance after the initial retreats.

German tank losses were enormous, and their industry proved incapable of replacing them at the necessary rate. But assault guns were coming off the assembly lines in more satisfactory quantities. The number of tank battalions in a Panzer division had already been reduced from four to three. Now it was further reduced to two, with the third battalion equipped with assault guns, or with *Jagdpanzers* ('tank-hunters'), built on the Panzer IV or Pz38(t) chassis.

The range of specialised anti-tank vehicles was expanded by mounting high velocity guns on a range of proven chassis—including the Panzer IV. The StuG IV was the same conversion as the StuG III, but built on a PzKpfw IV chassis, the difference in overall length being made up by fabricating a new roof section. It was popularly known as the *Guderian Ente* (Guderian Duck).

Giving the StuG III an anti-tank capability detracted from its performance in the infantry support role, so a further range of artillery models were built. The Ausf G models were equipped with a 105-mm. howitzer with the new *Saukopf* (pig's head) mantlet, now fitted to all the later models of the StuG III.

The *Sturmgeschütze* specialised assault guns were unique in the inventory of the German Army. They proved their worth in providing firepower in the attack and in the great defensive mobile battles the Germans fought, from the Western Desert to the snows of Russia.

Assault guns in Russia. Right: Driver wearing naval-type shell helmet. Far Right: Section advancing in the Caucasus. Below: StuG III shoots infantry into a blazing Russian village. Note the binocular range-finder

FIRE AND MOVEMENT

From the experimental machine-gun carriers produced by British designers in the 1930s evolved the Universal Carrier, its strength and versatility proven on every front from Dunkirk to the defeat of Germany.

The Universal Carrier did not look the most impressive of fighting vehicles. A simple lightly-armoured box with a bowed front and open at the top, was mounted on two narrow steel tracks. Nevertheless, the carriers went to war in 1939 and they were still fighting in 1945, serving in vast numbers with the British and Commonwealth armies. It was a highly manoeuvrable platform for infantrymen and their equipment and was the culmination of a stream of development that started in the 1890s.

During the Boer War the British were using a completely armoured self-propelled vehicle. This was the Fowler Steam Tractor, a 25-ton vehicle created to be a land locomotive pulling a train of armoured trailers. However, it was wheeled. Tracked military vehicles were slow in appearing.

Bren-gun platoon spring from their Universal Carrier on an exercise. The soldier to the left carries a spare Bren barrel

The authorities were not the least to blame, and it is ironic that the War Office rejected what might be described as the conceptual forerunner of the ubiquitous Universal Carrier. It was based on an idea submitted by L. A. de Mole, an Australian civil engineer, who built a working model of a tracked vehicle based on this idea and later found himself drafted into the British Army as an infantryman when he came to England during World War I to attempt again to promote his ideas.

Above: Double anti-tank gun raft mounted on Universal Carrier. The rafts could take a 6-pdr. gun. Right: Carrier, MG No. 2 Mk. I, designed in 1936 to take the .303 Vickers and three-man crew forward under fire

Even so, the potential of armoured vehicles as a means of troop mobility giving, at the same time, maximum protection, was realised in certain quarters well before de Mole's abortive attempts to interest the War Office. As far back as the 1890's, designers working for leading powers were concentrating on the development of armoured cars. Nevertheless, their effectiveness in battle was not put to the test until many thousands of Allied troops had been mown down by the numerical superiority of German machine-guns.

All this was to change during 1917-18. The French and British tanks which broke through the German trench lines harnessed fire power, protection and mobility in a war-winning team.

Fighting Vehicle Experiments

The Armistice put a stop to the intensive developmental work on tanks but experimentation picked up again in the early 1920's. Then, the firms of Carden-Loyd and Vickers-Armstrong started a development programme which did not cease until 1939.

The tracked Carrier concept, itself peculiar only to the British Army until well into World War II, was supplemented early on by another specialized vehicle, the 'Dragon', the name being a bastardised abbreviation of its function, that is, 'drag gun'. This was a tracked vehicle and in addition to carrying a gun detachment and supply of ammunition, could also tow a gun. It was to be the basis for the much later Vickers machine-gun carrier.

Ultimately, the development of Carriers and Dragons was to settle down, during the 1930s, to a programme of progressively improving designs, but prior to this many different types were the basis of experiment. For instance, a cross-country supply vehicle with a Ford engine, the diminutive Ammunition Carrier, emanated from Lt.-Col. P. H. Johnson's Tank Design Department. It was conceived as an amphibious craft, the hull was watertight and it propelled itself in water by a single rear screw. It seemed in every way a success and, demonstrated on a pond near Aldershot in June 1922, proved at home also in water. However, the Tank Design Department closed down at the end of that year and the two Ammunition Carriers which had been built were destroyed.

Due to a large extent to limited finance, work on tanks had to be kept to modest proportions. Thus, the Carden-Loyd Mark VI Carrier, predecessor of the famous Universal Carriers of World War II, were themselves based on the one man tankettes of 1925-26.

The Horstmann suspension was introduced in 1933 on the Dragon, Light, Mark II. Some saw service with the B.E.F. Below: Carden-Loyd Mark VI .303 Vickers machine-gun carrier with enclosed head-covers designed for export

Symptomatic of the financial restrictions of this time was the 'home-made' machine constructed by Maj. G. le Q Martel, in the garage of his own home during 1925. This was his own idea, built at his own expense and made from stock commercial components.

The engine was that of an old Maxwell car and a disused Ford lorry kindly supplied the back axle. Only the tracks were specially manufactured (Roadless Traction Company) and the outcome was War Office authorisation to build four modified factory-made machines. The initial one-man version was followed by a two-man version and eight of the latter were ordered in 1927.

Although the one-man tankette was dropped—it set an almost impossible task for its single occupant of having to drive *and* man the gun—further work on this original design was undertaken during 1927 by Crossley Motors. However, sheer lack of time, both on the part of Martel and the later developers, the Morris Motor Company, resulted in the idea being discarded by them. It so happened that John Carden, of Carden-Loyd, had also built a one-man tank and, on the strength of the Martel-Morris experiments, went forward with developing this project. The outcome was the Carden-Loyd Mark I, with a 3-sided rotatable open-rear shield which covered the driver's head and shoulders and also contained a stripped Lewis light machine-gun. This basic design underwent various developments and in 1928 the improved Mark VI was commencing manufacture by Vickers-Armstrong who had recently acquired the Carden-Loyd patents and appointed John Carden as principal designer for light tanks and tractors.

The excellent Carden-Loyd Mark VI

MG Carrier completed with hooded aperture for a Bren-gun

Carrier, Bren, No. 2 Mk. I kept the sloping rear hull

After Dunkirk some carriers were fitted with steel roofs as AA cover

Universal Carriers go into action. A top speed of 32 m.p.h. was possible

was, itself, to be the basis of a necessarily larger model and thus, the Vickers Carrier, was to become mother and father to a growing family, that of Bren and Universal Carriers, so important in the battles of World War II.

Novel Suspension

It was at the end of 1934 that the successful Carden-Loyd Mark VI was supplanted by a new carrier developed by Vickers-Armstrong. It had a new chassis using a suspension arrangement of two two-wheel 'Horstmann' type units with coil springs—one on each side—and the cross-tube running through the vehicle could be moved sideways, thus creating the possibility of lateral displacement of tracks for gentle turns.

Early in 1935 the first commercial machine incorporating the above developments was produced and a year later three further models saw the light of day, the Cavalry, Bren and Scout carriers, all of which, in due course, were to operate as part of the B.E.F. equipment in the early days of the War.

All three were highly successful, but all three were, also, the same basic vehicle with different types of hull. Obviously the position could be rationalised to advantage and thus, in April 1939, the first contracts were awarded for the latest, and best, type of carrier, incorporating all previous improvements—the Universal Carrier had arrived.

Wheel-cum-track Carden-Loyd Mk. V Tankette of 1927

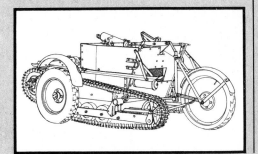

37-mm. PAK mounted by the Germans on captured carriers

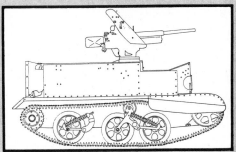

2-pdr. mounted on Carden-Loyd chassis, a dead-end design of 1935

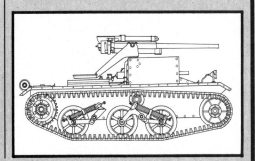

The Universal Carrier went into service during 1940. Its hull was an amalgam of both the Bren and Scout Carrier hulls with the addition of side and rear protective plates. The engine cover, too, had been modified with bullet-proof plates on top. It carried a crew of three, the driver and gunner in the front compartment, and a third man in a back seat placed to the right.

The gun housing could accommodate a variety of weapons, but those chiefly used were a .55-in. Boys anti-tank rifle, a .303-in. Bren LMG or a Vickers .303-in. medium machine-gun, more common on Australian carriers.

Extra Fire-Power

Such was its versatile use of equipment that the Universal Carrier became renowned for its appearance in so many areas of war. On the field, it could be re-armed to suit the current requirements and a 2-in. mortar was mounted on several carrier units to achieve extra fire-power, resulting, in 1943, in the standard fitting of a mounting in the gunner's department.

Although in military use during 1940, the Universal Carriers were not deployed in the dark days of the invasion of France and the Low Countries and the subsequent retreat. Their time of glory was not to commence until the campaigns in the Western Desert.

The price to be paid by the Universal

Above: Carrier at speed. The only overhead protection was the crew's helmets. Right: Scout Carrier and Light Dragon move through shattered Louvain, May 1940

Carriers for being so useful and adaptable was a lack of character, rather in the way a bicycle lacks character. They were there, everywhere, and shunted around to wherever they were needed, doing a vital job, being sent to strengthen pressure points wherever they may have been.

Such events were a day-to-day occurrence in the Western Desert and Middle East campaigns. One such encounter is mentioned by Capt. W. A. T. Synge in his book *The Story of the Green Howards.* Under the command of Maj. T. W. G. Stansfeld, a column of the 7th Green Howards was sent out in April 1942 to go to the rescue of a column of the Durham Light Infantry. Having contacted some of these men, they were then directed to a spot two miles away where the action had taken place. Arriving there, Maj. Stansfeld discovered a scene of carnage, with ruined tanks and dead crew. A message came through from Capt. H. J. D. Collett of the Carrier Platoon, revealing that fourteen enemy tanks were approaching rapidly from the North —Stansfeld and his men were right in the line of attack.

Popper

Musée Royal de l'Armée

Wasp I, Carrier flamethrower on firing trials. A tank within the Carrier's hull fuelled a flame projector with a range of over 40 yards of blazing petrol

As a result, Maj. Stansfeld gave orders to withdraw, and succeeded in so doing only by the gallant help of Capt. Collett who, with his Carrier platoon, gave notable and brave support to the withdrawal operation. This action enabled many guns to be salvaged before the German tanks arrived.

During the month of June 1942, Capt. Collett's Carriers were again involved in outstanding rescue, for which he was recommended for decoration. The 'D' Support Company had been formed on May 1 and as well as Capt. Collett's Carriers, consisted of a mortar platoon, anti-tank platoon, 63 other ranks and eight anti-tank guns. Details of the event are interesting and it appears that owing to mechanical breakdowns a column had lost its way and arrived at its objective late. As a result, confusion was caused, unplanned troop additions occurred and, ultimately, the column ran into barbed wire and a minefield and was fired on by artillery, machine-guns and anti-tank guns with tracers and flares, and forced to withdraw.

It was then decided to break through to Tobruk and Capt. Collett was instructed to return some way and to contact missing elements. This he did, but finding nobody, came back and caught up with the remainder.

By this time the column had caught up with the 9th Durham Light Infantry and, with other odd collections of troops collected en route, was being heavily shelled and machine-gunned. They shortly encountered enemy tanks and infantry, which they attacked, in the process being strongly supported by the Carrier platoon which fired more than fifteen thousand rounds.

Military Medal

Sgt. G. F. Usher, in charge of a section of the Carriers, led his vehicles into the attack and, by virtue of his courage and determination, forced the enemy to withdraw, taking prisoners at the same time. For this, the Sergeant was later awarded the Military Medal.

All of this day, Capt. Collett led his Carrier platoon into the attack again and again, destroying tanks and halting counter-attacks, a tireless man whose vehicles, darting about like flies, contributed in no small measure to the successful withdrawal of the British troops towards Egypt.

All during this campaign, the Universal Carrier was being subjected to further development and experiment

Above: King George VI and his Queen watch an exercise from Carrier. Right: Trial mounting of 25-pdr. on Loyd Carrier

at home. For instance, as early as 1940, it was fitted with a flame-projecting cylinder called the 'Adey-Martin Drain Pipe.' This was a piece of static equipment to be used in the defence of anti-tank ditches and, initially, was given a 'trial run' at Sandown Park, being manned by Welsh Guards.

Later, this device was developed further, becoming the Ronson, a pressure-operated flame thrower. So yet again, the Universal Carrier found itself supplemented, this time by two 60-gallon flame-fuel tanks, filled externally and thus enabling the tank to retain its regular crew. This device or 'flame gun' was attached to the superstructure, the fuel itself being carried via a pipe along the left flank of the tank and into the fuel containers placed at the rear.

There were, however, limitations to the effectiveness of the flame-throwing Carrier, including a throw-range of not more than 50 yards. This, plus the additional vulnerability caused by the external fuel tanks, resulted in the War Office turning it down although the Canadian Army thought differently and organised the production, in Canada, of 20 Ronson flame devices. The ultimate outcome of the Canadian

Above: Carrier Universal Mk. I. The armour was thin—only 12-mm. maximum. Right: Boys anti-tank gun armed Carriers support an infantry exercise, November 1940

development was the incorporation of the device into the M3AI light tanks of the U.S. Marine Corps, the tanks later being named 'Satan.'

One of the most individual developments of the Carrier was known as the 'Praying Mantis'. This incorporated an armoured driving and fighting compartment that, when mechanically operated, rose to a height of 12 ft. above the ground and, in appearance, resembled the insect which gave the tank its name.

Mantis Abandoned

The original idea on which the 'Praying Mantis' was based went back to World War I, when a machine-gun officer, E. T. J. Tapp, formulated the concept of the raised compartment. Not until 1937 was this concept made a practicality. During that year, Mr. Tapp contacted General Sir E. Swinton who was impressed with the idea. Because of his interest and promotion, work commenced on a prototype and in

October 1939, under the surveillance of General Martel, the 'Praying Mantis' was subjected to trials.

After this, it was decided to go ahead on the basis of a two-man compartment, but again there were delays due to more pressing military needs. A revival of interest in 1941 led, finally, to an order being placed and a year later Country Commercial Cars started production of the two-man version.

Tests continued until the end of 1943 when, once again, military needs changed and, finally, during the Summer of 1944, the 'Praying Mantis' idea went completely out of favour. Nevertheless, its planned function is yet one more indication of the basic elasticity of the design of the carrier.

The Germans thought so too! Of all the British tanks captured during the War, it was the Universal Carriers that the Germans made most use of. Nimble and practical, they did their duty in a way that was as unostentatious as their appearance.

MORTARS
BOMBARDING AT SHORT RANGE

While the infantry's task is generally accepted as being close-quarter fighting, the fact remains that they need to reach out to more than arm's length or grenade-throwing range in order to deal with long-range enemy weapons or to bombard a hostile strong point so that they can get closer to it. For this the standard weapon is the mortar, and a wide variety have been developed since the original Stokes mortar of 1915, though few have strayed very far from Stokes' original idea.

The typical mortar is a very simple contrivance; a smooth-bore barrel with a fixed firing pin at the bottom, resting in a baseplate which sits on the ground, with the barrel cocked up in the air by a bipod with some form of screw gear for elevating and traversing the muzzle. The bomb fired from such a weapon is usually tear-drop shaped, with fins at the rear and fuse at the front. The propelling charge is in two parts, called the 'primary' and 'secondary' cartridges; the primary is a cardboard and brass shotgun shell with a charge of fast burning powder which slips into the tail tube of the bomb, at the centre of the fins. The secondary charges, up to six in number, are celluloid containers of powder or sheets of explosive clipped between the fins.

When the bomb is to be fired, it is inserted tail first into the muzzle of the mortar and dropped. It slides down the barrel and the cap in the primary cartridge strikes the firing pin at the bottom of the bore with sufficient force to fire it; the powder in the cartridge fires, and flashes through holes in the tail tube to light the secondary charges; these explode and the rush of gas lifts the bomb and throws it from the muzzle.

It will be obvious from this description that the prime asset of a mortar is simplicity and cheapness; the thing can be made by almost any competent engineering shop without having to call on specialised gun makers, and the bombs are usually made of cast iron with sheet metal fins and one of the cheaper and less efficient explosives inside. As a result, accuracy and long range are not to be expected, but for what they are asked to do, they are ideal. The other virtue of the mortar is that it can be dismantled and carried by a three-man team to any place that a man on foot can go. Generally, they are taken on long marches by some form of transport, but once battle is joined, man-carry is most often the only way of moving them about.

For the simple soldier

Mortars fall into two groups. Firstly there are the small models which throw a light bomb for about 500 yards, mortars which some armies, with more honesty, call grenade dischargers; secondly the medium mortars, about three inches in calibre and having a range of about three thousand yards. There are mortars larger than this, but in most cases they are treated as artillery weapons, requiring the fire control and observation back-up usually found with artillery organisations.

Of the light mortars, the only ones of interest came from Russia and Japan, and they are of interest because of their system of operation. The Russian 50-mm mortars were designed with the idea of making them as simple to operate as possible, so that a few simply-memorised settings could produce almost anything needed. Instead of being adjustable to any elevation between

British infantrymen firing a 3-inch mortar

Imperial War Museum

A Japanese 81-mm mortar crew in action

Associated Press

40 and 85 degrees, which is the usual range for mortars, they could only be set at two fixed elevations, 45 and 75 degrees. Only one propelling charge, a heavy primary cartridge, was fitted to the bomb, and adjustment of range at the two fixed elevations was made by opening a vent in the bottom of the mortar which allowed a proportion of the gas to be released through an exhaust pipe, thus providing less thrust to the bomb. The maximum range was 800 metres, and the operation was very simple: if you wanted maximum range you set 45 degrees and closed the port; for other ranges there was a particular setting of the port and one of the elevations to be used, and that was that. It could all be carried in the head, and provided the mortarman made a good estimation of the range he couldn't miss.

By comparison the British 2-in mortar was an example of private enterprise. It had no sights except a white line painted up the barrel. The operator held it up at whatever he thought ought to reach the range he wanted, pointed it in the right direction by means of the white line, and fired. Like most small mortars it could fling bombs out so fast that adjustment could be done very quickly by eye and the bombs were soon dropping where they were wanted. But it demanded a certain degree of skill, and a good mortarman was a prized asset to the platoon.

The Japanese 'Type 89 Grenade Discharger' was another peculiar item which, for reasons which are difficult to explain, became almost a booby-trap to Allied troops. The weapon was a very simple device which was no more than a short barrel on the end of a long screwed rod, with a curved plate at the bottom. The plate was pushed into the ground and the barrel screwed down the rod until it was against a marker for the desired range. It was then held at 45 degrees, a simple

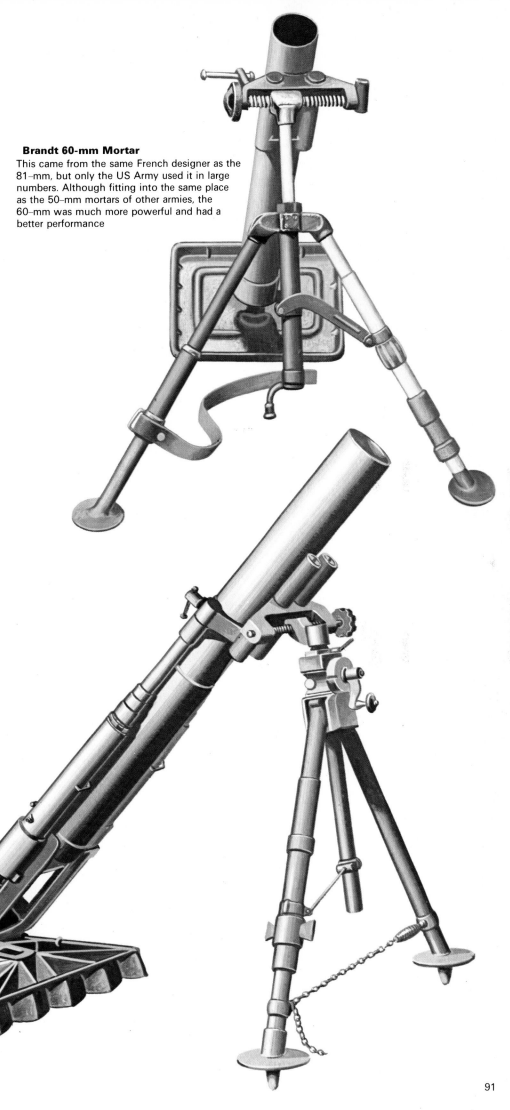

Brandt 60-mm Mortar
This came from the same French designer as the 81-mm, but only the US Army used it in large numbers. Although fitting into the same place as the 50-mm mortars of other armies, the 60-mm was much more powerful and had a better performance

Japanese 90-mm Mortar Model 94
Very heavy for its role, since it was fitted with an unusual hydraulic recoil system, the Japanese 90-mm weapon fired to over 4,000 yards. However, they were relatively few and far between

spirit bubble indicating the correct angle, and the bomb popped in and fired by a trigger and striker. Screwing the barrel down caused some of the rod to move into the barrel and reduce the space inside, so that the bomb was further up or down when fired and thus the gas pushed on it for a longer or shorter time; this governed the range of the bomb.

It was customary for the Japanese mortar-man to carry this mortar strapped to his leg; and probably due to a faulty translation of a Japanese document, the weapon became known in Allied circles as the 'Knee Mortar'. As a result, when specimens were captured and examined, one or two soldiers came to the conclusion that the shaped spade at the bottom was just the right curve to fit a man's leg and the approved method of using it was to kneel down and place the mortar on the thigh. After several Allied soldiers entered hospital with compound fractures of the femur, word got around.

In the medium mortar class there was much less scope for individuality; most mortars adhered strictly to the typical pattern, so much so that two nations on opposite sides had the same mortar firing the same design of bombs. In the 1930s both Italy and the USA had been in the market for a useful medium mortar and both had gone to the same place – a French designer named Edgar Brandt – and purchased manufacturing rights to his design of 81-mm mortar. There were very small differences between the two mortars when they finally reached the Italian and US Armies, largely due to modifications to suit their own style of use and their national manufacturing standards, but nevertheless the ammunition was based on the same designs and was interchangeable.

The heaviest infantry mortar of the war was the German 120-mm, a powerful weapon

British 2-in Mortar
The standard British mortar, one of these was issued to each platoon. It could fire a 2–lb bomb to 500 yards

NAME	CALIBRE	WEIGHT IN ACTION (lb)	BARREL LENGTH (in)	WEIGHT BOMB (lb)	MAXIMUM RANGE (yards)	RATE OF FIRE (R.P.M.)
Germany						
Granatwerfer 36	50 mm	31.0	19.3	2.0	500	40
Granatwerfer 34	81 mm	125.0	45.0	7.5	2,625	15
Granatwerfer 42	120 mm	628.0	73.2	35.0	6,600	10
Great Britain						
2 inch	2.0 in	19.0	21.0	2.0	500	10
3 inch	3.0 in	112.0	51.0	10.0	2,800	10
United States						
60 mm M2	60 mm	42.0	28.6	3.0	1,985	18
81 mm M1	81 mm	136.0	49.5	7.0	3,290	18
Italy						
Brixia 35	45 mm	34.0	–	1.0	580	25
Model 35	81 mm	129.0	–	–	4,425	18
Japan						
Model 89	50 mm	10.25	10.0	1.75	750	20
Model 99	81 mm	52.0	25.0	7.0	3,200	20
Model 94	90 mm	340.0	52.0	11.5	4,150	18
Soviet Russia						
Model 1941	50 mm	22.0	22.0	1.5	800	30
Model 41/43	82 mm	99.0	48.0	7.5	3,200	20
France						
50 mm	50 mm	21.0	21.0	1.75	650	30

MORTARS

which could throw a 35-lb bomb to 6,600 yards, and it was heartily disliked by everyone who came under fire from it. Yet this, too, had originated in France; the original model had been bought for evaluation by the Soviets and then modified to suit their purposes. It went into service with the Soviet Army in 1938, but so many were captured by the Germans in 1941–42 that they found it worth while to issue them to their own units. It proved so effective that eventually it was re-designed slightly to make it a little stronger and went into production in Germany as the *Granatwerfer* 42. In the Soviet Army it had been manned by artillery units, but the German infantry preferred it to their own 81-mm mortar because of its longer range and more lethal bomb. Although heavy, it was easily moved since each mortar was provided with a transporter which could be attached to the mortar in seconds.

French 50-mm Grenade Launcher
This weapon fired a bomb weighing 1·75 lb to a maximum range of 650 yards. It was not used a great deal during the war

Brandt 81-mm Mortar
This mortar was designed in France and bought by Italy, the USA and Japan, among others. As a result, they all had similar weapons during the war. Firing light or heavy bombs, its maximum range was generally about 3,500 yards

MINES
THE SILENT BATTLEFIELD

German Pot Mine

This simple anti–personnel mine was developed late in the war; it is basically a metal can holding about six ounces of explosive with a chemical igniter screwed into the lid. The igniter was simply a soft metal container with flash powder and a glass ampoule of acid inside; stepping on it crushed the ampoule and allowed the acid to contact the powder. The reaction was sufficient to set off the mine

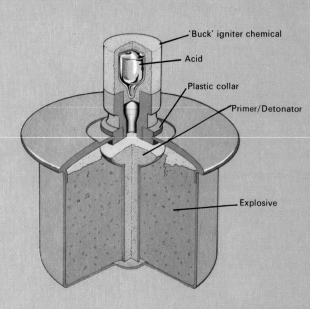

'Buck' igniter chemical

Acid

Plastic collar

Primer/Detonator

Explosive

Russian TM-41 Mine

This was a simple pressure–operated anti–tank mine; a weight of 350 lb would set off the 9–lb explosive charge

Operation of the S-Mine

S-Mine stood for 'Schrapnell-Mine', and this was the favourite German anti-personnel mine. It was buried so that only the prongs of the igniter were above the ground; a pressure of only 7-lb on these would cause the igniter to fire. This lit a propelling charge which fired the shrapnel container into the air; as it was launched, a delay fuse was lit which acted when the container was about 4 ft above the ground and detonated the charge of explosive in the container. This blasted the surrounding steel balls in all directions

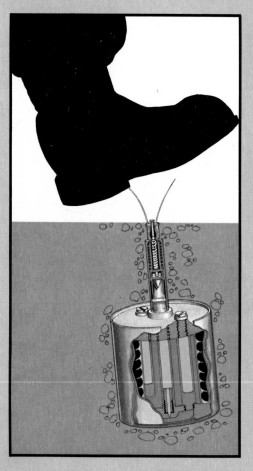

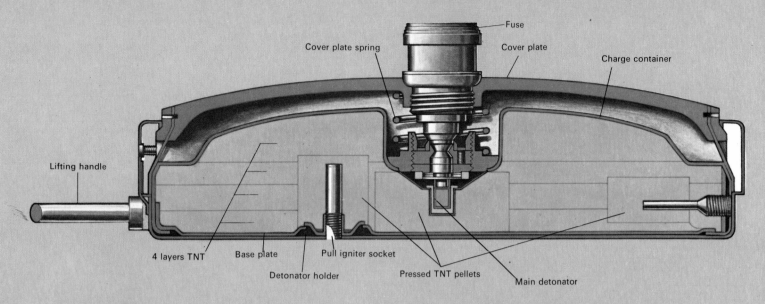

Fuse

Cover plate spring

Cover plate

Charge container

Lifting handle

4 layers TNT

Base plate

Pull igniter socket

Detonator holder

Pressed TNT pellets

Main detonator

Tellermine

The standard German anti–tank mine, this contained about eleven pounds of TNT and was activated by pressure on the fuse set in the centre. About 350 lb would set off the mine, and the blast would rip the tracks off any tank

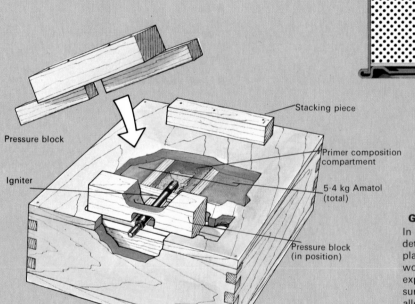

Stacking piece

Pressure block

Igniter

Primer composition compartment

5·4 kg Amatol (total)

Pressure block (in position)

British Anti-tank Mine Mark 7

Developed by Britain after the Second World War, this resembles the German Tellermine but contains almost twice as much explosive

German Holzmine 42

In order to defeat Allied magnetic mine detectors, the Germans began using wood, plastic and glass for their mines. This is a wooden anti–tank mine filled with 10 lb of high explosive. A 200–lb pressure on the upper surface sheared two wooden dowels inside and allowed the firing pin to be released, detonating the mine

German Riegel Mine 43

This anti–tank mine contained 8·8 lb of Amatol, and required a pressure of 440 lb on the ends or 880 lb on the centre to set it off. The explosive rested on the shear wires; when these were broken the striker was freed, and the detonator ignited

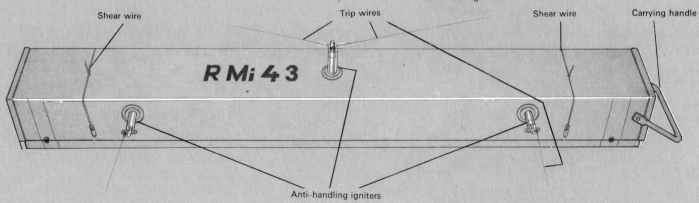

Shear wire

Trip wires

Shear wire

Carrying handle

RMi 43

Anti–handling igniters

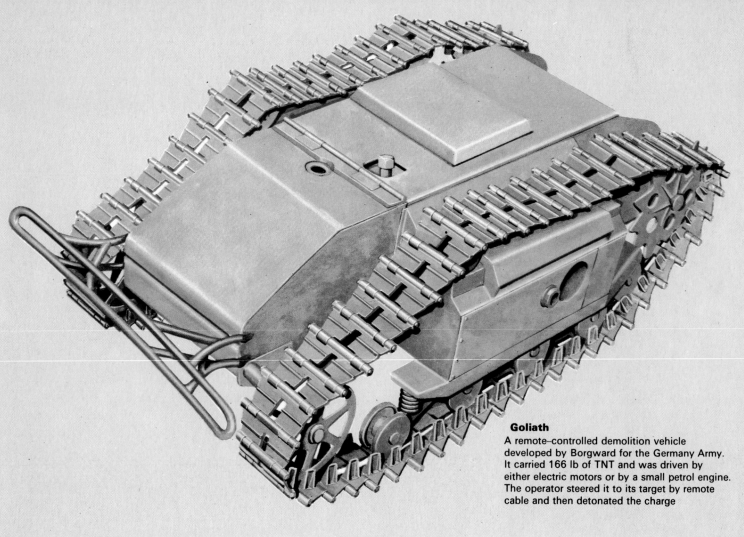

Goliath
A remote–controlled demolition vehicle developed by Borgward for the Germany Army. It carried 166 lb of TNT and was driven by either electric motors or by a small petrol engine. The operator steered it to its target by remote cable and then detonated the charge

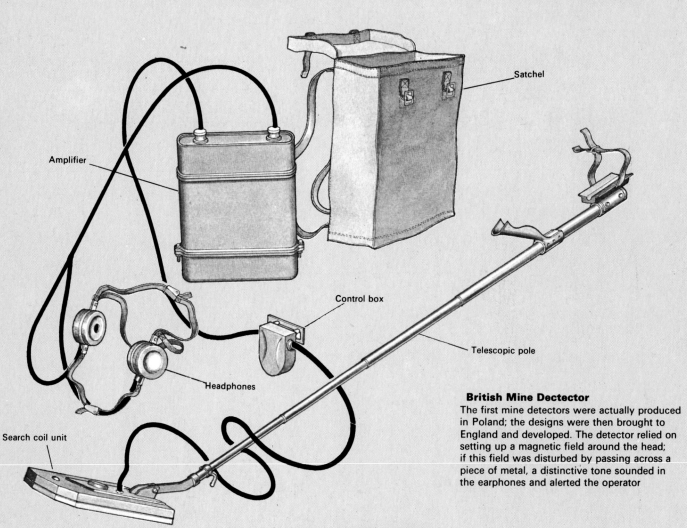

Satchel

Amplifier

Control box

Telescopic pole

Headphones

Search coil unit

British Mine Dectector
The first mine detectors were actually produced in Poland; the designs were then brought to England and developed. The detector relied on setting up a magnetic field around the head; if this field was disturbed by passing across a piece of metal, a distinctive tone sounded in the earphones and alerted the operator

A mine, part of the British defences along the Gazala Strip, explodes during Rommel's attack in June, 1942

ARTILLERY
BIG GUNS FOR INFANTRY

The mortar is generally considered to be the infantryman's private close support artillery; as a result it may come as a surprise to many people to find that infantry were often provided with genuine artillery guns and howitzers of their own. This practice was most common in continental armies, much less common among British and US troops. But sooner or later everybody had a try at it, some giving up quicker than others. In the British Army there was a period after the First World War when special light artillery batteries were attached to infantry battalions for close support, but in the late 1920s it was decided that the infantry would do better with their 3-in mortar and the light artillery was turned to other tasks. But during the war, probably spurred by consideration of what the German Army was doing, it was decided to give the infantry their own howitzer, a 95-mm model put together from a variety of bits and pieces in current production for other weapons. The barrel was 95-mm calibre since this was 3·7-in and they could be made on machinery set up for making 3·7-in anti-aircraft gun barrels. The breech mechanism was that of the 25-pounder, the recoil system that of the six-pounder. The whole thing was built up on a steel trail and had a large shield to give protection to the crew; it was towed by a Bren Gun Carrier.

Unfortunately, nobody had thought to ask the infantry if they wanted such a weapon in the first place, and when the idea was produced for their inspection they were distinctly cool about the whole scheme. It was simply a question of manpower. The battalions were already expected to man mortars, anti-tank weapons, machine-guns and even anti-aircraft weapons, and nobody was clear as to where the men were going to come from to man this new addition. In course of time the question resolved itself; the design of the gun ran into severe mechanical problems which were not satisfactorily sorted out until the war was almost over. By the time the answers had been found there was obviously no need for the gun, so it was quietly dropped.

The US Army had a very similar experience. Their idea was to produce a shortened and lightened version of the standard artillery 105-mm howitzer mounted on a 75-mm gun carriage. Infantry Cannon Companies were formed and trained in the use of this weapon, and were sent to North Africa in 1942. Again the manpower problem raised its head, and it became obvious that

Soviet 76·2-mm Gun
In the early months of the invasion of Russia, the Germans captured hundreds of Soviet 76·2-mm guns. These had their chambers reamed out to take a heavier cartridge, and were handed over to the infantry. They became very efficient anti–tank guns, and formed the basis for many post–war Russian designs

there were grave disadvantages to having one's own pocket artillery compared to being allocated a battery of regular artillery. One drawback was that if the cannon company didn't have the firepower to deal with a particular target that was the end of the story, whereas an artillery battery had lines of communication through the artillery set-up which could call in extra firepower to deal with such problems. For these and other reasons, the cannon company idea was abandoned after the North African campaign. But the howitzer was not a total loss, since it was found to be ideal for

A Russian sniper, the holder of three Soviet medals for valour in combat, leads a patrol on the Volkhov front

Robert Hunt Library

airborne artillery units, giving a combination of heavy firepower and light weight.

The German Army had the best co-ordination of infantry guns. Each infantry regiment had a gun company with six 75-mm light guns and two 15-cm heavy guns. In some regiments these proportions were varied, and it was common to find four 75-mm and four 15-cm. The 15-cm *Schwere Infanterie Geschutz* was an elderly design but it was quite efficient and stayed in service throughout the war. Firing an 83-lb shell to a range of 5,150 yards, it could provide excellent support and devastating shell-power on to any obstacle which stopped the advance of the forward troops. It was provided with a hollow charge anti-tank shell, and also a very unusual demolition bomb.

This weighed almost 200 lb and was a bomb with a tail rod and a set of fins attached to the body and clear of the rod. The rod was slipped into the gun muzzle so that the fins lay outside the barrel and the bomb's warhead was also outside the muzzle. It was launched by a special blank charge loaded into the gun breech and, after leaving the gun, the tail rod dropped off. The head contained 60 lb of explosive and could go to a range of 1,000 yards, and it was a highly effective device for breaching minefields, removing barbed wire, or demolishing pillboxes or other strong points. It was not supposed to be an anti-tank weapon, but from some accounts of battles on the Eastern Front it appears that it was so used in emergencies, with an astounding effect on the tanks that were hit.

Absolutely foolproof

The smaller weapons changed their design several times during the war. The original pattern was quite unique mechanically, being the only artillery piece ever to be built on the lines of a shotgun. The 75-mm *Leicht Infanterie Geschutz* 18 did not use the usual type of sliding wedge breech normal in German artillery, but instead held the barrel in a long box, the rear end of which acted as the breech block. When the lever was pulled to open the breech, the rear end of the barrel tipped up to expose the gun chamber, while the 'breech block' stayed still. Once opened, it was held there by a catch which was automatically released as the shell and cartridge were loaded, so that the loaded gun dropped back into position in front of the breech by its own weight. It was a clever idea, rapid to operate and absolutely foolproof. The rest of the weapon was quite normal, a two-wheeled equipment with a tiny shield, weighing 880 lb in action. It could fire its 13-lb shell to 4,150 yards, and as well as high explosive shell it was provided with an anti-tank shell and a blue smoke shell for signalling targets to dive bombers. Mountain units had a special lightweight version using a tubular steel carriage.

After the campaign in France in 1940 the infantry requested a more powerful weapon, but for various reasons they didn't get one until 1944. Then they got two, the IG37 and the IG42. These were identical as far as the gun barrel and breech went, but were on different mountings. The gun had been designed by Krupp in 1942 and used a normal sliding wedge breech with a semi-automatic action, which opened the wedge and threw out the empty cartridge case automatically as the gun recoiled, leaving the block open and held against a spring. As soon as the next round was loaded the block closed automatically.

This was a useful device since it saved one man in the crew; without it, it would have been necessary to have one man doing nothing but open and close the breech. The IG37 model was mounted on the carriage of the obsolete PAK 37 anti-tank gun, while the IG42 was on a carriage which was in production for the 8-cm PAW 600 anti-tank gun. In 1944 the problem confronting the Germans was production, and by adapting the design to items which were already in production they simplified matters and also speeded up the introduction of new weapons.

The new gun fired the same ammunition as the old IG18 but due to having a longer barrel and an extra part to the propelling charge it could reach out to 5,600 yards.

The Germans also obtained one more infantry gun, known as the 7·5-cm *Infanterie Kanone* 290(r). The (r) indicates 'russian' and shows that it was a captured Soviet gun; it was originally the 76·2-mm Regimental Gun Model 1927, which is said to be the first artillery gun designed by the Soviets after the Revolution. Vast numbers of these were captured in the early months of the German invasion in 1941 and, since the German artillery weren't particularly interested, they were given to the infantry to reinforce their gun strength. It was very popular with its new owners, since, like most Russian weapons, it somehow managed to get more range for its weight than anybody else ever managed. It weighed 1,720 lb, but it reached out to 9,300 yards with a 14-lb shell, which was a very useful performance. It was so well received that the Germans found it worthwhile to produce their own ammunition for it when stocks of captured Soviet ammunition were used up. (In fact, although the Germans called it '7·5 cm' it was actually 76·2-mm in calibre; misleading, to say the least.)

In the Japanese Army the business of artillery support was treated a good deal differently than in other armies; a lot of this may have been due to the fact that they had, for several years, been engaged in fighting in China where the use of large amounts of artillery was never necessary. Consequently the infantry relied much more on their own infantry guns for support, using them in ones and twos and handling them very boldly, bringing them close to the front where they could fire over open sights at short range as well as deploying them further back to give long range indirect covering fire.

One of the most common was the 70-mm 'Model 92', a tiny gun weighing less than 500 lb. It could fire an 8-lb shell to just over

German PAK 38
This 5-cm gun, produced by Rheinmettal, a rough equivalent of the British 6-pounder, was used by German troops throughout the war

German PAK 40
The 75–mm PAK 40 was simply Rheinmettal's scaled–up version of the PAK 38, produced in 1940 to meet the demand for more powerful guns to combat more heavily armoured tanks

3,000 yards however, and was ingeniously designed with wheels mounted on cranked stub axles so that the gun could be set low down for direct shooting – or swung up to give clearance beneath the breech for the gun to recoil when fired at high angles as a mortar. Although some reports claim that it was unreliable and flimsy, the fact remains that it was always in evidence throughout the war and was in use for years afterwards by the Chinese Communist Army, who captured vast stocks of them in Manchuria and used them as late as 1952 in Korea. So it couldn't have been all that ineffective.

The other Japanese infantry gun was a hand-me-down which began life as the

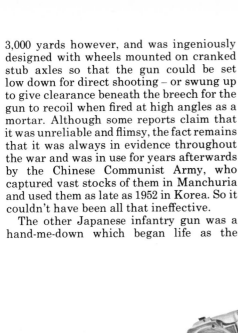

German PAK 41
Krupp's answer to the need for a more powerful anti-tank gun, this was a brilliant design. The barrel tapered from 75-mm at the breech to 55-mm at the muzzle, and its overwhelming performance enabled it to defeat any tank in the world. Unfortunately, the shortage of tungsten, needed for the special shot, limited its life

US 105-mm 'Priest'
The US Howitzer Motor Carriage M7, called Priest because of its pulpit-like machine-gun mount, used the M4 tank chassis as its base. The first models produced went to the British 8th Army in the Western Desert, where they proved highly successful

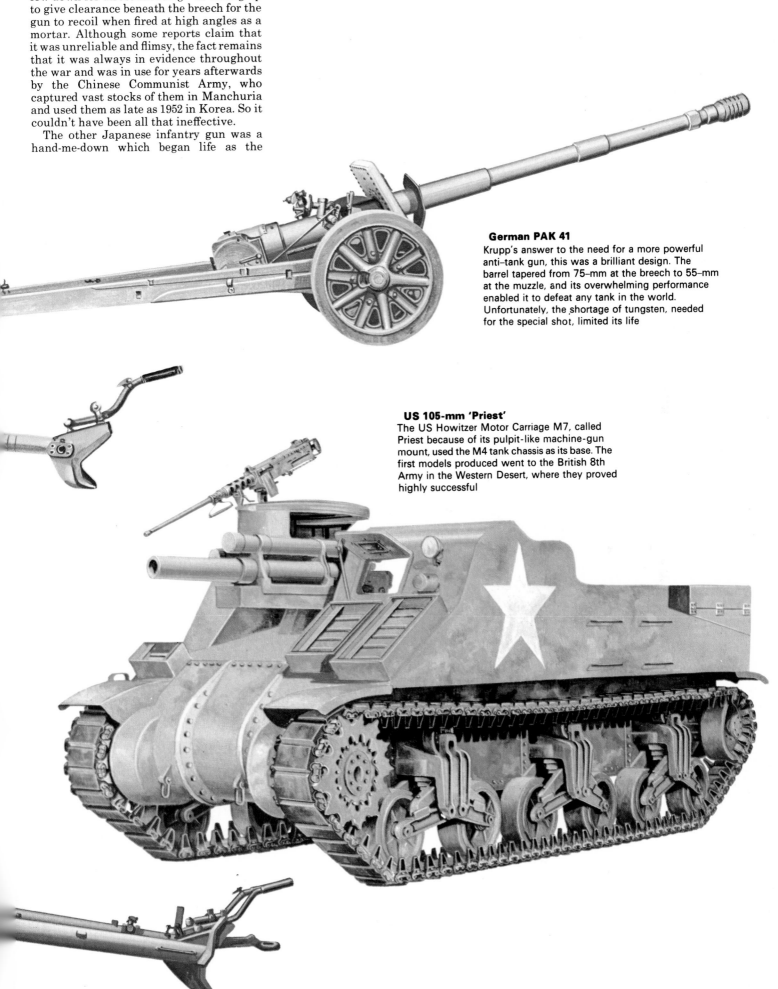

standard field artillery 75-mm gun in 1908. When the field artillery got a better gun they passed the 'Type 41' across to the Mountain Artillery, and in 1935, when they were in turn issued with something more modern, they gave the guns to the infantry. Consequently this weapon was a full-sized artillery piece which weighed almost a ton and fired a 12½ lb shell to almost 12,000 yards. Four of these guns were issued to each infantry regiment, and were kept at regimental headquarters under the Commander's control to be sent as heavy support to points where they were most needed.

The other class of gun which normally fell to the infantry's lot was, of course, the anti-tank gun. For some years it was held that the proper instrument to deal with a tank was another tank, and all the infantry needed was an anti-tank rifle for use in emergency. But as the tank became better understood it was realised that the original vision of grand fleets of tanks battling it out like naval fleets, with the rest of the army standing aside, was unlikely to happen. Tanks instead would be likely to drive through the front and fan out in small parties to do whatever damage they could,

and it looked as if it was up to the people in the front line – in other words, the infantry – to stop them. As a result of this re-thinking, infantry anti-tank guns began to be developed.

It might be said at this point that the British Army, while generally agreeing with the principle, found themselves up against the manpower problem and solved it by issuing their anti-tank guns to specialised artillery regiments and not to infantry. Later in the war infantry regiments did, at last, get anti-tank guns, but not until the artillery regiments had had their full issues.

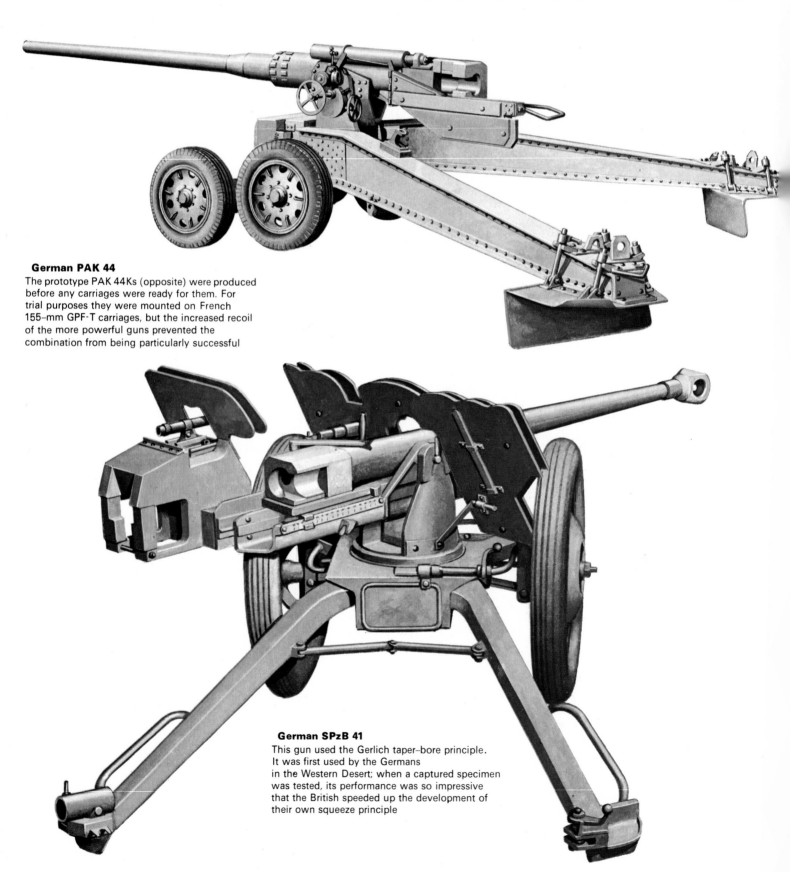

German PAK 44
The prototype PAK 44Ks (opposite) were produced before any carriages were ready for them. For trial purposes they were mounted on French 155–mm GPF-T carriages, but the increased recoil of the more powerful guns prevented the combination from being particularly successful

German SPzB 41
This gun used the Gerlich taper-bore principle. It was first used by the Germans in the Western Desert; when a captured specimen was tested, its performance was so impressive that the British speeded up the development of their own squeeze principle

In general, everybody's ideas about a suitable anti-tank gun were similar; something of about 37- to 40-mm calibre, firing a shell of about 2 lb in weight. Rheinmettal of Germany produced a very good design of 37-mm gun which entered the German Army as the PAK (*Panzer Abwehr Kanone* – Tank defence gun) 37, and this design was more or less copied by several other nations. The American equivalent was the 37-mm gun M3, weighing 990 lb and firing a 2-lb shell at 2,900 feet per second to penetrate two inches of armour at 1,000 yards range. Its use was mainly in the Pacific Theatre of

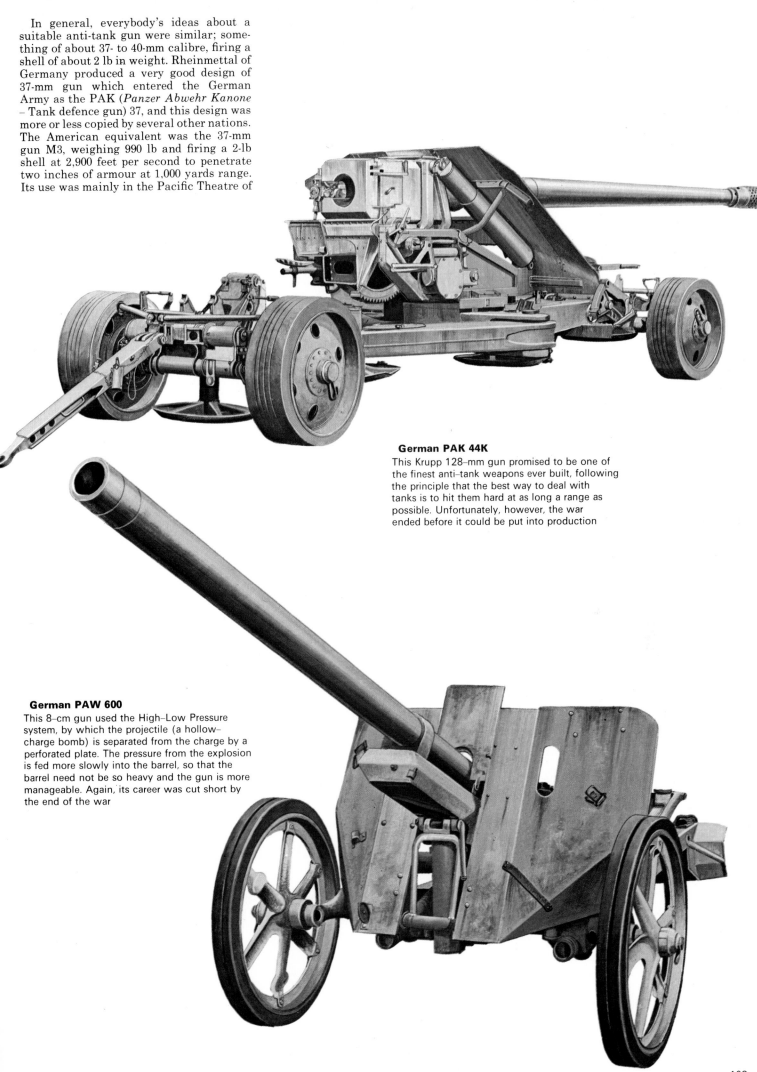

German PAK 44K
This Krupp 128–mm gun promised to be one of the finest anti–tank weapons ever built, following the principle that the best way to deal with tanks is to hit them hard at as long a range as possible. Unfortunately, however, the war ended before it could be put into production

German PAW 600
This 8–cm gun used the High–Low Pressure system, by which the projectile (a hollow–charge bomb) is separated from the charge by a perforated plate. The pressure from the explosion is fed more slowly into the barrel, so that the barrel need not be so heavy and the gun is more manageable. Again, its career was cut short by the end of the war

operations, since by the time the US Army entered the war in Europe and Africa a 37-mm gun was useless against the current German tanks, but it could still cope with the less well-armoured Japanese vehicles.

The Japanese for their part also had a 37-mm gun of very similar performance, but later replaced it with a more powerful 47-mm gun based on a Russian design which they had captured on the Manchurian border in 1939. This weapon fired a 3-lb shell to penetrate 70-mm of plate at 500 yards, but fortunately for the US Army there were never enough of them and for the most part the Japanese had to rely on their older 37-mm which had much less performance and was less of a threat.

Shattering impact
The Russians first equipped their infantry with the German 37-mm PAK 36 which they bought from Germany in 1937. But the Russians were very skilled at tank design, as the Germans found to their cost, and they were of the opinion that a 37-mm gun would not stay superior for very long if a war broke out. They therefore designed a new barrel of 45-mm calibre to fit the German carriage and then redesigned the carriage to produce an entirely new weapon, the Model 42. As well as firing a standard type of piercing shell, this was provided with a special high velocity shot known as an 'Arrowhead' shot, the name coming from its distinctive shape. The body of the shot was of mild steel, but concealed inside was a core of tungsten carbide.

The reason behind this type of shot was a problem which was met by every nation in turn; in fact it was the Germans who solved it first, and the Russian projectile was a copy of a German design. Ordinary anti-tank shell and shot were made of hard steel so as to smash their way through the armour, and the harder they were fired, the more likely they were to penetrate, which was why anti-tank guns had large cartridges and fired at high velocity. But this is only true up to a point. At a point where the shell strikes the armour at about 2,700 feet per second, the force of the impact is such a

shock to the projectile that the point breaks off and the shell simply smashes to pieces without penetrating. It is possible to get some results by placing special protective caps on the tip of the shell, but this only defers shatter to a slightly higher velocity and is not much of a solution.

The only real solution is to use tungsten carbide, a very hard composition which can penetrate without breaking at almost any velocity a gun can reach. But tungsten carbide is three times heavier than steel, is difficult to machine and expensive, so that it would not be practical to make an entire shot out of it. Which all led up to the idea of making a slender core of tungsten and surrounding it in a light steel body of the required calibre. Then, in order to cut down the weight as much as possible, so as to be able to drive the shot at the utmost velocity, the excess steel around the centre of the shot was machined away, leaving two bands at front and rear to support the shot in the gun barrel and a pointed nose to cut through the air; and that in turn leads us to the reason for the shot being called 'Arrowhead' – because of its shape after the cutting away of the centre section.

The Russian 45-mm arrowhead travelled at 3,500 feet per second as it left the muzzle and cut through 54 mm of armour at 500 yards; which brings out another odd point. The ordinary steel shot could penetrate 50 mm at the same range, and the obvious question is "Why go to the trouble for an extra 4 mm of performance?" The answer lies in ballistics and is somewhat involved, but put simply it is that a light projectile (the arrowhead weighed just under 2 lb) 'carries'

less well than a heavy one – one can compare this by throwing a golf ball and a ping pong ball and seeing which goes furthest. So at longer ranges the performance of the arrowhead shot soon fell off. Below 500 yards, (and shooting below 500 yards was preferred anyway since the gunner had more chance of scoring a hit) the arrowhead was superior.

But even with the 45-mm arrowhead it proved impossible to stay ahead of the game, and in 1943 the Soviets produced a 57-mm gun. This was the same calibre as similar weapons in use in the British and US Armies, but had a longer barrel, was more powerful and had better penetration; again, it was

given arrowhead shot. However, the jump from 45-mm to 57-mm was not really enough to get the anti-tank gun well ahead. By this time everybody else was using 75-mm or more, in the hope of producing a gun which would see the next generation of tanks taken care of as well as the current crop. As a result of not thinking big enough, the Russians had to start thinking about a new gun almost as soon as the 57-mm was in service, but the lesson had been learned, and they took a big jump to produce a 100-mm weapon. This was, as might be imagined, exceptionally potent, but very few were produced before the war ended, and eventually it became the standard divisional anti-tank gun for several years after the war.

The Americans had realised the 37-mm was out of date before they ever got into the war, and took an intelligent short cut; they obtained drawings and jigs for the British 6-pounder, converted them as necessary to

Japanese 70-mm Model 92 Howitzer
Maid-of-all-work for the Japanese infantry was this weapon, which could function either as a direct-fire gun or as a mortar, since it had a maximum elevation of 70°

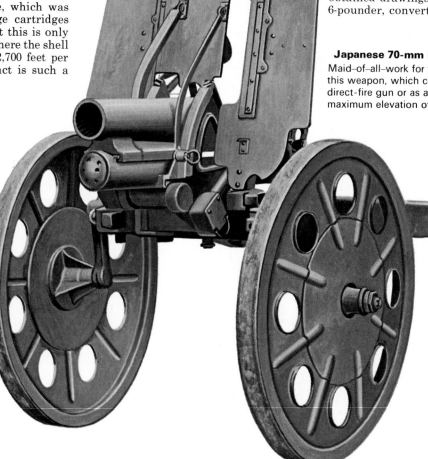

suit American manufacturing methods and standards, and put it into production as the 57-mm Gun M1. As with the British, this was the largest anti-tank gun provided for the infantry, heavier weapons being reserved for special 'Tank Destroyer' battalions. In fact, although the US Army did have some heavier anti-tank guns, there were not very many of them because their policy was to put their anti-tank guns on tracks and go chasing the tanks. This was slightly modified in the latter part of the war, but nevertheless the major US anti-tank strength was in self-propelled weapons.

As befitted a country which had put the tank on the map of modern war, Germany

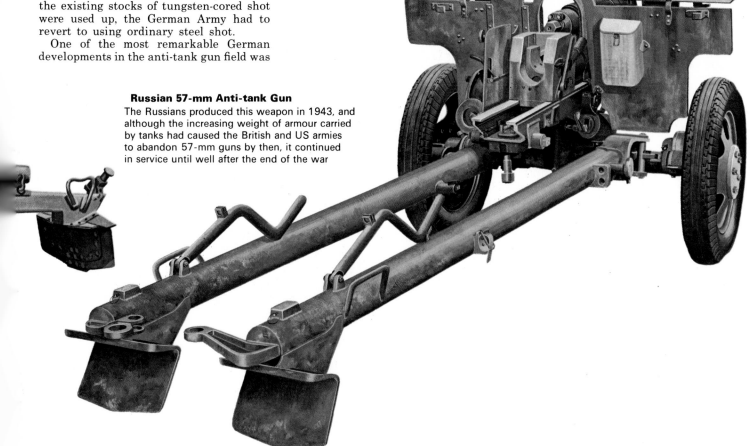

Japanese 47-mm Anti-tank Gun
Japanese tanks were poorly armoured and generally inferior. Consequently, their anti-tank weapons, like this one, were somewhat under-powered

had the most impressive line-up of anti-tank guns. They had begun by a rational programme of increases in calibre to keep up with the estimated improvement in tanks, but their calculations were upset when the Russian T-34 appeared on the scene and from then on their programme was somewhat patchy, as design after design was rushed into service in order to try and beat the Soviet armour back. They were the first to put tungsten-cored projectiles to use, but they were also the first (and only) country to abandon them, due to the pressure of economic warfare.

Tungsten was not native to either Germany or its possessions, and all supplies had to be imported. Consequently there was a shortage, which in the middle of 1942 became so acute that the decision had to be made whether to use the available supplies for machine tools or for ammunition. Finally, the decision was taken to reserve the scarce material for machine tools, and when the existing stocks of tungsten-cored shot were used up, the German Army had to revert to using ordinary steel shot.

One of the most remarkable German developments in the anti-tank gun field was

the 'taper-bore' gun. In this design the calibre of the gun barrel gradually decreased as it reached the muzzle; thus, since the base area of the shot grew smaller, the pressure behind it increased and the shot was propelled faster. The first weapon to use this was the 'Heavy Anti-tank Rifle 41' in which the barrel tapered from 28-mm to 21-mm, pushing the shot out at over 4,000 feet per second. As might be imagined from the calibre, the shot wasn't very big, but it had good penetrating power at short range. A similar weapon tapering from 42-mm to 30-mm was also produced, just in time for the tungsten shortage to put it out of action.

To replace their 37-mm gun, a 50-mm had been designed but did not appear until 1940. This was quite a useful weapon, and although bigger guns appeared later on it stayed in service throughout the war and was still giving a good account of itself at the end. It was superseded by a 75-mm model which was little more than an enlargement of the 50-mm, so much so that it is hard to tell them apart at a casual glance. But the contract for the 75-mm was put out to two companies, Rheinmettal-Borsig and Krupp; Rheinmettal produced the scaled up model, but Krupp developed a brilliant taper-bore gun, in which the calibre dropped from 75-mm to 50-mm. This had an overwhelming performance and would have been one of the finest anti-tank guns of the war, but, like the other taper-bore weapons, the tungsten

Russian 57-mm Anti-tank Gun
The Russians produced this weapon in 1943, and although the increasing weight of armour carried by tanks had caused the British and US armies to abandon 57-mm guns by then, it continued in service until well after the end of the war

FROM THE JAPANESE ARSENAL

The Japanese army was primarily an infantry force, and consequently its field units were relatively well supplied with artillery. The equipment compared well with that in other armies, being soundly constructed, reliable in action, and with good range and hitting power. All these howitzers had their gun counterparts, but these were less widely used because the terrain made the plunging fire of howitzers and mortars of higher value in the Pacific War

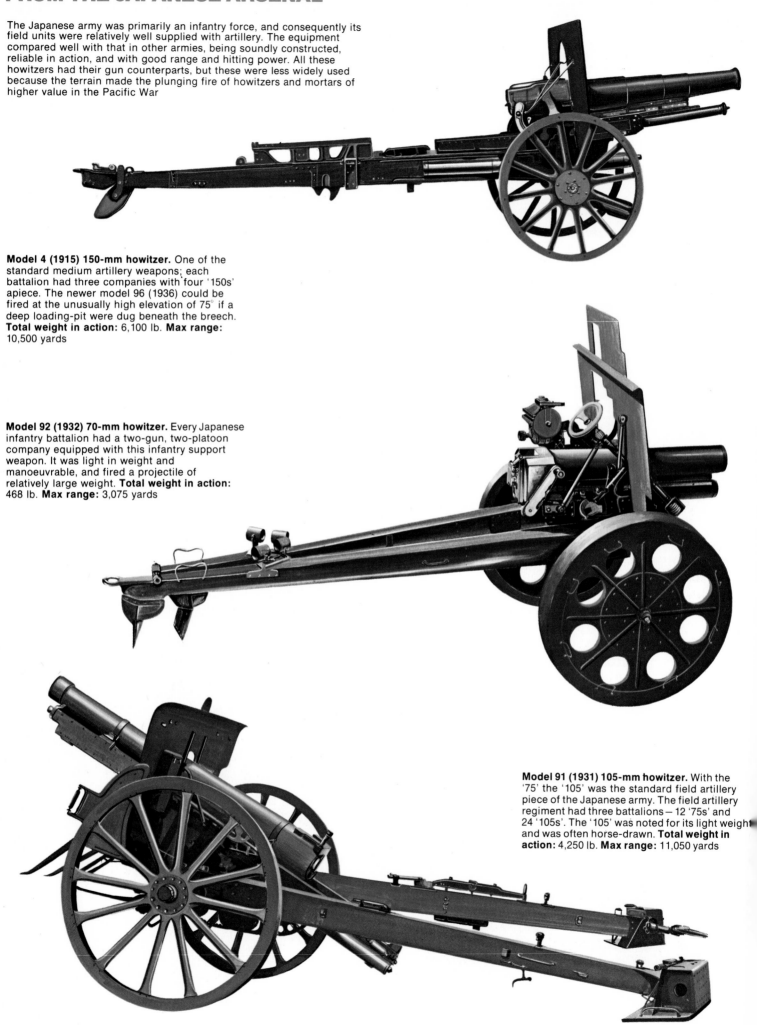

Model 4 (1915) 150-mm howitzer. One of the standard medium artillery weapons; each battalion had three companies with four '150s' apiece. The newer model 96 (1936) could be fired at the unusually high elevation of 75° if a deep loading-pit were dug beneath the breech. **Total weight in action:** 6,100 lb. **Max range:** 10,500 yards

Model 92 (1932) 70-mm howitzer. Every Japanese infantry battalion had a two-gun, two-platoon company equipped with this infantry support weapon. It was light in weight and manoeuvrable, and fired a projectile of relatively large weight. **Total weight in action:** 468 lb. **Max range:** 3,075 yards

Model 91 (1931) 105-mm howitzer. With the '75' the '105' was the standard field artillery piece of the Japanese army. The field artillery regiment had three battalions — 12 '75s' and 24 '105s'. The '105' was noted for its light weight and was often horse-drawn. **Total weight in action:** 4,250 lb. **Max range:** 11,050 yards

BRITISH PANZER KILLER

The 17-pounder anti-tank gun was the 'next generation' after the 6-pounder. Since the height to the top of the gunshield was over 5 feet, the bulk of the 17-pounder posed problems of manoeuvre into and out of position, and also of concealment. But there was no doubt about its punch: it could knock out a German Tiger at 1,000 yards' range. *Overall length:* 24 feet. *Crew:* six. *Max range:* 3,000 yards

KANGAROO-BATTLEFIELD TRANSPORT

The Kangaroo armoured troop-carrier was another Allied improvisation. It was produced by removing the turret from a Canadian-built Ram tank (a machine developed from American and British components, but which was never used in action as a tank). As usual, there were many variants. depending upon workshop facilities. This variant carried a section of ten infantrymen, and was armed with a single ·50-inch machine-gun

US Self-Propelled Howitzer M37
Infantry depend on artillery, and a good example of the standard support weapon is this 105–mm howitzer. Firing a 32–lb high explosive shell to 12,200 yards, it could also fire smoke and anti–tank shells. The equipment weighed 20 tons and could move at 35 mph on roads

CHI HA Type 97 (1937) Medium Tank. Used in China during the latter part of the war, this tank embodied features learned from tankette and light-tank designs. It was also encountered in Burma and on Guadalcanal. *Weight:* 15 tons. *Length:* 18 feet. *Armour:* 25-mm maximum. *Crew:* Four. *Armament:* One 57-mm gun, two 7·7-mm MG. *Speed:* 25 mph. *Range:* 120 miles.

The Gerlich Squeeze Principle
The squeeze principle involves using a barrel tapering towards the muzzle. As the shell travels along the barrel, the supporting studs are forced into their recesses and the steel sealing band is compressed. Since the shell is smaller at the muzzle than at the breech, the force of the explosion is more concentrated, and the tungsten–cored shot attains a higher velocity

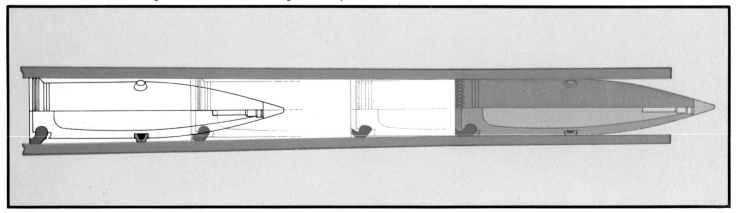

US M8 Self-propelled Howitzer
The M2 75–mm howitzer mounted on a tracked chassis, and given a remarkable 1½ in of armour protection. In general, self–propelled guns did away with such heavy armour; after all, their function was to give guns flexibility and mobility, not to become armoured fighting vehicles

ban finished it. Tungsten was necessary for the ammunition of these taper-bore guns since the tungsten core could be fitted with mild steel skirts which deformed as the barrel tapered; and of course, it was of little use to shoot steel projectiles at velocities over 4,000 feet per second knowing they would shatter on the target.

The most famous German anti-tank gun was, of course, the Eighty-eight. The original '88' was an anti-aircraft gun which was found to have a useful performance against tanks. As a result of this Krupp were asked to produce a purely anti-tank Eighty-eight, which they did in 1943. This was known as the PAK 43 and, instead of being the usual two-wheeled pattern, was carried on a four-wheeled mounting. In action the wheels were removed and the gun sat on a girder platform so that it could swing completely round in a circle and thus fire in any direction. Unfortunately this platform was difficult to make, and since things on the Russian Front were looking bad, the barrel was mounted on to a normal two-wheel pattern put together from stocks of spare parts for other guns. The result looked odd and was heavy and cumbersome to move, but it had an excellent performance. It was claimed by some troops on the Russian Front that they habitually stopped T-34 tanks at ranges up to 3,000 yards; even allowing for exaggeration in telling the tale, it was still a remarkable performance.

Towards the end of the war came the most potent anti-tank gun ever developed, a 5·9-in monster firing a 60-lb shell. Its performance was twice that of the Eighty-eight, but fortunately for the Allies only a handful were made before the war ended.

ANTI-TANK GUNS

NAME	CALIBRE	WEIGHT IN ACTION (lb)	SHELL WEIGHT (lb)	VELOCITY MUZZLE f.p.s.	PENETRATION	REMARKS
Germany						
S.Pz B 41	28 mm	500	0.26†	4,595	94 mm @ 100 m	Taper bore
PAK 36	37 mm	950	1.5	2,500	65 mm @ 100 m	
PAK 41	42 mm	1,400	0.75†	4,150	120 mm @ 100 m	Taper bore
PAK 38	50 mm	2,175	1.81†	3,925	120 mm @ 500 m	
PAK 40	75 mm	3,150	7.04†	3,250	154 mm @ 500 m	
PAK 41	75 mm	2,990	5.72†	3,700	209 mm @ 500 m	Taper bore
PAK 36(r)	76.2 mm	3,800	8.9†	3,250	158 mm @ 500 m	Ex-Russian field gun
PAW 600	81 mm	1,325	5.9*	1,700	140 mm	Smoothbore
PAK 43	88 mm	8,150	16.0†	3,700	274 mm @ 500 m	PAK 43/41 similar
PAK 44	128 mm	22,500	6.20	3,200	230 mm @ 1,000 m	Very few made
Great Britain						
Six-pounder	2.244 in	2,525	6.25	2,693	80 mm @ 500 m	
United States						
37 mm M3	37 mm	990	1.92	2,900	60 mm @ 500 m	
57 mm M1	2.244 in	2,810	7.3	2,700	80 mm @500 m	
Italy						
Model 37	47 mm	660	3.25	2,100	43 mm @ 500 m	Czechoslovakian design
Japan						
Model 94	37 mm	815	1.42	2,300	32 mm @ 500 m	
Model 1	47 mm	1,660	3.08	2,700	70 mm @ 500 m	
Soviet Russia						
Model 36	37 mm	896	1.8	2,500	51 mm @ 500 m	Purchased from Germany
Model 42	45 mm	1,257	1.9†	3,500	54 mm @ 500 m	
Model 43	57 mm	2,550	3.8†	4,200	100 mm @ 500 m	
Model 44	100 mm	7,620	20.0†	3,600	181 mm @ 500 m	

General Note: † signifies tunsten-cored ammunition * signifies hollow charge shell

INFANTRY GUNS

NAME	CALIBRE	WEIGHT IN ACTION (lb)	SHELL WEIGHT (lb)	VELOCITY MUZZLE f.p.s.	MAXIMUM RANGE (yards)	REMARKS
Germany						
1e 1G 18	75 mm	880	13.2	690	3,775	
IG 37	75 mm	1,124	12.2	918	5,625	IG 42 had same performance
sIG 33	150 mm	3,750	84.0	790	5,150	
Geb G 36	75 mm	1,654	12.75	1,560	10,000	Mountain gun; 8 mule loads
Geb G 43	75 mm	1,282	12.75	1,575	10,375	Mountain gun; 7 mule loads
Geb H40	105 mm	3,660	32.0	1,870	18,300	Mountain how; 5 mule loads
Inf K 290(r)	76.2 mm	1,720	13.75	1,270	9,350	Ex-Russian
Great Britain						
95 mm inf How	3.7 in	2,100	25.0	1,083	10,000	Never issued
United States						
105 How M3	105 mm	955	33.0	1,020	7,250	
Japan						
Inf How M92	70 mm	468	8.3	650	3,050	
Regtl Type 41	75 mm	2,158	12.5	1,672	11,900	

Although these ever-larger guns gave ever better performance, they also got heavier and heavier, until they got past the stage where the crew could manhandle them in battle. Where the guns were handled by artillery this was less important, for they usually managed to provide more men and have a tractor of some sort handy, but where it was an infantry weapon, operating with the absolute minimum crew, the escalating size became a severe problem. The Germans had, however, produced the answer a long time before, and suddenly everybody began to move in the direction that they had indicated – towards the recoilless gun.

The heaviest part of a normal gun is not usually the actual gun, but the mounting which goes underneath it. This has to be heavy and strong to withstand the shock of recoil, and a lot of the weight comes from the complicated hydraulic system used to check recoil. If recoil could be done away with, it would be possible to dispense entirely with this weighty system and make the rest of the mounting a lot lighter. In fact it had been done in the First World War in a design for an aircraft gun in which the chamber was between two barrels, and firing the cartridge shot a shell out of the front and a balance weight out of the back. Since both articles weighed the same amount and were travelling at the same speed, they recoiled equally and cancelled each other out. But although this weapon worked, it was scarcely practical on the ground.

Surprises in Crete
When the German Air Force began putting their airborne parachute troops together they cast around for some lightweight form of artillery with which to arm them. After some trials, the Rheinmettal company produced a recoilless gun working on new principles: instead of shooting a counter-weight out of the back of the gun at the same speed as the shell, they shot a stream of gas out at very much higher speed. The weight and speed of the gas came to the same product as the weight and speed of the shell, so the gun balanced without recoil. To get the stream of gas, a special cartridge was built which had the base made of thick plastic material, and the gun breech had a hole in it leading to a rearward-pointing jet pipe. When the cartridge fired, the pressure built up and started the shell moving and then blew out the plastic disc and allowed gas from the cartridge to blow out through the jet.

Obviously, since some of the charge was being used to produce gas, it meant that the shell would not go so far as it would have done with a conventional gun of the same calibre. Moreover it was necessary to make a larger charge, since about four-fifths of the cartridge actually went back in flame and gas, and only one-fifth was pushing the shell. But the idea worked, and the resulting 'Light Gun' (so called as a security cover) had quite enough performance for the Parachute Infantry. It was designed so that it could be taken to pieces and carried either by individual jumpers or dropped in containers; once on the ground it could be quickly put together on a simple tripod mount with small wheels. The first 75-mm model was so successful that 105-mm models were produced next, and all these guns were revealed when the parachute troops attacked Crete in 1941.

Until then, although the Allies knew about the original counterweight type of

RECOILLESS GUNS
MORE POWER LESS KICK

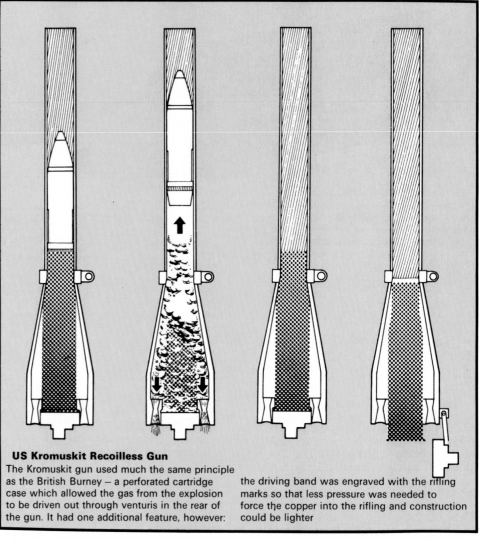

US Kromuskit Recoilless Gun
The Kromuskit gun used much the same principle as the British Burney – a perforated cartridge case which allowed the gas from the explosion to be driven out through venturis in the rear of the gun. It had one additional feature, however: the driving band was engraved with the rifling marks so that less pressure was needed to force the copper into the rifling and construction could be lighter

gun, they had not given much thought to recoilless guns, and the performance of these weapons in Crete gave them a surprise. They therefore began work on their own designs. The British models were generally called 'Burney' guns after their inventor, and they operated on a different system. The breech of the gun was quite normal, but the gun chamber was perforated and surrounded by a second chamber which led back to jets alongside the breech. The cartridge case was pierced by a number of large holes in its side, closed with thin metal sheet. When the charge fired, the metal sheet held up long enough for the shell to start moving, then blew out allowing gas to pass into the outer chamber and then through the rear jets. The end result was the same, though the method of reaching it slightly different.

The British weapons were much longer than the German, but were intended solely for direct shooting at short range, the

principal intention being to use them in the jungles of Burma where such a weapon would allow heavy fire power to be carried through the jungle to otherwise inaccessible places. A 3·45-in gun was first developed; this acquired the nickname of the "twenty-five pounder shoulder gun" as it was the same calibre as the 25-pounder field gun, though firing a much lighter shell. A 3·7-in on a lightweight wheeled carriage was also designed, and a large 95-mm howitzer intended as an artillery weapon for air-borne troops. But before any of these could be produced in quantity the war ended, and only a few were issued to selected infantry units so that they could evaluate them and come to some decisions as to the future use of this type of gun.

The American development of recoilless guns was on similar lines to the British and they developed a 57-mm and a 75-mm model, choosing these calibres because they could adapt ammunition already in production for other guns and thus speed things up by having something less to worry about. These also use perforated cartridge cases, and the 57-mm was fired from the shoulder or from a tripod while the 75-mm had a tripod mounting only. Numbers of these were produced in time to be flown to the South Pacific with both high explosive and anti-tank ammunition to be tried out in combat. They were highly successful, and were to remain in service for many years before being replaced by improved designs.

The backlash

But the recoilless gun had two drawbacks: one was the large amount of propellant powder it consumed, and the other was the huge flash and blast which came from the back end when it was fired, and which made an area up to one hundred yards behind the gun very dangerous to be in. No army liked this latter problem, though they have learned to live with it, but it was the former problem which worried the German Army because, by 1944, there was a growing shortage of the chemicals needed for the production of powder, and propellant was practically rationed. It became imperative to try and find some system which would still give the infantry the lightweight gun

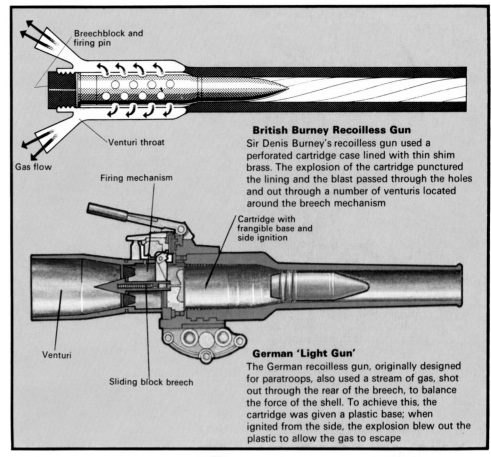

British Burney Recoilless Gun
Sir Denis Burney's recoilless gun used a perforated cartridge case lined with thin shim brass. The explosion of the cartridge punctured the lining and the blast passed through the holes and out through a number of venturis located around the breech mechanism

German 'Light Gun'
The German recoilless gun, originally designed for paratroops, also used a stream of gas, shot out through the rear of the breech, to balance the force of the shell. To achieve this, the cartridge was given a plastic base; when ignited from the side, the explosion blew out the plastic to allow the gas to escape

they demanded, still give a respectable performance against tanks, but do it more economically.

The answer to this seemingly impossible compromise was the PAW (*Panzer Abwehr Werfer* – Tank defence discharger) 600 (see page105). (see page105) It was called 'Werfer' rather than 'Kanone' because it had a smooth-bore barrel and fired a fin-stabilised hollow charge bomb of 81-mm calibre. The unusual thing about it was the fitting of a steel plate pierced with jets in front of the cartridge case; when the charge was fired it generated high pressure inside the case which then leaked out into the barrel to propel the bomb. This meant that only the area of the gun chamber had to be strong and heavy, the rest of the barrel could be much thinner as it had less pressure to withstand. This 'High-and-Low Pressure System' was one of the few really new ballistic discoveries to come out of the Second World War, but it has seen relatively little employment since.

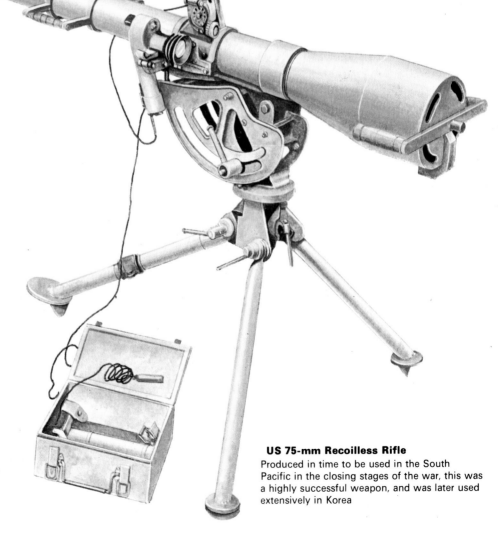

US 75-mm Recoilless Rifle
Produced in time to be used in the South Pacific in the closing stages of the war, this was a highly successful weapon, and was later used extensively in Korea

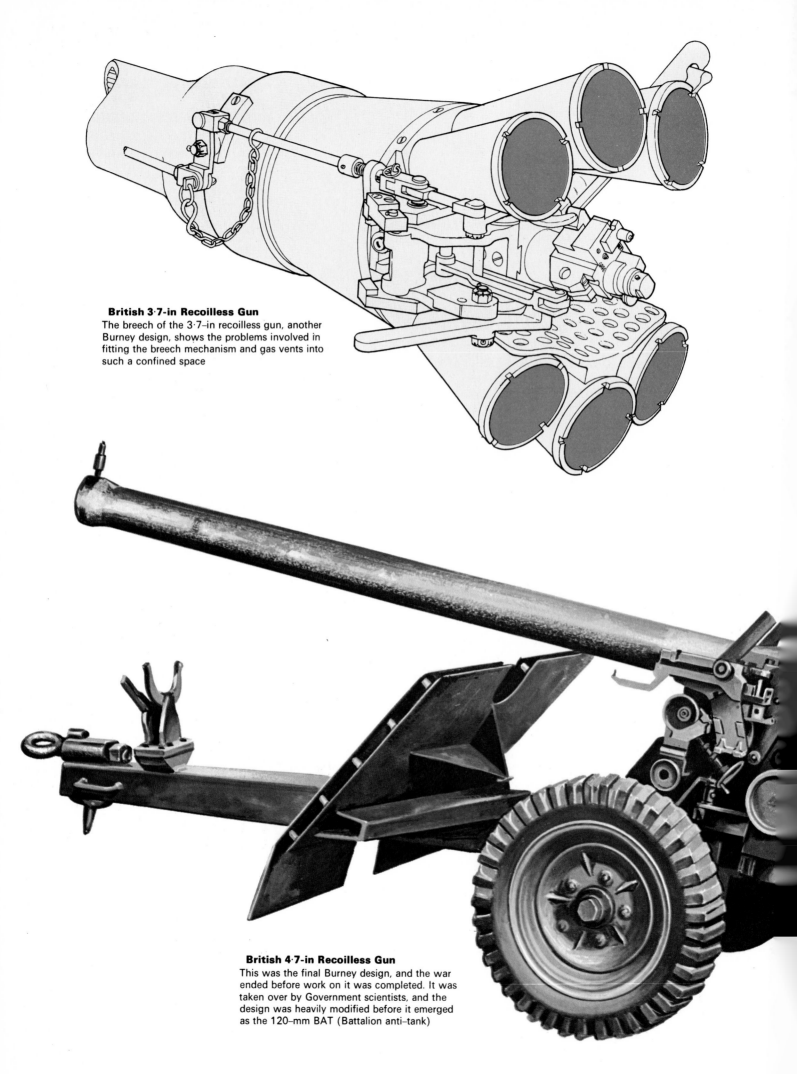

British 3·7-in Recoilless Gun
The breech of the 3·7-in recoilless gun, another Burney design, shows the problems involved in fitting the breech mechanism and gas vents into such a confined space

British 4·7-in Recoilless Gun
This was the final Burney design, and the war ended before work on it was completed. It was taken over by Government scientists, and the design was heavily modified before it emerged as the 120–mm BAT (Battalion anti–tank)

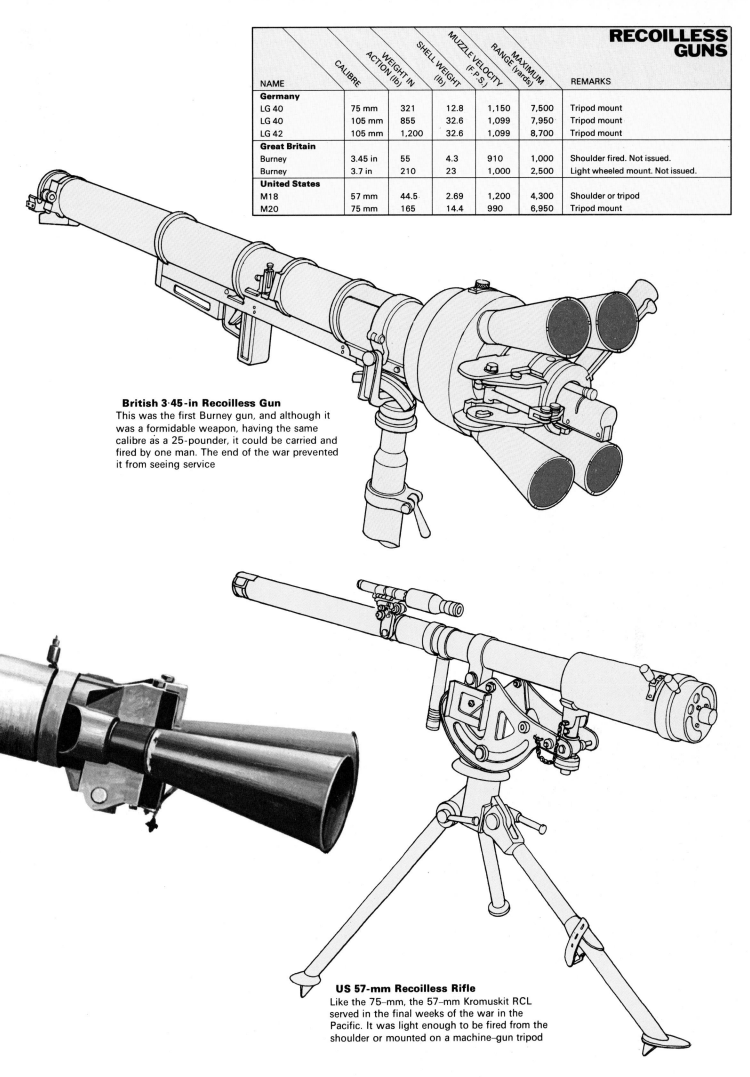

NAME	CALIBRE	WEIGHT IN ACTION (lb)	SHELL WEIGHT (lb)	MUZZLE VELOCITY (F.P.S.)	MAXIMUM RANGE (yards)	REMARKS
Germany						
LG 40	75 mm	321	12.8	1,150	7,500	Tripod mount
LG 40	105 mm	855	32.6	1,099	7,950	Tripod mount
LG 42	105 mm	1,200	32.6	1,099	8,700	Tripod mount
Great Britain						
Burney	3.45 in	55	4.3	910	1,000	Shoulder fired. Not issued.
Burney	3.7 in	210	23	1,000	2,500	Light wheeled mount. Not issued.
United States						
M18	57 mm	44.5	2.69	1,200	4,300	Shoulder or tripod
M20	75 mm	165	14.4	990	6,950	Tripod mount

British 3·45-in Recoilless Gun
This was the first Burney gun, and although it
was a formidable weapon, having the same
calibre as a 25-pounder, it could be carried and
fired by one man. The end of the war prevented
it from seeing service

US 57-mm Recoilless Rifle
Like the 75–mm, the 57–mm Kromuskit RCL
served in the final weeks of the war in the
Pacific. It was light enough to be fired from the
shoulder or mounted on a machine–gun tripod

ARTILLERY
THE HEAVIES

We have already seen that the infantryman was sometimes given his own artillery for close and immediate support, usually firing over open sights at something directly in front. But the proper handling of artillery demands specialist troops and a specialist organisation, a manpower problem which the infantry could not face from within its own ranks. This section therefore covers the big guns, guns for the long-range support of infantry, for the destruction of tanks, for the defence of coastlines and for anti-aircraft defence.

A thorough discussion of the history and development of every artillery weapon used in the Second World War would need several volumes, for the sheer size of the subjects is incredible; the German forces alone disposed over 200 land service weapons in 51 different calibres, without considering experimental models. Britain and America between them fielded about 100 artillery weapons, again not counting experimental models but only those which found their way into the hands of troops. Instead of trying to catalogue every weapon used, therefore, this section merely outlines the principal features of the research which developed during the war, and also brings to light one or two of the more unusual and less well-known weapons which were produced.

There are three main subjects to be explored:
● The routine improvement of weapons, in order to bring them into line with changing tactics and concepts of employment or to counter improvements in enemy defences;
● The improvements in ammunition introduced to step up the performance of existing weapons;
● The application of hitherto untried scientific principles.

In many cases these topics tend to overlap, but rather than try to develop a chronological story with these three aspects jumbled together, it is best to consider them as separate fields.

First, routine improvement. A good example of this in action is the history of the celebrated German 88-mm Flak Gun. This was originally conceived in the late 1920s by Krupp designers attached to the Bofors Company in Sweden. When in 1931 they returned to Essen with the design, the political climate seemed right. A prototype was built in 1932; and due to thorough paperwork it was an immediate success and was issued in 1933 as the 8·8-cm Flak Model 18. It should be stressed, in view of the exaggerated tales which became current in later years, that there was nothing unorthodox about this weapon at all—it was simply a good, sound, conventional anti-aircraft gun. It was taken to Spain by the Kondor Legion during the Civil War and tested in action; its potentialities as an anti-tank gun were also seen, though not advertised. This experience showed that there were a few weak points in the design and as a result, minor modifications were made in the mounting to improve stability and facilitate mass-production. This modified version became known as the Flak 36. In the following year an improved sighting and fire-control system was fitted, and the gun became the Flak Model 37. The 36 and 37 remained in service throughout the Second World War, being used in their primary role as anti-aircraft guns; as anti-tank guns, when fitted with shields and direct-fire sights; fitted to coastal craft and U-boats; used as coast defence guns, and even mounted on 12½-ton half-tracks as self-propelled guns (though this was not one of their most successful applications).

By early 1939 though, in spite of its excellence, it became obvious that bombers were going to fly faster and higher than before, and the gun's performance would have to be improved. And so in 1939 Rheinmettal-Borsig were given a contract for an improved model, to be known as the Flak 41. Prototype trials began in 1941 and it was found that the gun, although a most efficient design, had a lot of teething troubles which were going to take time to eliminate. Since no one else had a contract for the gun, the Luftwaffe (which was responsible for Germany's anti-aircraft defences) was forced to use it or else do without. Consequently the next year saw a great deal of effort thrown in and by March 1943 the first issues were made.

The Flak 41, as finally produced, was a considerable improvement over the 18, 36, and 37. By using a turntable to carry the gun, instead of the more usual pedestal mounting, a much lower silhouette was achieved. The muzzle velocity and ceiling were both improved by adopting a more powerful cartridge, and the stability in action was excellent. The only fly in the ointment was the difficult extraction of the fired cartridge case, which is a flaw of major proportions in a quick-firing anti-aircraft gun. Different designs of barrel were produced in an effort to overcome the trouble, and a special brass cartridge case was developed; but none of these palliatives made much impression and the gun was never the success it might have been.

Some time after Rheinmettal had received their contract, a similar specification had been given to Krupp. Their development, sometimes referred to as the Flak 42, became more and more entangled with their concurrent development of 88-mm tank and anti-tank guns in the hopes of producing a family of weapons which would use interchangeable parts and common ammunition. Before the Krupp version had got off the drawing board, the Luftwaffe was demanding more performance than the design could produce, and in February 1943, not without a certain amount of relief, one feels, Krupp dropped the Flak 42 to concentrate on the tank and anti-tank weapons.

While the 88 shows an example of improvement of a particular calibre, the more common approach was to improve a particular class of weapon by raising the calibre; most anti-tank weapons display this technique. The British army began the war with a 2-pounder; followed it by a 6-pounder and then a 17-pounder; and finally had a 32-pounder in preparation when the war ended, having toyed briefly with a possible 55-pounder. America began with a 37-mm, took over the British 6-pounder and called it the 57-mm; then moved to a 3-inch based on a redundant anti-aircraft gun; then a 90-mm, also based on an AA gun, and was working on a 105-mm when the war ended. Germany also began with a 37-mm and progressed through 28, 42, 50, 75 and 88-mm to arrive at a 128-mm as the war closed.

All these series show steady progression in conventional guns, all intended to beat the forthcoming increases in enemy armour. However, the flaw in this system becomes apparent on looking at the British 32-pounder or the German 12.8-cm Pak 44 — bigger calibres may mean a bigger punch, but they invariably mean bigger guns as well, and this means more weight to move about. This is a considerable drawback for an anti-tank gun which usually has to be emplaced by manpower, and certainly the 32-pounder was too big for its task; even had the war continued, it is doubtful whether it would have been accepted into service.

Anti-aircraft guns tend to show a similar pattern among all nations, always striving to extract more ceiling and greater velocity; the increased ceiling meant that higher-flying aircraft could be engaged, while higher velocity meant a shorter time between firing the gun and the shell arriving at the target, and hence less room for error in the prediction of the target's position at the time of the shell's arrival. The two groups of anti-aircraft weapons in common use were the light guns, such as the German 37-mm and the British and US-employed Bofors 40-mm, and the heavy guns, such as the German 88, 105, and 128-mm guns, the British 3.7-inch, 4.5-inch, and 5.25-inch guns, and the American 90-mm, 105-mm, and 120-mm types. The light guns relied on throwing up a heavy volume of fire at a high rate, to counter the low-flying attacker. The heavies fired at slower rates, threw heavier shells, and had higher ceilings to deal with the high-level bomber. But strangely enough, all the combatants had a gap in their defences, which lay between the maximum ceiling of the light guns — about 6,000 feet — and the minimum effective ceiling of the heavies — about 10,000 feet. Below this figure the heavy gun could not swing fast enough to follow a fast low flyer. In an endeavour to fill this gap, development took place in both Britain and Germany to provide a medium AA gun.

As far as Britain was concerned, a paramount feature of any weapon proposed in 1940 was to avoid usurping production already hard at work with the more basic weapons needed for simple survival. In view of this, the first question the designers asked themselves was: 'What existing gun can be worked over to fill the bill?' After a few false starts the design coalesced around the existing coast artillery 6-pounder gun, the same calibre as the anti-tank gun but using a heavier cartridge and capable of greater range. This was adapted to a twin-barrel mounting on a three-wheeled trailer, and work then began on designing a suitable automatic feed system to get the rate of fire thought necessary, and a fire-control system to put the shells where they were needed. Since the guns were originally designed for hand loading, the adaptation to autofeed turned out to be more difficult than had at first been imagined; then Allied air superiority gave the project less priority; and, in the event, the twin 6-pounder never entered service and Britain never had a medium AA gun.

The German development was not restricted to an existing weapon, since the 'gap' had been appreciated before the war, and in 1936 Rheinmettal was given a contract to develop a 50-mm gun. This was eventually introduced in 1940 in limited numbers for an extended troop trial to assess whether such a weapon was desirable and whether the Flak 41, as it was known, would fill the requirement. For a variety of reasons the gun was not a success, but the experience showed that the medium AA gun was needed, and a great deal of thought went into the design of a completely integrated weapon system, probably the first such system to be conceived as a complete entity. It was to comprise a 55-mm automatic gun, with matched radar, predictor, displacement corrector, and full electro-hydraulic remote control of a six-gun battery. By the time all these theories and designs had been put together it was mid-1943, and the production of such a far-reaching concept was so difficult that the war ended before the weapon was completed. To act as a stop-gap, the now-obsolescent 50-mm anti-tank gun was fitted with an automatic loading system, but this idea fell by the wayside, and it is doubtful if any were ever made. All in all, the medium AA gun story is remarkable in the similarity of British and German experience.

The much-feared German '88'. Disliked equally by Allied armour and infantry the Pak 43 was both versatile and hard-hitting

US crewmen fire a 120-mm AA gun. The largest American AA gun, it could be fired by remote control as well as manually

The British 4·5-inch static AA gun is seen here being loaded by its crew, its 55-pound shells ready to hand

During a period of bitter jungle fighting in December 1943, US marines at Cape Gloucester on the Pacific island of New Britain pass ammunition to the gun crew of a 75-mm howitzer

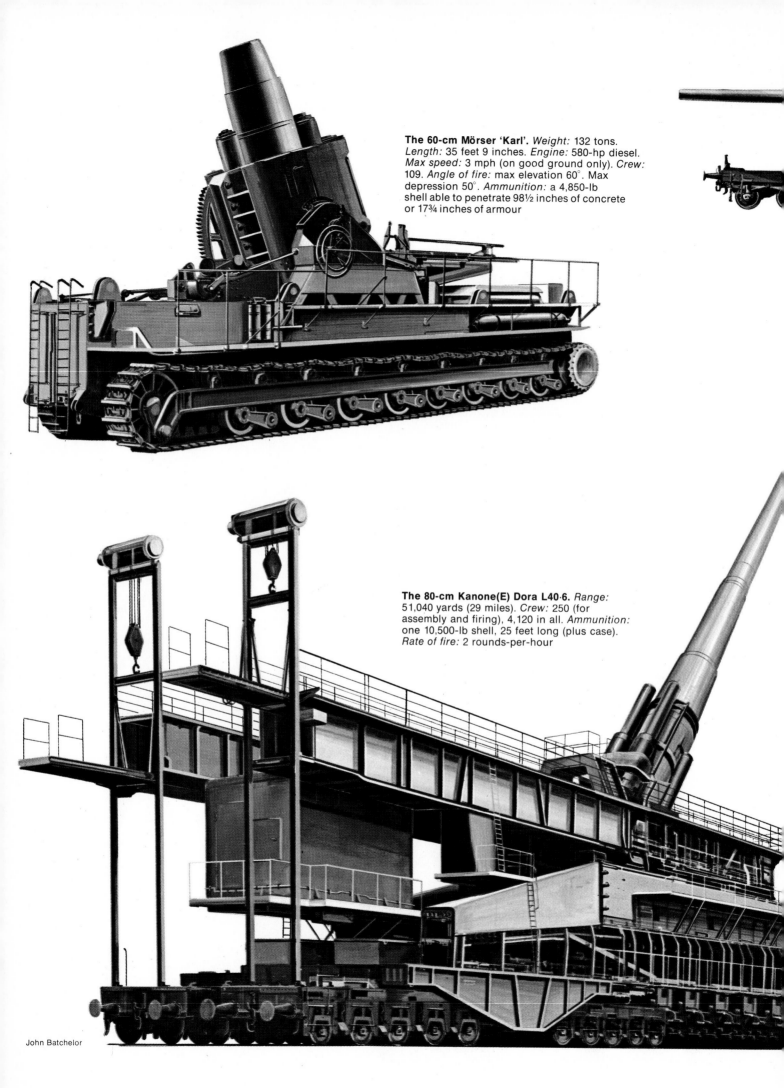

The 60-cm Mörser 'Karl'. *Weight:* 132 tons. *Length:* 35 feet 9 inches. *Engine:* 580-hp diesel. *Max speed:* 3 mph (on good ground only). *Crew:* 109. *Angle of fire:* max elevation 60°. Max depression 50°. *Ammunition:* a 4,850-lb shell able to penetrate 98½ inches of concrete or 17¾ inches of armour

The 80-cm Kanone(E) Dora L40·6. *Range:* 51,040 yards (29 miles). *Crew:* 250 (for assembly and firing), 4,120 in all. *Ammunition:* one 10,500-lb shell, 25 feet long (plus case). *Rate of fire:* 2 rounds-per-hour

John Batchelor

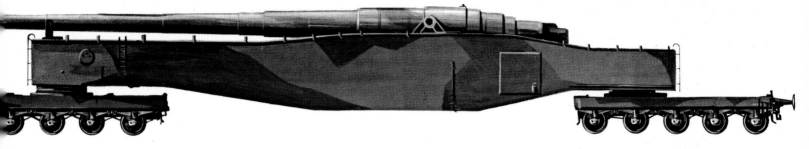

The 28-cm K5(E). *Weight:* 479,600 lb. *Length:* 96 feet. *Range:* 66,880 yards (38 miles). *Crew:* 10 (for firing)

RAILGUNS AND REGULARS FROM HITLER'S ARMOURY

The 10·5-cm Leichte Feldhaubitze 18M L/28. *Weight:* 4,488 lb. *Range:* 13,377 yards. *Crew:* 6. *Rate of fire:* 6-8 rounds-per-minute

The 10·5-cm Leichte Feldhaubitze 43 L/28. *Weight:* 5,060 lb. *Crew:* 6. *Range:* 17,875 yards. *Rate of fire:* 6 rounds-per-minute

In the field artillery world practically all development was simply a matter of improvement on existing designs. No nation in its right mind would attempt a major re-equipment of its standard weapons in the middle of a war. The British 25-pounder served valiantly, and modifications to meet special demands included the self-propelled 'Bishop' (on a Valentine chassis) and 'Sexton' (on a Ram chassis); the Australian-developed 'Short' or 'Baby' 25-pounder with a truncated barrel, no shield, short trail and castor wheel for easy manoeuvring in the jungle; it was tried as a self-propelled gun (SP) in many vehicles including the Lloyd carrier, which was asking too much of such a light vehicle; it was strapped to the cargo bed of a DUKW for supporting amphibious landings; and it was even considered for the armament of submarines. Similarly, the American 105-mm howitzer was tried in a variety of SP mountings, starting with a half-track, until the Sherman-based M-7 became standardized as the 'Priest'; it was shortened and placed on a light carriage for use by airborne units; it was mounted in tank turrets as a close support gun; and, like the 25-pounder, mounted on the long-suffering DUKW.

The German 1E FH 18, more or less the equivalent of the 25-pounder and 105 howitzer, suffered similar, though more drastic, changes. First it was given a muzzle brake and a heavier charge with a long-range shell; then in an attempt to reduce the weight, like the 'Baby 25-pounder', the barrel and recoil system were mounted on the carriage of the 75-mm Pak 40 anti-tank gun; the wheels were removed and it was dropped bodily into a tank hull to provide an assault gun; it was grafted on to a variety of tracked mountings. But eventually a complete re-design was called for and Rheinmettal was given a contract. Before their offering was ready, the experiences of the Russian Front had shown that certain features were mandatory in the next generation of field guns. Briefly, these were that the gun must have a good anti-tank performance for self-protection; at the same time it had to be capable of hiding in forests and firing out at high angles; the range had to be at least 8 miles without demanding special ammunition; it had to have all-round traverse, since Soviet partisans could attack from any direction; and it had to weigh less than 2,200 pounds. Now even today a designer would have a hard time meeting that specification, but in 1943 both Krupp and Skoda rose to the challenge.

The Skoda version, the 10.5-cm 1E FH 43, was most ingenious: the carriage had virtually a normal split trail at the rear, plus another split trail at the front, beneath the barrel, and a firing pedestal beneath the axle. In action, the equipment rested on the two rear trails and the pedestal, and the front trails were laid on the ground to form a cruciform stable platform above which the gun could rotate through 360 degrees, the four legs giving stability at any angle of the barrel. The novelty of this carriage lay in the fact that the two front legs were not rigidly attached to the carriage; to compensate for uneven ground they were permitted to lie at any convenient angle. A hydraulic system was arranged so that slow movement of the legs—as during folding and unfolding to and from the travelling position—was freely permitted, but fast movement—as the firing shock—would cause the legs to lock rigidly to the carriage and give the desired stability.

Krupp, under the same nomenclature, produced two models; one was very similar in general design to Skoda's, though without the hydraulic system, while the other was based on a more or less conventional cruciform platform of the type familiar in AA guns. However, none of the designs, Krupp or Skoda, were ready for production before the war's end, and only prototypes existed.

The German super-guns

The heaviest field equipments seen during the war were the German self-propelled howitzers generically known as 'Karl Mörsers'. These were of two calibres, 540-mm and 600-mm, mounted on the same type of carriage. Six carriages were made and the exact disposition of barrels between them is in some doubt; the carriages were numbered I to VI; Vehicle V was captured by the US 1st Army and found to have a 540-mm barrel, yet photographs captured later showed this same carriage to have a 600-mm barrel. It is probably safe to assume that three of each calibre were made. The date of introduction is also a little vague, but it seems fairly certain that the 600-mm version was introduced in 1942 and the 540-mm in 1944.

The carriage of 'Karl' was a simple rectangular box, divided into three compartments. The first held the Mercedes-Benz engine and transmission; the second carried the gun; and the third held the carriage raising and lowering gear. After driving into position on its tracks the engine was used to drive the lowering gear, which rotated the anchorages of the suspension torsion bars so as to allow the chassis to be lowered to the ground until the suspension and track were relieved of the weight. For long-distance moves the gun and recoil system were removed from the carriage, dismantled, and loaded on to special trailers; the carriage was then winched on to a special tank-transporter. For very long distances the complete gun and carriage assembly could be slung between two railway flat wagons by means of special trusses.

In the use of railway artillery Germany virtually had the field to herself. This class of weapon is really the prerogative of the Continental nation with a well-developed rail system by which it can readily deploy them to any front. In contrast, Britain and the USA, while possessing railway guns, used them solely as mobile coast defence units, since the problem of transporting two or three hundred tons of railway mounting across the Channel was not a trick to be undertaken lightly. Indeed, the British and American weapons were almost entirely relics of the First World War which had been in mothballs. 1940 saw a few more mountings hastily cobbled together from available spares and hurried to cover the Channel, just as in similar fashion American guns were mobilised and deployed in 1941. In 1944 reports from France indicated that heavy railway artillery might be of use in demolishing strongpoints to be expected in the final assault in Germany, and designs were hastily prepared by the Americans for a number of 16-inch guns, but within a few weeks it was seen that heavy artillery of this class had been rendered superfluous by the quality and quantity of air support available, and the demand was cancelled.

The German army had a vast range of railway guns from 150-mm upwards, but two were really outstanding and deserve closer examination. The first was the 28-cm K5(E)—Kanone, Model 5, *Eisenbahnlafette*—which became their standard super-heavy railway gun and was probably the finest design of its kind in the world. The basic arithmetic and paperwork had been done in the late 1920s and early 1930s, and work began on the gun in 1934. (It is worth noting that every German railway gun was designed and built by Krupp—Rheinmettal did design two, but they were never made.) First, a 150-mm barrel was produced for tests; it had been decided that to obtain the great range demanded, a conventionally rifled barrel was out of the question. A design was prepared with 12 deep grooves and having a shell carrying 12 ribs, or splines, to match. The theory behind this was that the engraving of a conventional copper driving band on the shell gave rise to very high pressure in the gun chamber; by using the spline and groove method to spin the shell, this resistance was removed, and the shell would step off more smartly, allowing a bigger propelling charge to be used without over-straining the gun. The 150-mm test barrel proved that the theory was right, and a full-calibre 280-mm barrel was built.

The mounting was a simple box-girder assembly carried on two six-axle bogies, with the front bogie slung so as to allow the front of the box-girder to be swung across it for aiming the gun. For large angles the whole weapon was mounted on a special portable turntable built at the end of a short spur of track laid at the desired firing point. Each gun was supplied with a special train which included wagons for carrying the turntable, light-anti-aircraft guns for local defence, air-conditioned ammunition wagons, living quarters and kitchen for the gunners, and flat wagons to carry their entitlement of motor transport.

By 1940 eight of these complete equipments were in service, and production continued throughout the war, 25 being built in all. The German gunners called them 'Slim Bertha', but to the Allies in Italy one at least became famous as 'Anzio Annie'.

With the 561-pound pre-rifled shell the gun could reach to 68,000 yards. A rocket-assisted shell was later developed which increased this range, with a certain loss of accuracy, to 94,000 yards. Finally, the Peenemünde Research Establishment designed a 300-pound dart-like projectile which was fired from a special 310-mm smooth-bore barrel and which ranged to 170,000 yards. Although coming too late for general issue, these 'Peenemünde Arrow Shells' were issued for troop trials in the field, and some were fired against the US 3rd Army at ranges of about 70 miles.

The second railway gun, 'Gustav', was the biggest gun the world has ever seen—the Krupp-designed 800-mm Kanone. The idea was conceived in 1937 of a pair of super-guns; they were of quite conventional design, except for their immense size. Too large to be moved in one piece, they were transported piecemeal in special trains and assembled at the selected sites by travelling cranes. When assembled, the mounting straddled two sets of standard-gauge rails, with 80 wheels taking the 1,350-ton weight. An armour or concrete-piercing shell of 7 tons was propelled by a 1¾-ton charge to a range of 23 miles, or a 5-ton high-explosive shell to 29 miles. The first equipment, 'Gustav', was proved at the Rugenwalde range in March 1943, in Hitler's presence. The only record of its use was at the siege of Sebastopol; the gun was sited at Bakhchisary and fired some 30 to 40 rounds. One shot is recorded as having penetrated through 100 feet of earth to destroy a Soviet ammunition dump at Severnaya Bay. The subsequent history of the gun is un-

A German 105-mm howitzer hammers back at Soviet forces during the battle for the Orel salient in the summer of 1943

'NEBELWERFER' 150-MM ROCKET-LAUNCHER: The most widely used of the family of launchers developed by the Germans, the six-barrelled Nebelwerfer ('fog-thrower') was used to lay down extremely heavy short-range bombardments or smoke screens. As compared with conventional artillery, the Nebelwerfer fired a heavy projectile (below) from a light carriage, and was thus very manoeuvrable, but it was far less accurate. The six barrels had to be fired separately (this took 10 seconds) to prevent the carriage overturning; the tubes could be reloaded in 90 seconds. *Weight of launcher:* 1,195 lb. *Range:* 7,330 yards with high explosive, 7,750 yards with smoke shells. *Weight of rocket:* 75·3 lb (high explosive), 78 lb (smoke)

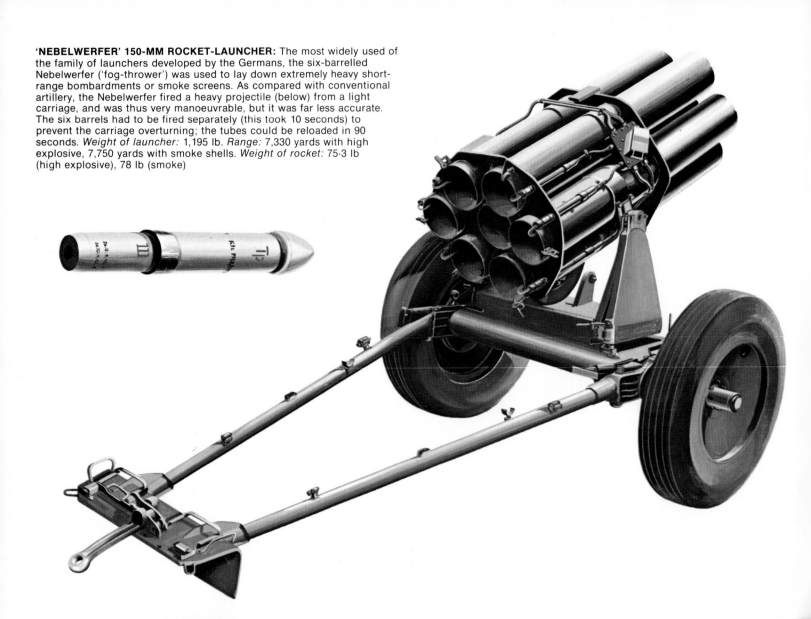

▷One of Rommel's deadly '88s' dug in along the Egyptian/Libyan frontier following the Afrika Korps' eastward push of early 1941. Before its transfer to Rommel's desert army, this particular gun (as indicated by the rings on the barrel) had fought in the Polish, Belgian, and French campaigns, with an impressive total of kills to its credit

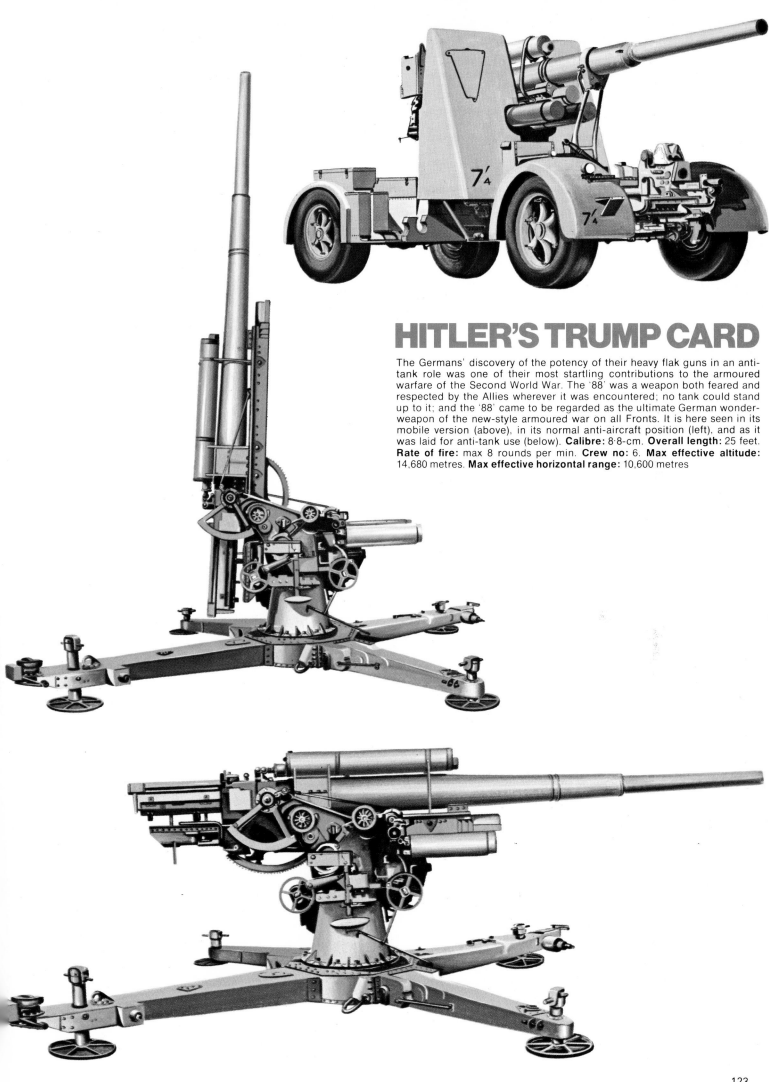

HITLER'S TRUMP CARD

The Germans' discovery of the potency of their heavy flak guns in an anti-tank role was one of their most startling contributions to the armoured warfare of the Second World War. The '88' was a weapon both feared and respected by the Allies wherever it was encountered; no tank could stand up to it; and the '88' came to be regarded as the ultimate German wonder-weapon of the new-style armoured war on all Fronts. It is here seen in its mobile version (above), in its normal anti-aircraft position (left), and as it was laid for anti-tank use (below). **Calibre:** 8·8-cm. **Overall length:** 25 feet. **Rate of fire:** max 8 rounds per min. **Crew no:** 6. **Max effective altitude:** 14,680 metres. **Max effective horizontal range:** 10,600 metres

SHOT AND SHELL-HOWITZER AND GUN

The main difference between guns and howitzers is that guns fire 'directly' at their targets, while howitzers fire 'indirectly' at high angles, dropping their shells on to targets which are hidden by hills or fortifications in the target area. The plunging fire of howitzers is also ideal for cracking open heavy gun emplacements and defences. Howitzers usually fire at shorter ranges than guns, which means that the propellent charges of howitzer shells are comparatively small. And this in turn means that howitzers have shorter barrels than guns, for howitzer charges have a shorter-burning fuse.

This basic distinction was narrowed by 1939 with the appearance of the multi-purpose gun howitzer, of which the classic example is the British 25-pounder: it had exactly the same calibre as the German 88-mm gun, and could serve as an efficient anti-tank gun with a 20-pounder shot. The chart below shows the comparative ranges of guns and howitzers of various calibres; note the longer reach of the gun. At the foot of the page is an array of some of the most used shells of the war—from the armouries of the main combatant powers—compared to a standard rifle round*, to show the scale

M = Mortar
H = Howitzer
G = Gun

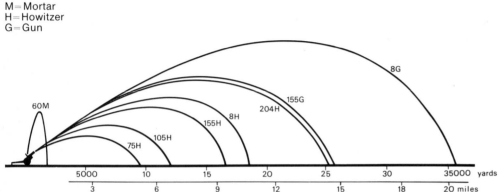

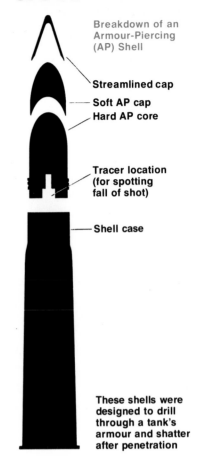

Breakdown of an Armour-Piercing (AP) Shell

— Streamlined cap
— Soft AP cap
— Hard AP core

— Tracer location (for spotting fall of shot)

— Shell case

These shells were designed to drill through a tank's armour and shatter after penetration

AA = Anti-aircraft
AP = Armour-piercing
A/TK = Anti-tank
HE = High-explosive
Chem = Chemical

1. Italian 20-mm AA, AP
2. Italian 47-mm AP, HE
3. German 37-mm AA, HE
4. British 95-mm A/TK, HE
5. British 6-pdr AP
6. British 25-pdr (chem)
7. German 88-mm AA, AP
8. British 3.7-inch AA, HE
9. US 90-mm AA, HE
10. Russian 76.2-mm HE
11. Russian 57-mm AP
12. German 47-mm AP, HE
13. Italian 65-mm shrapnel
14. Italian 37-mm AA, HE
15. Italian 47-mm A/TK, HE
16. US 37-mm AP

known (it was presumably captured by the Red Army).

The second equipment, 'Dora', so far as is known, never left the proving ground, though what happened to it at the end of the war is a minor mystery (some ammunition and a spare barrel were found at Krupp's proof establishment at Meppen near the Dutch border).

The detachment necessary to man, maintain, and give local protection to Gustav was 4,120 men strong, commanded by a major-general. The actual fire-control and operation of the gun demanded a colonel and 500 men, and the construction or dismantling of the weapon took between four and six weeks. A long-range 'Peene-münde Arrow Shell' was developed for Gustav, but, so far as is known, was never fired. This was to weigh 2,200 pounds and range to 100 miles. There was also a proposition to mount a 520-mm gun on the same carriage to fire rocket-assisted shells and 'Peene-münde Arrow Shells' to a range of 118 miles for cross-channel bombardment, but this never got past the drawing-board.

If it is accepted that it is not a good idea to tamper with a good gun design in the middle of a war, then the only way to render the gun more effective is to improve the ammunition, and this technique was frequently adopted during the war. And in no field is this seen to greater effect than in the battle against the tank. The reason for this is fairly self-evident: personnel targets remain more or less the same—once the anti-personnel projectile is perfected it can stay as it is. On the other hand, once a new anti-tank projectile appears, it is only a matter of time before the enemy put thicker armour on his tanks.

At the outbreak of war there were two types of anti-tank projectile: the armour-piercing (AP) shot, and the AP shell. The difference is basic. Shot are solid, with no explosive filling, and rely purely on their speed to smash through the armour and do damage inside the tank by their impact, the fragments of plate they knock off during penetration, and their own effect when they penetrate the plate and bounce around inside the tank. AP shells, on the other hand, have a small cavity filled with high explosive and are fitted with a fuse in the base. The shell penetrates, similarly to shot, by brute force, but the fuse is activated by the impact and, after a short delay to allow the shell to pass through the plate and enter the tank, the explosive is detonated, shattering the shell into fragments and adding to the shot-like damage already caused. On paper the shell is the better proposition, since there is the bonus of the explosive filling. But paper figures tend to be deceptive, and in fact the shot is probably the more practical projectile, because the high-explosive (HE) cavity weakens the shell, and the fuse is precariously supported against the hammer-blow of impact. Britain held firmly to the shot theory for anti-tank work, though many years of experience in producing AP shells for naval use was available. Several other nations preferred AP shell, bewitched by the HE bonus.

Most of the belligerents entered the war with a plain shot or shell and relied on throwing it hard enough to penetrate the opposing tanks. So long as the target was relatively lightly armoured this was successful; but, naturally, each side began to increase armour thickness on each succeeding generation of tank. The quick answer to this was to increase the gun charge or even the calibre, and thus throw the projectile harder, but there comes a time when the impact is too much for the projectile, and instead of piercing, it merely shatters on the outside of the target without doing any damage.

The answer to this was to protect the tip of the shot or shell with a softer cap, which tended to spread the impact stresses over the shoulders of the projectile, instead of concentrating them into the tip. This preserved the piercing action to higher velocities, and the gun was again winning the battle. The next move belonged to the tank designers who made their armour thicker, and so it went on until the projectile was once more shattering, cap or no cap. At this point the projectile designers were faced with a new problem: if it was futile to throw the projectile harder, might it not be possible to throw a harder projectile? And what was harder than an armour-piercing projectile? Tungsten carbide, a diamond-hard alloy, provided an answer, but it was about one-and-a-half times as heavy as steel, so that it could not easily be made into a projectile. Furthermore, it was expensive and in short supply.

The first application of tungsten to an anti-tank projectile was by the German army in their 28-mm *Schwere Panzerbüchse* 41, a weapon with a unique tapered barrel. The shot consisted of a small core of tungsten carbide held in a light alloy casing of 28-mm calibre. As the shot was fired down the gun barrel, so the calibre diminished and the light alloy casing was ground down, until it emerged as a 21-mm shot. This squeezing enhanced the velocity and changed the ratio of shot diameter to weight. The velocity reached was 4,000 feet per second, and, on impact with the target, the hardness of the core was impervious to impact shock and penetrated successfully.

About the same time—late 1940—a similar idea had been put forward by a Mr Janáček, a Czechoslovakian weapon designer working in England. While his idea was still under consideration, a specimen of the German weapon was captured in North Africa and flown home for trials: the idea was seen to be feasible. The British version was in the form of a taper-bore adapter to be fitted to the existing 2-pounder gun, together with a special tungsten-cored shot, known under the code name of 'Littlejohn', an Anglicised version of Janáček. The advantage here was that the adapter could be removed to permit firing normal explosive shells, but could be refitted quickly for the special shot, whereas the German design required a special pattern of high-explosive shell to be developed, a difficult feat in such a small calibre. The 'Littlejohn' attachment and its shot were not used in towed artillery, since by the time they were ready for service the anti-tank units were armed with 6-pounders, but it was used on 2-pounder and American 37-mm guns mounted in armoured cars.

To use tungsten in a conventional gun, a different approach was needed. The first attempt, for the 6-pounder, was the 'AP Composite Rigid' (APCR) shot, a tungsten core mounted in an alloy sheath of approximately the same dimensions as the conventional steel shot for the gun. By virtue of its light alloy content the APCR shot was somewhat lighter and thus had a higher velocity when fired. Unfortunately the ratio of weight-to-diameter was unfavourable, giving a poor ballistic coefficient or 'carrying power', and while the short-range performance was impressive, the velocity soon dropped, and at ranges over 1,000 yards, steel shot was just as good, sometimes better. Some German weapons were also provided with the same type of projectile, and one was designed for use in the Soviet 76.2-mm field gun which the Germans captured in large numbers and converted into an anti-tank gun. Unfortunately for them, by early 1942 the shortage of tungsten in Germany began to be felt, and in the middle of that year a ban was placed on the use of tungsten in ammunition; what scarce supplies there were had been earmarked for machine tool production, not for throwing about the Russian steppes. After strong remonstrations, the 5-cm Pak 38 anti-tank gun was specifically exempted from this ban, since at that time it was the only weapon capable of stopping a Russian T-34 tank, provided it had a tungsten-cored shot.

Although the 6-pounder APCR shot seemed reasonably successful, it was not the ideal answer. The ideal, in fact, sounded ridiculous: what was wanted was a shot which in the barrel was large-calibre and light, so as to pick up speed quickly and leave the gun at high velocity, but which outside the barrel should be small in diameter and heavy, so as to have good 'carrying power' and keep up its high velocity for a long range. These two conflicting requirements were fused into one projectile by two British designers, Permutter and Coppock, of the Armaments Research Department. Even before the 6-pounder had received its APCR shot they were at work, and in March 1944 their 'AP Discarding Sabot' shot was provided for the 6-pounder. In this design, the tungsten core is contained in a streamlined steel sheath or sub-projectile; this in turn is carried in a light-alloy framework or 'sabot' of the full gun calibre. On firing, this sabot holds the sub-projectile centralised in the bore and gives the whole thing the combination of light weight and large area which is wanted for velocity. But firing actually 'unlocks' the sabot, and as the shot leaves the gun muzzle, so the sabot is thrown clear, allowing the sub-projectile to race to the target at velocities of the order of 3,000 feet per second. Now, since the sub-projectile's sheath is virtually a skin round the tungsten core, it follows that the weight is high in relation to the cross-section—the ideal condition for good carrying power and thus long-range performance. A similar projectile for the 17-pounder followed in September 1944, and one was under development for the 20-pounder tank gun when the war ended.

More punch from the hollow charge

Running parallel with this unfolding story of piercing projectiles was the development of the hollow-charge principle into a viable weapon. This illustrates the adaptation of a well-documented scientific phenomenon to a weapon of war: almost 200 years ago a Norwegian engineer had observed that hollowing out the face of an explosive charge made it cut deeper into rock when blasting. In the 1880s an American experimenter, Monroe, found that when firing guncotton slabs against armour plate, the initials 'USN' engraved in the guncotton reproduced themselves in mirror-like form in the face of the armour plate. From his observations and reports the phenomenon became known as the 'Monroe Effect' and was a scientific curiosity for many years. Just before the First World War one or two inventors toyed with the idea of employing this effect in mines and torpedoes, but since no one really understood why it did what it did, it was difficult to engineer the idea into a practical form.

THE UBIQUITOUS 25-POUNDER

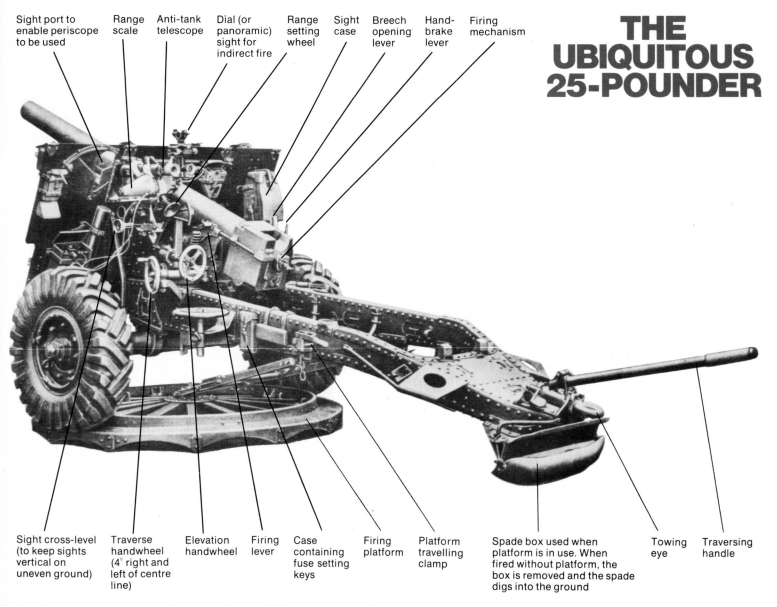

Sight port to enable periscope to be used • Range scale • Anti-tank telescope • Dial (or panoramic) sight for indirect fire • Range setting wheel • Sight case • Breech opening lever • Hand-brake lever • Firing mechanism

Sight cross-level (to keep sights vertical on uneven ground) • Traverse handwheel (4° right and left of centre line) • Elevation handwheel • Firing lever • Case containing fuse setting keys • Firing platform • Platform travelling clamp • Spade box used when platform is in use. When fired without platform, the box is removed and the spade digs into the ground • Towing eye • Traversing handle

The 25-pounder gun-howitzer. Manoeuvrable, hard-hitting—it was one of the most reliable artillery pieces of the war

Australian gunners, 'the elite troops of the empire' man a 25-pounder in the Western Desert

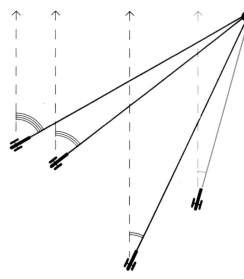

When an artillery target was identified only one gun of the battery would 'range in' on it. When this gun's fire registered, the battery command post would make the calculation to bring all the other guns onto the target. This principle could be extended to include any number of guns, the key to success being good communications

The 25-pounder was originally called the 'Universal Field Artillery Equipment' when it was being designed, and its subsequent career lived up to that description. It was a gun-howitzer, capable of flat-trajectory fire as a gun or, by using a multi-part cartridge, it could act as a howitzer, lobbing shells high into the air to drop them into otherwise inaccessible places. Its maximum range was 13,400 yards — over 7½ miles — and with a special 'Super-Plus' cartridge and a 20-lb piercing shot it proved to be a formidable anti-tank gun. Early models (known as the 18/25 pounder) used the 25-pounder barrel in the carriage of the older 18-pounder gun, but the 'proper' carriage, with its unique circular platform beneath allowing a 360° traverse, appeared in 1940 and first saw action in Norway. The gun was later fitted to Valentine and Ram tank chassis to become self-propelled; a shortened version was developed by Australia for use in the jungle; and a narrow-track model with a hinged trail (to allow greater elevation) became the standard British airborne gun.

A 25-pounder in action in Vichy Syria in the spring of 1941

The short 25-pounder Mark I was developed by the Australians. Its lighter construction allowed its use in jungle terrain

Several versions of a self-propelled 25-pounder were produced. This version, mounted on a Loyd carrier, was not adopted

THE RED ARMY'S GOD OF WAR

As Stalin's saying, 'Artillery is the God of War', shows, the artillery has always been the élite arm of the Red Army. But it was not until the beginning of the Second World War that the Russians were forced to incorporate major innovations in their use of artillery. They were the first to develop the concept of the 'artillery division'—a large independent unit with guns of all calibres, which could be used en masse to bring great pressure to bear on a selected part of the front. And the Red Army was the first to use mortars (such as the regimental 120-mm illustrated below) as the standard support weapon for large infantry formations. These developments were precipitated by the enormous losses of the first months of the war: the remaining equipment had to be husbanded and used to the greatest effect; and production had to be concentrated on a few simple designs which would be easy to mass-produce, and which could be operated by the inexperienced and ill-educated conscripts who now formed the mass of the army

122-mm Type 31/37 Howitzer
Range: 22,000 yards
Weight of shot: 55 lb
Firing weight: 15,500 lb

45-mm Type 32 Anti-tank Gun
Range: 9,850 yards with anti-tank shot
5,200 yards with high-explosive
Weight of shot: 3·25 lb (anti-tank)
4·75 lb (high-explosive)
Firing weight: 950 lb

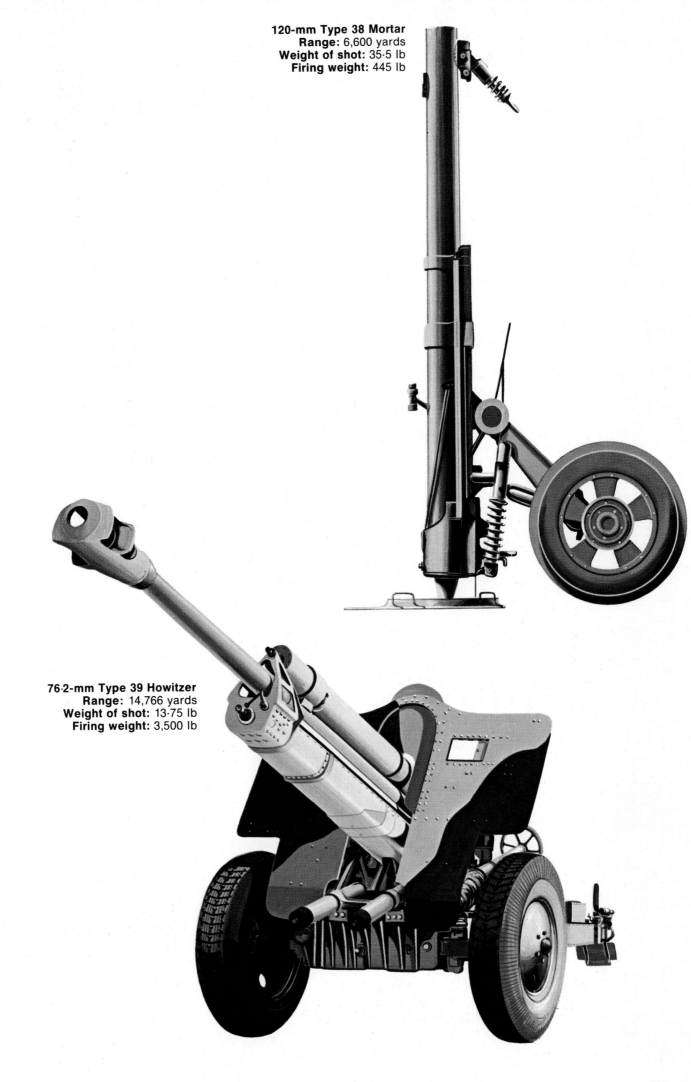

120-mm Type 38 Mortar
Range: 6,600 yards
Weight of shot: 35·5 lb
Firing weight: 445 lb

76·2-mm Type 39 Howitzer
Range: 14,766 yards
Weight of shot: 13·75 lb
Firing weight: 3,500 lb

Two sorts of armour-piercing shot. *Left and centre:* the British Armour-Piercing Discarding Sabot which shed its lightweight casing and *(right)* the Armour-Piercing Composite Rigid, which kept it until impact

The German airborne 28-mm PzB-41 gun had a barrel which tapered from 28-mm to 20-mm, giving its tungsten steel shot a muzzle velocity of 4,600 feet per second

Recoilless: the British 3·7-inch RCL saw no service in the war

Just before the Second World War broke out, a Swiss consortium approached the British government to offer a 'new and powerful explosive' for anti-tank use—at a high price. The inventors refused to divulge any information until cash was forthcoming, but were prepared to demonstrate their projectile being fired. An astute observer from the Research Department of Woolwich Arsenal went to Switzerland to watch the firing; being a well-read expert on ammunition development and history, he realised that what he was watching was not a new and powerful explosive so much as a practical application of the Monroe Effect. Upon his return to Woolwich he duly reported this, and, since it appeared that the Monroe Effect could be made to work, research immediately began into applying it to a light anti-tank grenade which the infantry soldier could fire from his rifle. Before the outbreak of war, this '68 Grenade' had been perfected and was in production, and carries the distinction of being the first weapon ever to reach the hands of troops which relied on the Monroe Effect, or as it came to be known, the Hollow-Charge Principle.

Hollow-Charge Principle

What is this Hollow-Charge Principle? Put simply, it consists of forming the forward surface of the shell's explosive charge into a cone or hemisphere and then lining this with a thin metal liner. The shell is then fitted with a suitably shaped nose, for ballistic effect and also to give the vital 'stand-off' distance. This is the distance from the target—a matter of a few inches—at which the explosive must be detonated in order for the hollow charge to work effectively. On detonating the explosive at its rear end, the detonation wave exerts an immense pressure on the metal of the liner; the cone shape virtually 'focusses' the explosive energy and causes the metal of the liner to be shaped into a jet of finely-divided metal and explosive gas, shooting toward the target at speeds of up to 20,000 feet per second. The stand-off distance is necessary in order to allow this jet to form and accelerate. When the jet strikes the target plate, the pressure exerted is so great as to blast a hole through the armour, blowing splinters of metal from the inside and permitting the white-hot jet to pass into the tank where it will set fire to fuel or ammunition, and, of course, kill or injure the crew.

The great virtue of the hollow-charge shell is that its performance is always the same, irrespective of the velocity at which it strikes. Even if the shell were standing still when detonated, the penetration would be the same. Because of this, it could be fired from guns too small to fire the large cartridges needed to give the necessary velocity to normal piercing projectiles. As soon as the 68 Grenade was seen to be successful, design began on other hollow-charge projectiles. A great deal of work went into producing one for the 25-pounder, though in the end it was never issued, since the AP shot issued for that gun was quite satisfactory and there was no real need for a hollow-charge shell. Then came a request from India to produce an anti-tank projectile for the 3.7-inch Pack Howitzer, the modern version of Kipling's immortal 'screw-gun'. This gun, a small and portable weapon, could not be made to fire a piercing projectile at anything like the velocity needed to defeat even Japanese tanks, and a hollow-charge shell was designed and placed in production. The same shell was used in the 95-mm howitzer, an abortive infantry support gun which never saw service as a towed weapon, though it was employed as a self-propelled support weapon by the Royal Marines in Normandy.

By 1944, though, sufficient basic research had been done into this principle for it to be seen that a spinning shell was not the ideal method of employing hollow charges, since the spin tended to spread the jet out and give poor penetration. Finned projectiles were more effective, and consequently no more artillery shells were designed around the hollow charge; it was extensively employed, instead, for infantry weapons such as the PIAT, the Bazooka, and a variety of rifle grenades.

The Germans, and later the Russians, embraced the hollow-charge shell wholeheartedly. The Germans began issuing shell in late 1940 and eventually almost every German field and tank weapon had a hollow-charge shell, thus giving every gun or howitzer an anti-tank capability. Indeed, so short were the Germans of anti-tank guns after the Russian invasion got under way, that they hastily collected up all the French army's 75-mm guns and assembled hundreds of them on to redundant anti-tank gun carriages of German design. A hollow-charge shell was produced and these makeshift weapons were deployed in Russia to stem the advancing Soviet tanks until 75-mm and 88-mm anti-tank guns were in sufficient supply. Judging from appearances, the Soviet hollow-charge shells were developed as virtual copies of German designs which had been captured.

In addition to artillery shell Germany also used the principle for infantry weapons such as the *Panzerfaust*, rifle grenades, and even a small shell which could be fired from a signal pistol. They also employed the principle in an ingenious attempt to prolong the life of the prewar 37-mm anti-tank gun, whose piercing projectile was, by 1942, no longer effective against current tanks. A large hollow-charge bomb was fitted with a hollow tail carrying fins; within this tail was a stick which fitted snugly into the barrel of the 37-mm gun, allowing the tail and fins to slide over the barrel. A blank cartridge completed the outfit, and this was used to fire the stick bomb to ranges of 300 to 400 yards. The bomb's warhead was about 6 inches in diameter and carried about 8 pounds of explosive, giving a devastating effect at the target. In all fairness, it must be pointed out that Lieutenant-Colonel Blacker, inventor of the PIAT and the 'Black Bombard' of Home Guard fame, had proposed a similar 60-pound stick bomb in 1940, to be fired from the 25-pounder, but the idea was turned down on the grounds that it might lead to mis-employment of the gun as a purely anti-tank weapon. (This mis-employment theme was not confined to the British side: many German Flak commanders bewailed the loss of their valuable 88-mm Flak guns as they were whittled away to provide anti-tank defences.)

The third subject is the application of new principles to gun design. The first of these to be unveiled was the taper-bore anti-tank gun, which has already been touched upon. This was the child of a German engineer called Gerlich, who, advocating his principle of attaining high velocity without attracting any buyers, had been stumping the world for several years. He was briefly employed by both the US War Department and the British War Office at various times, but his ideas on improving shoulder arms were felt to be impractical. He eventually settled in Germany and saw his idea accepted as an anti-tank weapon. The 28/21-mm came first, then a 42/30-mm and finally a 75/50-mm. Unfortunately, the lack of tungsten carbide for the special projectiles spelled the demise of these weapons, but experiments continued with coned bores and coned muzzle-adapters for guns of various calibres up to as large as 280-mm, in order to boost velocity and range. These were intended to use high-explosive shells, which were more practical in the larger calibres, though the development of a shell which would stand up to being squeezed down the gun barrel was no easy task.

The second, and more widespread, new line of thought was the recoilless gun. Like most weapon ideas, there was nothing really new about it: Commander Davis of the US Navy had produced a recoilless (RCL for short) gun during the First World War which was adopted by Britain as an anti-Zeppelin aircraft weapon. The virtue of an RCL gun is that by having no recoil one needs no complicated hydraulic buffer system to absorb the firing shock: one need only make the gun-carriage strong enough to take the weight of the gun, instead of being strong enough to withstand being fired from—an ideal state of affairs for an aircraft weapon, particularly in the stick-and-string era. Davis's idea is worth looking at, although outside our time scale, since it is the classic recoilless weapon. He simply provided the gun with two barrels, one pointing forward which fired a normal shell, and one pointing rearward which fired an identical weight of grease and buckshot. When the central cartridge was fired the shell and countershot departed at equal speed in opposite directions and cancelled each other's recoil. From this it can be seen that if you make the countershot (say) one-fifth of the weight of the shell and fire it out at five times the speed, then the gun will still be in balance. Taking this idea to its logical conclusion one finishes up firing out of the back of the gun a fast, light stream of gas, still balancing the recoil since the weight times speed of the gas is the same as the (greater) weight times (slower) speed of the shell.

Cutting down the recoil

This was the principle which the Germans revealed in Crete when their troops appeared armed with a 75-mm RCL gun. The shell was the standard 75-mm shell, but the cartridge case had a frangible plastic base which held for long enough to allow pressure to build up and start the shell moving, then blew out through a hole in the breech-block, releasing the balancing stream of gas. The all-up weight of the gun, on its ex-machine gun tripod, was only 320 pounds, whereas the weight of the standard 75-mm field gun was about 1½ tons—no mean saving for airborne carriage. A 105-mm version soon followed, weighing 855 pounds as opposed to the 105-mm 1E FH18's 4,312 pounds, and many more developments began in this field to provide light weapons for mountain troops and infantry, particularly for anti-tank use. (It ought perhaps to be pointed out that the *Panzerfaust* was in fact a recoilless gun, and not, as generally supposed, a rocket launcher). Eventually RCL guns of up to 380-mm calibre were under development, including many for slinging beneath aircraft to carry artillery aloft for the battle against the Allied bombers, but none of these came to fruition.

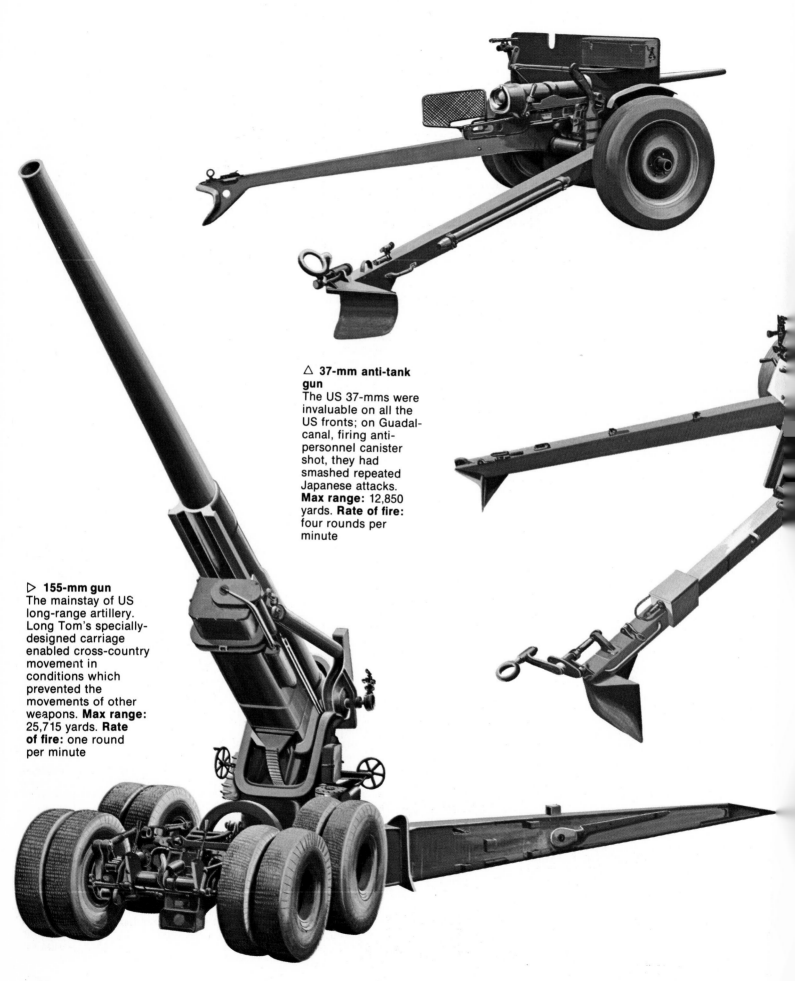

△ **37-mm anti-tank gun**
The US 37-mms were invaluable on all the US fronts; on Guadalcanal, firing anti-personnel canister shot, they had smashed repeated Japanese attacks. **Max range:** 12,850 yards. **Rate of fire:** four rounds per minute

▷ **155-mm gun**
The mainstay of US long-range artillery. Long Tom's specially-designed carriage enabled cross-country movement in conditions which prevented the movements of other weapons. **Max range:** 25,715 yards. **Rate of fire:** one round per minute

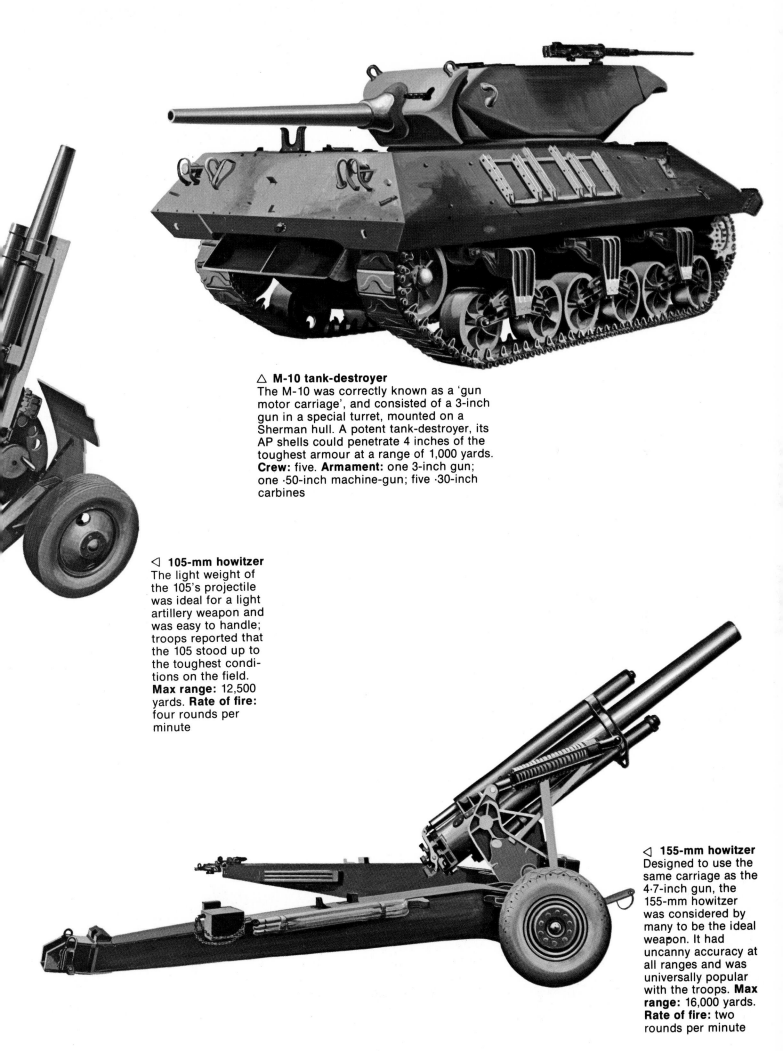

△ **M-10 tank-destroyer**
The M-10 was correctly known as a 'gun motor carriage', and consisted of a 3-inch gun in a special turret, mounted on a Sherman hull. A potent tank-destroyer, its AP shells could penetrate 4 inches of the toughest armour at a range of 1,000 yards.
Crew: five. **Armament:** one 3-inch gun; one ·50-inch machine-gun; five ·30-inch carbines

◁ **105-mm howitzer**
The light weight of the 105's projectile was ideal for a light artillery weapon and was easy to handle; troops reported that the 105 stood up to the toughest conditions on the field.
Max range: 12,500 yards. **Rate of fire:** four rounds per minute

◁ **155-mm howitzer**
Designed to use the same carriage as the 4·7-inch gun, the 155-mm howitzer was considered by many to be the ideal weapon. It had uncanny accuracy at all ranges and was universally popular with the troops. **Max range:** 16,000 yards. **Rate of fire:** two rounds per minute

A cheap substitute for the field gun was the mortar, with its high rate of fire. This specimen is the American 155-mm, seen in action in the Pacific theatre. It could throw a 60-lb bomb with great accuracy between 200 and 2,205 yards' range

In Britain, the RCL gun development during the war is a scarcely-known story of one man's persistence. Sir Denis Burney, airship designer and prolific inventor-engineer, began to be interested in the recoilless principle early in the war. In order to prove his theories he converted a four-bore gun into a recoilless weapon and proceeded to fire it from the shoulder with ease; it must have been the world's most comfortable duck gun. Having proved his point he proceeded to design a series of RCL guns ranging from 20-mm to 8-inch calibre. In addition to designing the guns, he expanded his theories and designed special ammunition to take advantage of the ballistic peculiarities of the weapon. He argued that since the rearward blast was taking place, the pressure within the gun would be less than with a conventional type, and the shell would be subjected to a more steady thrust. In which case it would be possible to make shells with thinner walls, which would carry greater charges of explosive than previously possible. He then went further, and reasoned that, since the shell walls were thin, if the shell were to be filled with the then new plastic explosive, it would spread on to the surface of the target like butter; a fuse fitted in the base of the shell would then detonate this plaster and blast in the target. His envisaged target was either the concrete emplacements of the European coast, or the palm-reinforced Japanese bunker, and he called his shell the 'Wallbuster'.

In 1944 his designs were accepted and a 3.45-inch (the same calibre as the 25-pounder) shoulder-fired gun, a 3.7-inch towed gun, a 95-mm towed howitzer, and a 7.2-inch towed howitzer were prepared for production. The 95-mm was also jeep-mounted—the first application of what has since become a standard method of carrying these guns. The 7.2-inch soon fell by the wayside, since it had been intended solely as a means of defeating the Atlantic Wall emplacements, but other weapons were found to do all that was needed. The 3.45-inch was intended as an infantry weapon in the jungle, enabling one man to carry what was virtually a 25-pounder punch on his shoulder. The 3.7-inch was proposed as the future infantry anti-tank weapon, and the 95-mm was contemplated

as the airborne field gun to replace the US 75-mm howitzer and the 25-pounder. However, before the guns were produced in sufficient quantity for issue, the war came to an end; some 3.45-inch and 3.7-inch guns were issued to selected units to obtain their reaction to RCL guns and the 95-mm was abandoned altogether.

The principal difference between the Burney guns and the German type was that the Burneys had much longer barrels, and used cartridge cases which, instead of the plastic blow-out base, used many perforations in the sidewall to release the gas into a surrounding chamber, from whence it was passed back to a number of vents around the breech.

Concurrently with Burney's work in Britain, American designers began on similar weapons. A 105-mm howitzer T-9 was developed on similar lines to the German 105-mm, having a blow-out base to the cartridge. Another team developed 57-mm and 75-mm weapons which used perforated cases similar to the Burney pattern but having more and smaller holes, and also had the shell driving band pre-engraved in order to reduce the pressure inside the gun. Both these latter weapons were accepted for service early in 1945, saw service with the US Army in the Pacific theatre, and remained in service for many years. A third team, this time under the auspices of the National Research and Development Council, developed a 4.2-inch RCL mortar, an unlikely-sounding weapon which, so as to be able to fire direct at the target at low angles, carried a small rocket on the nose of the shell to push it down the barrel and fire the propelling cartridge in the usual mortar fashion. Due to the blast of the rearward jet, it could only be fired at low elevations; there was a certain amount of enthusiasm for this weapon but it never entered service.

Perhaps the best summing up of all wartime development on RCL weapons was made in a wartime report: 'Undoubtedly a number of effective recoilless weapons have been developed, but they are being accepted with reserve, and will only be considered as supplementary to older and more orthodox weapons which have proved their accuracy and reliability in service.'

Below: A German gun crew engages the enemy on the streets of Zhitomir during the Axis advance into the Ukraine in the summer of 1941.
Right: A large German coastal gun looks out to sea in anticipation of the Allied invasion of Western Europe

ANTI-AIRCRAFT GUNS

Left: A German anti-aircraft post maintains its silent vigil in the twilight of a Norwegian fiord. The silhouette on the left is a 20-mm AA gun and the one on the right is a range finder

Right: German 88-mm AA guns nestle in a snow-clad Norwegian valley. *Below:* An '88' in action in Bulgaria, 1941

he German '88' was probably the best-publicised gun of the war, but it was only one of a varied armoury of anti-aircraft guns used by the Germans. Their standard light weapon was the 20 mm cannon, usually mounted as a twin or quadruple-barrel assembly, which delivered an impressive volume of short-range fire. The '88' was the medium gun, and there were also 105 mm and 128 mm heavy guns, principally retained in Germany for home defence. The gap between the 20 mm and the '88' was difficult to fill, the requirement being for a gun small enough to swing rapidly to keep up with low-flying raiders, but with enough power to reach up to 6000 feet or so with a lethal-sized shell. A 50 mm gun was tried, but was a mechanical failure, and it was followed by an excellent 55 mm model . . . but this was never finished in time.

The British and American forces, in contrast, relied less on the 20 mm calibre. Their light weapon was the famous 'Bofors' 40 mm gun. The British used the 3.7 inch and the Americans the 90 mm as their medium guns, while the heavy class was covered by the British 4.5 inch and the American 105 mm and 120 mm models. The Americans never tried to develop an 'intermediate' gun, and the British attempt – a 57 mm 6-pounder – did not meet with success.

Left: Armed with a Fiat 1935 8-mm machine gun fitted with AA sights, this Italian gun-crew awaits enemy aircraft along the sun-drenched Mediterranean shores of Cyrenaica during the early stages of the Desert War. *Below:* Their AA-sighted MG34 pointed to the skies, these German SS gunners on the Channel coast await airborne Allied interlopers in 1940

GERMANY'S ANSWER TO THE BOMBERS

Just as the Germans had been the first to realise and exploit the offensive power of aircraft, so they were among the first to provide their forces with a wide range of anti-aircraft equipment, ranging from the multiple 20-mm cannon to the legendary 88 and even larger weapons. All the guns illustrated below in their mobile versions could also be used to provide static defence for strategic targets, and combined with radar and searchlights to form a series of defensive belts

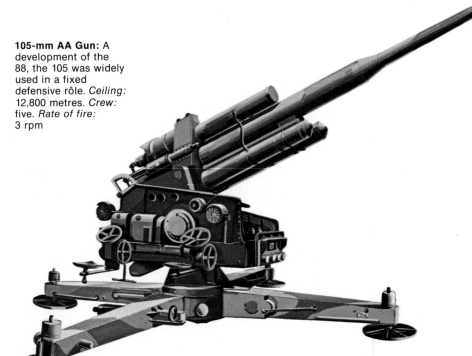

105-mm AA Gun: A development of the 88, the 105 was widely used in a fixed defensive rôle. *Ceiling:* 12,800 metres. *Crew:* five. *Rate of fire:* 3 rpm

128-mm AA Gun: When used in a static rôle this heavy AA gun looked very similar to the 105. It is shown here mounted on a railway car. *Crew:* six. *Ceiling:* 14,800 metres. *Rate of fire:* 2 rpm

37-mm Flak 43: The German equivalent of the Allied Bofors 40-mm light AA gun, mounted on a Sdkfz-251 chassis. *Crew:* four. *Rate of fire:* 150 rpm

20-mm Flakvierling 38: This version of the quadruple 20-mm was mounted on a small trailer and could be towed behind a light vehicle

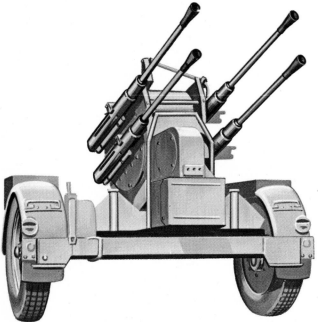

▽ There could be no relaxation for the flak crews on the Channel coast, many of whom had scores dating back for over two years

20-mm Flakvierling 38: The quadruple version of a standard light AA gun, armoured and mounted on a Pzkw-IV chassis. *Ceiling:* 6,230 metres. *Rate of fire:* 700/800 rpm

88-mm Grille 10: The most tested and feared German anti-tank and AA gun, mounted on a Pzkw-IV chassis. *Crew:* six. *Ceiling:* 10,800 metres. *Rate of fire:* 3 rpm

141

La Panne beach: the British Expeditionary Force destroyed many of their AA guns before they left.

FROM THE ALLIED AA ARMOURY

40-mm BOFORS ANTI-AIRCRAFT GUN. The Bofors, designed in Sweden, was one of the most widely used weapons of the war. It was not only an extremely effective anti-aircraft gun, but was also used during night attacks—such as Alamein—to fire tracer as a guide-line for advancing infantry. **Weight in action:** 2·4 tons. **Weight of shell:** 2 lb. **Rate of fire:** 120 rounds per minute. **Effective altitude:** 12,000 feet. **Crew:** Average of six.

Light Flak for the Allies
The 20-mm Oerlikon cannon, here shown on its naval mounting, was one of the most valued guns in Allied use. It served on land and sea, in all theatres, defending the ships on the 'Black-Out Route' to Russia and the Malta convoys, in the Atlantic and the Pacific. It was used to give teeth to amphibious landing-craft. It was mounted in anti-aircraft tanks such as the Skink and the AA Crusader—and it was one of the weapons 'blooded' in the European theatre that was most willingly adopted by the US armed forces. *Crew:* three. *Rate of fire:* 650 rounds per minute. *Magazine capacity:* 60-round drums

TANKS
KNIGHTS OF THE BATTLEFIELD

British Matildas on the move: the desert battle for Halfaya Pass in the summer of 1941 ended their reputation as 'the invulnerable queen of the battlefield', for the German 88s, used as anti-tank guns, penetrated their thick armour with ease'

PANZERS GO TO WAR

The tanks which thundered across the Polish border on September 1, 1939, were the product of years of development and probably represented the best armoured force in the world at that time. Of the models in use, the Panzer I design had begun in 1933, the Panzer II in 1934, the Panzer IV in 1935 and the Panzer III in 1936. The first Panzer Division was formed in 1935; in the years which followed more divisions were equipped and trained, and a number of tank battalions gained valuable experience in the Spanish Civil War. In addition to the German-designed tanks, the Panzer divisions entering Poland deployed a number of Czechoslovakian TNHP tanks. These were known as the Panzer 38(t), were extremely good light tanks, and formed a useful addition to German fighting strength.

In the campaign which followed the crossing of the border, however, several important facts emerged. The Panzer I — weighing just over 5 tons, with two machine guns, a two-man crew and thin armour — was soon seen to be more or less useless, and in fact had been obsolete before the war began. But 1500 had been built, and they made up a large portion of the German strength. As a result of Poland, most of them were withdrawn from service and the chassis used for building self-propelled guns and command tanks (the 'Panzer-befehl' type of vehicle). The Panzer II, a three-man tank of 7½ tons, mounting a 20 mm gun, was also obsolete as a fighting tank, but was useful for fast reconnaissance and scouting and was retained in some numbers as well as becoming a source of chassis for other types of fighting vehicle. The two tanks which bore the brunt of the action were the Panzer III, with a 37 mm high-velocity gun, and the Panzer IV with a short-barrelled 75 mm gun. These two were similar in appearance and design except for the armament, but battle showed that their weaponry could stand improvement: the 37 mm had become marginal as an anti-tank gun, while the 75 mm was too short and could not develop the velocity necessary to defeat armour. Consequently, the Panzer III was given a new, 50 mm gun which was a shortened version of the standard anti-tank gun, but the unfortunate Panzer IV remained unchanged with its 75 mm weapon.

As a result, when the offensive against France and the Low Countries opened in May 1940, the German Army had 329 Panzer IIIs and 280 Panzer IVs, as well as 381 Czech 35(t) and 38(t) models. With the remaining Panzer Is and IIs, the total strength in the field was 2514 tanks.

The French and British, between them, could muster more than this, but the German training and organisation was superior to that of the French, and the Panzers were concentrated in force while the Allied tanks were strung out along the whole length of the Franco-German frontier. Once again the German armour triumphed, except for a memorable setback when they met the British Matilda tanks at Arras. From then on, confident in their designs, the Germans rested rather on their laurels, only to be given a severe shaking in 1941 when they discovered that their products were inferior to the latest Russian designs pouring off the production lines by the hundred.

Panzer I A *(right)*. First used in the Spanish Civil War, this German light tank served in great numbers during Hitler's Blitzkriegs of Czechoslovakia, Poland and the West. **Weight:** 5.4 tons **Speed:** 25 mph **Crew:** 2 **Armour:** 13 mm max **Armament:** 2×7.92-mm mg

Panzer 35(t) *(below)*. 106 of these Czech TNHP light tanks served with the *Wehrmacht* following the take-over of 1939, and the model was produced until 1942. **Weight:** 9.9 tons **Speed:** 25 mph **Crew:** 4 **Armour:** 35 mm max **Armament:** 37.2-mm gun; 2×7.92-mm mg

Below: Tank pincers against Poland, 1939

Panzer II B *or* **C.** The backbone of the German armoured forces that invaded Poland and the West, this light tank went on to suffer a terrible mauling in Russia. **Weight:** 9.5 tons **Speed:** 25 mph **Crew:** 3 **Armour:** 30 mm max **Armament:** 20-mm cannon; 1×7.92-mm mg

In Poland, a Panzer I leads two Panzer IIs past a dead symbol of a bygone age

Ullstein

Panzer III B *or* **C** *(above).* These models
appeared during 1937. Only 15 of each were
ever built, and despite seeing service in
both Poland and the West they were only
ever a step on the way to future mass-
produced Panzer IIIs. **Weight:** 15 tons
Speed: 20 mph **Crew:** 5 **Armour:** 14.5 mm
max **Armament:** 37-mm gun; 3 mg

Panzer IA *(above, right).* Illustrated here
to show clearly the twin-machine-gun turret.
Once superseded by Panzer IIIs and IVs,
this tank went on to perform many general
duties including towing, reconnaissance,
etc. *(See page 146 for specifications)*

Panzer 38(t) *(right).* One of the best German
light tanks, this was a further product of
the Czech arms industry taken over in 1939.
During the invasion of France two Panzer
divisions were equipped with this model,
which formed 25 per cent of the German
tank force during 1940/41. **Weight:** 8.5 tons
Speed: 20 mph **Crew:** 4 **Armour:** 25 mm max
Armament: 37.2-mm gun; 2×7.2-mm mg

A waterproofed German Panzerbefehlswagen III scales the eastern bank of the River Bug (demarcation-line between the USSR and Nazi-occupied Poland) on June 22, 1941 — the first day of Hitler's invasion of Russia, Operation Barbarossa

THE BLITZKRIEG STYLE

The success of the Panzer divisions in 1939 and 1940 was due to early German recognition of one fundamental fact: that tanks by themselves could do little more than penetrate an enemy line, and penetration by itself was not sufficient to win battles. This basic fact had been revealed during World War One when tanks frequently got through the German lines, but since they were unable to consolidate their gains, and since support did not reach them, they achieved nothing lasting. In the inter-war years two principal Allied schools of thought arose: the British tank enthusiasts called for an independent tank force, hoping that in some way they would make such a hole in the enemy front that support would have no difficulty in reaching them. The French, on the other hand, tied their tanks firmly to the infantry, allowing the foot soldiers to determine the speed of advance.

The Germans, largely due to the guidance of Guderian, opted for a different solution. They prepared their tank force for penetration, but then attached to it a motorised support of infantry, artillery and engineers, together with a reconnaissance force of armoured cars and motorcycles. Thus their armoured division became a self-sustaining force of all arms, all units of which were on wheels or tracks and could keep up with the tanks in an advance, prepared to take advantage of any gains the tanks made.

The paper strength of the 1939 Panzer Division was 561 tanks, two two-battalion infantry regiments, 24 105 mm field howit- zers, 48 37 mm anti-tank guns, 16 75 mm infantry guns, together with light anti-tank and anti-aircraft weapons, mortars, and 84 armoured cars. Altogether this represented a force which could act quite independently and which was sufficiently well-balanced to be able to fight almost any sort of battle. Unfortunately, as with every other army through the ages, what the planners planned and what the soldiers actually had were two different things. In fact the Panzer Division generally had about 320–350 tanks instead of the planned 561, though the support element was normally up to strength.

It was these balanced, autonomous forces which carried out the German successes in Poland and France, aided to some degree by fortunate circumstances. In Poland the

Panzer III E *(below)*. The first mass-produced Panzer III, this model—by far the best tank of its kind—was rushed into service in France in 1940. **Weight:** 19.5 tons **Speed:** 25 mph **Crew:** 5 **Armour:** 30 mm basic **Armament:** 37-mm gun; 2 mg

Panzerbefehlswagen I *(above)*. This armoured command vehicle equipped with radio and map tables was built on a Panzer I hull, and served in the forefront of almost every German armoured assault of the War. Later models were built on the Panzer III hull.

speed and strength of the Panzer attack, supported by tactical air forces, soon smashed the Polish defences, and this rapid campaign had a psychological effect which is frequently overlooked. The new elements of warfare – tanks, the armoured spearhead, the Stuka and the lightning speed of advance and multi-pronged attack – appeared to the rest of the world both fearsome and apparently invincible. Skilfully made German propaganda films, playing on these points, were widely distributed through neutral countries and helped to build up the picture of German might. So, when the Panzers attacked again, in 1940, their reputation had gone before them, being magnified in the process. This reputation, together with the political atmosphere in France, was a considerable factor in the subsequent campaign: with such a ferocious war machine attacking, what was the use of trying to withstand it?

By the outbreak of war the British armoured division had moved away from the original all-tank idea to a formation closer to that of the Germans. The British division contained 321 tanks, with a supporting force of one motorised infantry battalion, a 16-gun artillery regiment and a company of engineers. The French, having clung far too long to their theory of the tank as a mechanised infantryman, were on the point of changing their ideas as war broke out, and their armoured division consisted of 158 tanks, a battalion of infantry and 24 light field guns.

The subsequent course of the war saw the British armoured division move closer to the German form, while the Panzer Division was reorganised and supplemented in various ways dependent upon the theatre of war in which it operated, being given a massive augmentation of firepower by the addition of assault guns, rocket launchers, heavy mortars and tank destroyers at various times. In their assessment of the requirement and their organisation to meet it, the Panzer Divisions were always ahead of their opponents, and most of the world's armoured forces of the present day can trace their organisational theories back to Guderian's 1939 Panzer Divisions.

General Rommel – VII Panzer Division's brilliant commander in France, 1940

Panzer IV D (below). Originally designed to support the Panzer III, the IV D soon became a main battle tank itself. **Weight:** 17.3 tons **Speed:** 26 mph **Crew:** 5 **Armour:** 30-mm max **Armament:** short 75-mm gun; 2 mg

After the Allied evacuation at Dunkirk, Rommel and his VII Panzer Division wheel south, crushing all French opposition

EARLY ALLIED TANKS

The principal defect of the tanks of the Allies in 1940 lay less in their construction than in their conception. The British and French armies believed that the coming war would be a continuation of World War One, an affair of trench lines and slow advances by masses of infantry accompanied by tanks at walking pace. In addition, the tank theorists of the 1930s had managed to convince people of the need for mobility, but they had done it so well that they had gone rather too far, raising visions of hordes of light and speedy tanks dashing all over the battlefield in the role of cavalry. As a result, by 1940 there were two distinct types of tank in service: the fast 'cruiser' with negligible armour and armament, and the ponderous 'infantry tank' with powerful armour but still with poor armament. The right balance between speed, protection and gunpower, as exemplified by the German Panzer III and IV, had eluded the Allies – an inevitable result of their faulty tactical thinking.

The British light 'cruiser' tanks – the A9 Cruiser Mk 1, A10 Cruiser Mk 2 and A13 Covenanter – were all thinly plated and armed with the two-pounder gun, which could fire only anti-tank solid shot and was quite useless against any other sort of target. A number of A10s tried to balance this by carrying a 3-inch low-velocity gun (known for some reason as a 'mortar'), but this had absolutely no anti-tank capability and merely erred in the other direction. The 'infantry' tank, the Matilda 2, was a strongly armoured

A British Cruiser Mk IV training 'somewhere in England' prior to service with the 1st Armoured Division in France

Cruiser Mk IV. Also known as the A13 Mk II, this tank served in both France and Libya. Its speed was an asset, but it was lightly armoured and prone to break down. **Weight:** 14.75 tons **Speed:** 30 mph **Crew:** 4 **Armour:** 30 mm max **Armament:** 2-pounder gun; 1mg

vehicle which could shrug off most German anti-tank gun projectiles, but it too carried nothing better than the totally inadequate two-pounder.

The French line-up began with the 10-ton Renault R-35 and the similar Hotchkiss H-35, both fairly agile and speedy, with armour up to 40 mm thick, but armed with only a 37 mm gun which was even less potent than the two-pounder. The worst feature of these tanks was that they carried only two men, the driver and the commander-gunner-wireless operator, who had more than enough to do. The medium tank, the 20-ton Somua 35, was a rather more formidable vehicle with heavier armour and a slightly better 47 mm gun. This carried a three-man crew, but still left the commander alone in the turret to act as gunner as well as trying to control the tank in action. The 'infantry' tank was the renowned Char B, a collection of anomalies which combined to make it useless. On paper it was brilliant, with a 75 mm hull-mounted gun, a 47 mm turret gun, 60 mm cast armour and good cross-country performance; but still the commander was alone in the turret, working like a one-armed paper hanger, while the 75 mm gun had no traverse and could only be aimed by swinging the whole tank on to the target, which called for some remarkably fine cooperation between driver and gunner. While the Char B's armour gave the Germans some difficult moments, this was insufficient to balance out its other undesirable features.

Infantry Mk I *(left)*. Also known as the A11 and nicknamed 'Matilda', 139 of these tanks were built before being superseded by the infantry Mk II, officially called 'Matilda'. Although invulnerable to all German anti-tank guns in 1940, their slow speed allowed the Panzers to outflank them with ease and great numbers were abandoned as the BEF evacuated from Dunkirk. **Weight:** 11 tons **Speed:** 8 mph **Crew:** 2 **Armour:** 60 mm max **Armament:** 1 mg

Light Mk VIB *(below)*. The most widely used British light tank of the war, this model formed a high proportion of the tank strength in France in 1940. **Weight:** 5.2 tons **Speed:** 35 mph **Crew:** 3 **Armour:** 14 mm max **Armament:** 2 mg

Cruiser Mk I *(above)*. Also known as the A9, this model served in France in 1940 and in the Middle East until 1941. Although a useful tank, economies in armour and armament made it no match for the Panzers of the day. **Weight:** 12 tons **Speed:** 25 mph **Crew:** 6 **Armour:** 14 mm max **Armament:** 2-pounder gun; 3 mg

The Matilda – 'Queen of the battlefield' in both France and the Desert

Char B-2 Well armed, heavily armoured and relatively fast, this French battle tank set German gunners quite a problem in 1940. Its one-man, non-traversing turret, though, cancelled out much of its advantage. **Weight:** 32 tons **Speed:** 17 mph **Crew:** 4 **Armour:** 60 mm max **Armament:** 75-mm gun; 47-mm gun; 2 mg

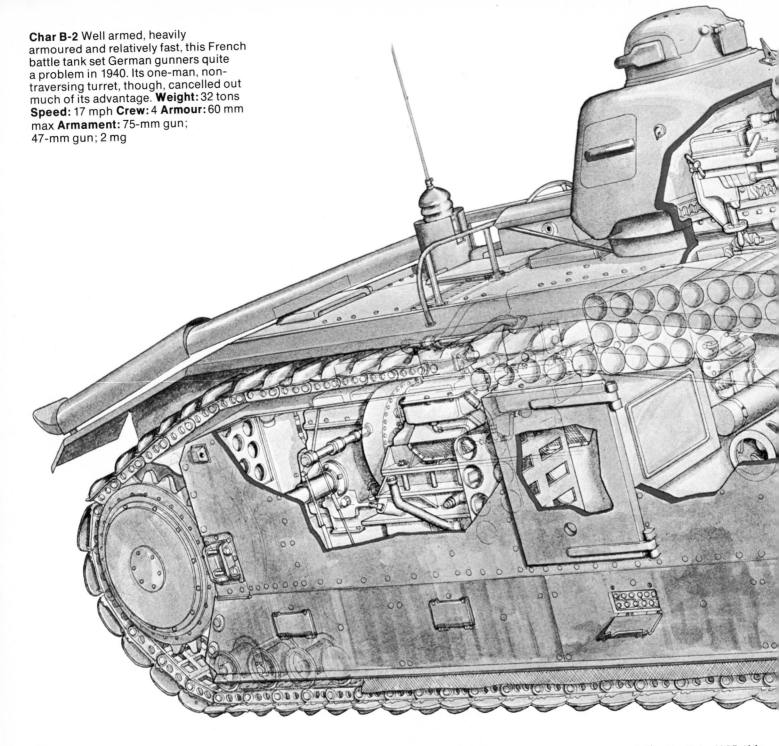

In northern France, 1940, Renault R-35s and crews await the advancing Panzers

Somua S-35 *(below)*. First built in 1935, this powerful French tank appeared the statistical equal of its main opponent, the German Panzer III. Both in its interior layout and in the training and tactical approach of its crews, however, it was unsuited to the new, flexible style of armoured warfare. **Weight:** 20 tons **Speed:** 25 mph **Crew:** 3 **Armour:** 55 mm max **Armament:** 47-mm gun; 1 mg

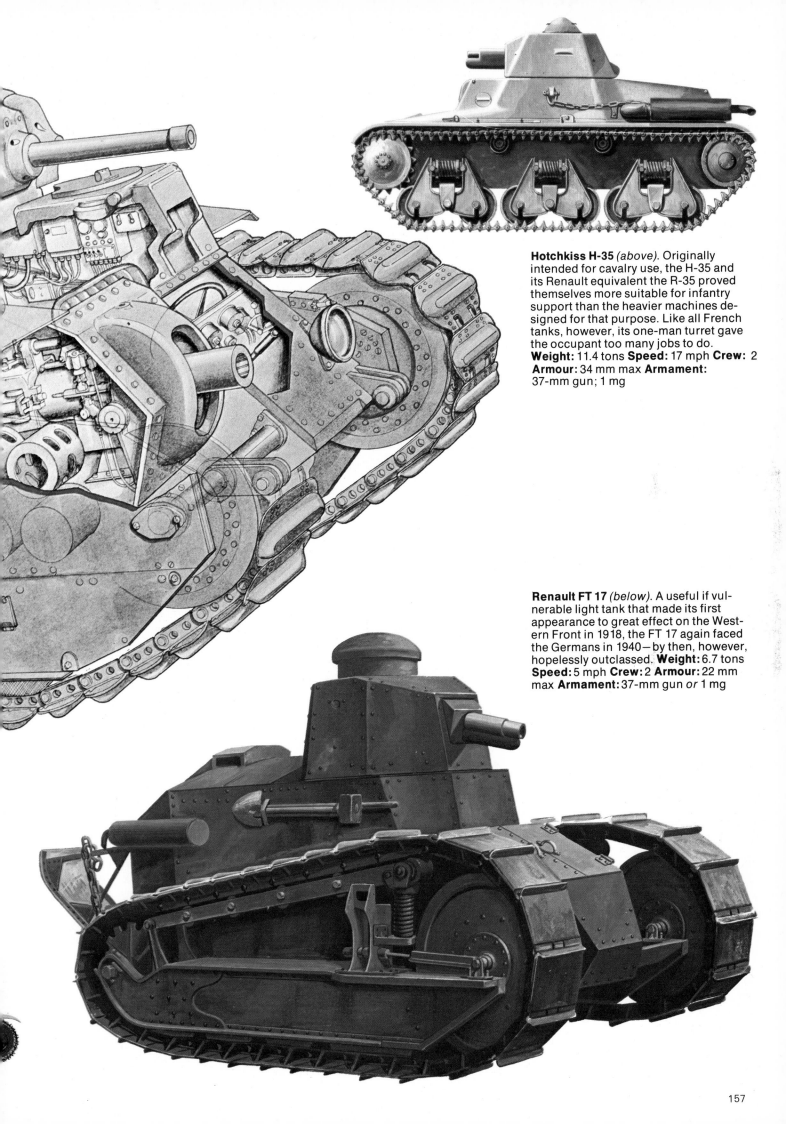

Hotchkiss H-35 *(above)*. Originally intended for cavalry use, the H-35 and its Renault equivalent the R-35 proved themselves more suitable for infantry support than the heavier machines designed for that purpose. Like all French tanks, however, its one-man turret gave the occupant too many jobs to do. **Weight:** 11.4 tons **Speed:** 17 mph **Crew:** 2 **Armour:** 34 mm max **Armament:** 37-mm gun; 1 mg

Renault FT 17 *(below)*. A useful if vulnerable light tank that made its first appearance to great effect on the Western Front in 1918, the FT 17 again faced the Germans in 1940—by then, however, hopelessly outclassed. **Weight:** 6.7 tons **Speed:** 5 mph **Crew:** 2 **Armour:** 22 mm max **Armament:** 37-mm gun *or* 1 mg

A patrol of the Long Range Desert Group: although intended mainly as a recon- naissance force, it also created confusion in the enemy's camp, forcing him to hold back vital troops to guard his communication lines

WEAPONS OF
THE DESERT WAR

THE EARLY DAYS

The British Army in Egypt was equipped with a mixture of tanks when the campaign began in 1940. There was the elderly Vickers Mark VI, mounting nothing heavier than a .303 machine gun or a .50 anti-tank rifle; the Crusader, a continuation of the A13 design with the same Christie suspension and two-pounder gun; and the Matilda infantry tank. These were later supplemented by the American M3 Stuart, called the Honey in British circles.

Their opposition on the Italian side consisted principally of the L/3, M/11 and M/13 models. The L/3, built by Ansaldo, was a 3-ton, two-man vehicle armed with twin machine guns and capable of nearly 28 mph. As a fighting vehicle, however, it was outclassed and outdated, principally because the machine guns were mounted in the hull and did not allow all-round fire. The M/11 was a three-man 11-tonner with a 37 mm gun, optimistically called a 'breakthrough' tank. In practice, though, it suffered from the same defect as the L/3: the main gun was in the hull and could cover only a restricted zone. One critic in fact described the L/3 as the worst design of the period. The M/13 was an improvement on the M/11, and used a turret to mount its 47 mm gun. While it was a considerable advance on the previous model it arrived too late to have any significant effect on the campaign.

The advantage was thus on the British side, since although their tanks were not particularly outstanding they were certainly better than the Italians', and the British crews were better trained. But the Crusader and Matilda were both prone to mechanical trouble, the Crusader being especially prone to breaking its tracks at critical moments. The thickness of the Matilda's armour made it the 'Queen of the Battlefield,' and was responsible for keeping it, and the whole idea of 'infantry tanks', in existence long after the theory should have been exploded.

The American Stuart was the latest in a line of designs which went back several years, so that by 1940 most of the mechanical problems had been overcome and it proved extremely reliable in action. Powered by a 9-cylinder radial diesel or a 7-cylinder radial petrol engine, both of which were air-cooled, it could travel at 36 mph. Armament was a 37 mm gun which fired both

Over the top. Pith-helmeted infantrymen of Graziani's Italian desert army attack during their initial, hesitant thrust of 65 miles to Sidi Barrani in Egypt

Light field-gun support for the advancing Italian troops

Right: **Autoblinda 41:** medium armoured car of the Italian desert army. Turret gun: 20-mm Machine-gun: 8-mm.

Below and left: **Italian M15/42 medium tanks moving across ideal terrain into Egypt. Badly designed and poorly armed, they proved no match for the British Matildas of the day**

Paul Popper

The Italian C-in-C: Marshal Graziani

M13/40 (left). This was the standard Italian medium tank during and after the 'Wavell campaign'. Unfortunately, despite good armour and armament, the tank's maximum cross-country speed of 7 mph caused it to fall into Allied hands by the score. **Weight:** 14 tons **Speed:** 20 mph max **Crew:** 4 **Armour:** 40 mm max **Armament:** 47-mm gun; 3 mg

Light Tank CV33/5 (below). This Italian design was little more than an infantry-accompanying machine-gun carrier. In this role it was quite useful; when used as a light tank it invariably came off worst. **Weight:** 3 tons **Speed:** 25 mph **Crew:** 2 **Armour:** 10 mm **Armament:** 2 mg

armour-piercing shot and high explosive shell, and it mounted six .30 Browning machine guns.

The wide open spaces of the Western Desert also gave considerable scope for the employment of armoured cars, and the British Army was still able to put a number of 1924-model Rolls-Royce cars into action. These carried a Vickers machine gun and a .50 Boys anti-tank rifle in the turret, and the legendary reliability of the Rolls-Royce motor was their strongest feature. A more modern vehicle, albeit less reliable, was the Humber car, armed with the 7.92 mm Besa machine gun, and this was later reinforced by the Daimler car which mounted the same two-pounder gun as used on the tanks. The South African Army used the Marmon-Herrington, assembled in South Africa from parts supplied from the United States. The Italians used the Fiat Autoblinda 40, with a turret-mounted machine gun, and later replaced it by the Model 41 which carried a modified tank turret holding a 20 mm cannon and a machine gun. These cars were valuable for reconnaissance and raiding, but they were at a distinct disadvantage when set upon by tanks.

A British Vickers Mark VIB light tank speeds on patrol in the Western Desert in 1941

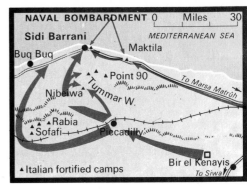

Left: A British armoured vehicle crosses the wire into Libya. *Above:* The Italians began the war in the Desert with a slow, hesitant advance to Sidi Barrani in Egypt, where they stopped and dug in. The British counterattack was the first of a series of engagements that took O'Connor's Western Desert Force all the way to El Agheila *(see map, below).* Classically, the main tactic used by the British tanks was to outflank the defence by wide sweeps through the desert to the enemy's rear, severing communications and spreading confusion

Universal Carrier *(left).* The ubiquitous British Bren-gun Carrier was well-suited to conditions in North Africa. **Weight:** 3 tons **Speed:** 25 mph **Crew:** 2 **Armour:** 11 mm max **Armament:** 1 mg

Rolls-Royce Armoured Car *(below).* A handful of these First World War relics saw action in Cyrenaica in 1940/41. **Weight:** 3.5 tons **Speed:** 45 mph **Crew:** 3 **Armour** 7 mm max **Armament:** 1 mg

Matilda II *(Below:).* Also known as the Infantry Tank Mk II, this British tank was built in 1938 to support men on foot, resist the fire of current anti-tank guns and destroy enemy troops, weapons and tanks. After a brief but glorious career in France and the Desert in 1940/41, the tank's offensive and defensive capabilities were outclassed by newer German and Russian designs. **Weight:** 26 tons **Speed:** 15 mph **Crew:** 4 **Armour:** 80 mm max **Armament:** 40-mm gun; 1 mg

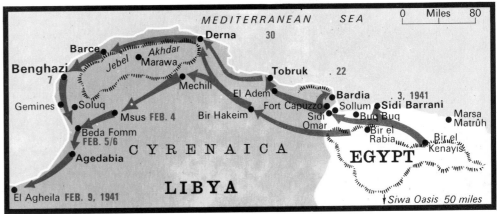

THE AFRIKA KORPS

With the arrival of the German Army in the Western Desert, the British superiority in tanks suffered a setback. Then when improved Panzers made their appearance, things began to look very black indeed. The Panzer IIIs and IVs had been bad enough, but the latter end of 1941 saw the arrival of the Panzer III Special and the IVG, both of which mounted much-improved armament. The III Special now had a long-barrelled 50 mm gun firing the same ammunition as the old model but at a higher velocity to defeat armour at a longer range; while the IVG now had a long 75 mm gun of much

greater power than the original short-barrelled version. Moreover, the anti-tank capability of the Afrika Korps was greatly reinforced by the use of its 88 mm anti-aircraft guns as long-range tank destroyers.

Simply speaking, the Crusaders and Matildas were outclassed. While the Crusader could manoeuvre, its armour was too thin and vulnerable to German fire long before it could get close enough to succeed with its two-pounder gun. The Matilda, in spite of its heavier plate, had the same defect and, being slower, was an easier target into the bargain. But then, late in 1941,

the American M3 General Lee and General Grant tanks appeared. These both mounted a 75 mm gun in a limited-traverse turret on the right side of the hull and a 37 mm gun in a fully traversing turret on top. The Lee also had a small cupola, or sub-turret, on top of the main turret, in which a machine gun was mounted; the Grant did not have this cupola, and this is the only difference between the two. The 75 mm gun, while not as powerful as that in the Panzer IVG, nevertheless gave the Germans a surprise when they first met the M3 tanks, while the reliability of these American products was

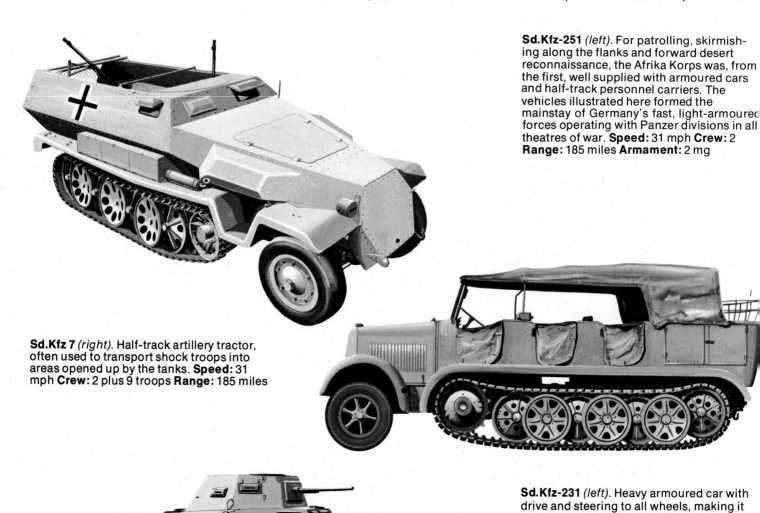

Sd.Kfz-251 *(left)*. For patrolling, skirmishing along the flanks and forward desert reconnaissance, the Afrika Korps was, from the first, well supplied with armoured cars and half-track personnel carriers. The vehicles illustrated here formed the mainstay of Germany's fast, light-armoured forces operating with Panzer divisions in all theatres of war. **Speed:** 31 mph **Crew:** 2 **Range:** 185 miles **Armament:** 2 mg

Sd.Kfz 7 *(right)*. Half-track artillery tractor, often used to transport shock troops into areas opened up by the tanks. **Speed:** 31 mph **Crew:** 2 plus 9 troops **Range:** 185 miles

Sd.Kfz-231 *(left)*. Heavy armoured car with drive and steering to all wheels, making it a fast, highly mobile desert weapon. **Weight:** 6 tons **Speed:** 50 mph **Crew:** 4 **Armour:** 14 mm max **Armament:** 20-mm gun; 1 mg **Range:** 187 miles

Sd.Kfz-222 *(right)*. Light armoured car. **Speed:** 50 mph **Crew:** 3 **Armament:** 20-mm cannon; 1 mg **Range:** 180 miles

△ German armoured cars in a night battle for Tobruk: 'scurrying through the night', says the original German caption

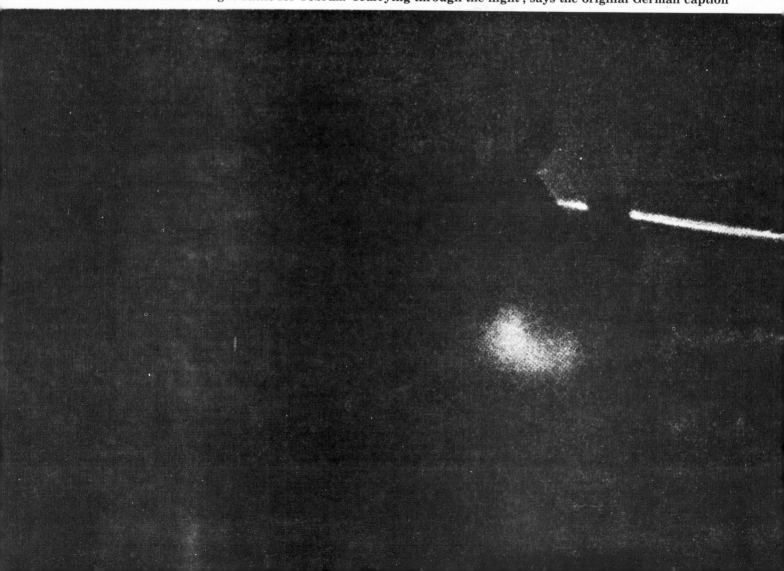

▽ German tracer strikes home: 'our shells hit them', says the caption; 'munitions explode, sparks fly'

outstanding. Their principal defects were the limited arc of the 75 mm gun and their high silhouettes, which made them good targets.

Experience in North Africa had taught the British something about the desirable features of tanks, and all these lessons were passed to the Americans who incorporated them in their next design, the M4 General

This page: An MG34-armed BMW motorcycle combination negotiates the desert sands of North Africa. Such motorcycle units were an important part of the German army's scouting and reconnaissance forces in all theatres

Sherman, which appeared in time to go into action at El Alamein in October 1942. This design put the 75 mm gun into the main turret, did away with the hull turret, and lowered the silhouette. From then on the Sherman became the standard American tank, some 49,000 being built during the war. The German reply to this new threat was to bring some Tiger tanks to North Africa late in 1942. Weighing 56 tons, with armour 100 mm thick and carrying the formidable 88 mm gun, the Tiger could move at 25 mph and was indeed a dangerous opponent. It suffered, however, from poor engine design and so demanded constant maintenance, and as it frequently broke down some of its potential was never realised.

The Germans also brought armoured cars to the desert, and the 8-wheeled SdKfz 231

of eight tons is the model usually associated with the Afrika Korps, but there were also numbers of the smaller 4-wheeled 4½-ton SdKfz 222. Both these were armed with a 20 mm cannon as standard, though a small number of 8-wheelers had the turret removed and the hull fitted with a 75 mm short-barrelled gun.

Right: Unkempt British SAS (Special Air Service) members of a LRDG pose in their battered jeeps prior to setting off on patrol. Liberally armed with Vickers 'K' machine guns and equipped to spend weeks in the wastes of the desert, these roving units performed valuable scouting and raiding duties far behind enemy lines

CUSTOM-MADE FOR DESERT RAIDS

Chevrolet 30-cwt truck: the first few of these, which formed the basic equipment of the LRDG[*] patrols, had to be bought in Cairo or begged from the Egyptian army. There was never any attempt at standardisation, each vehicle being modified as its commander thought fit. They were given a high fire-power, using Lewis machine-guns and Boyes anti-tank rifles to begin with, and Brownings, Vickers K's, and ·5-inch Vickers machine-guns later. The first machines had a 37 Bofors A/T gun mounted in back, but this was often replaced with captured Italian 20-mm Bredas. Normal range was 1,100 miles, carrying three weeks' supply of food and water

ALLIED TANKS – THE SECOND GENERATION

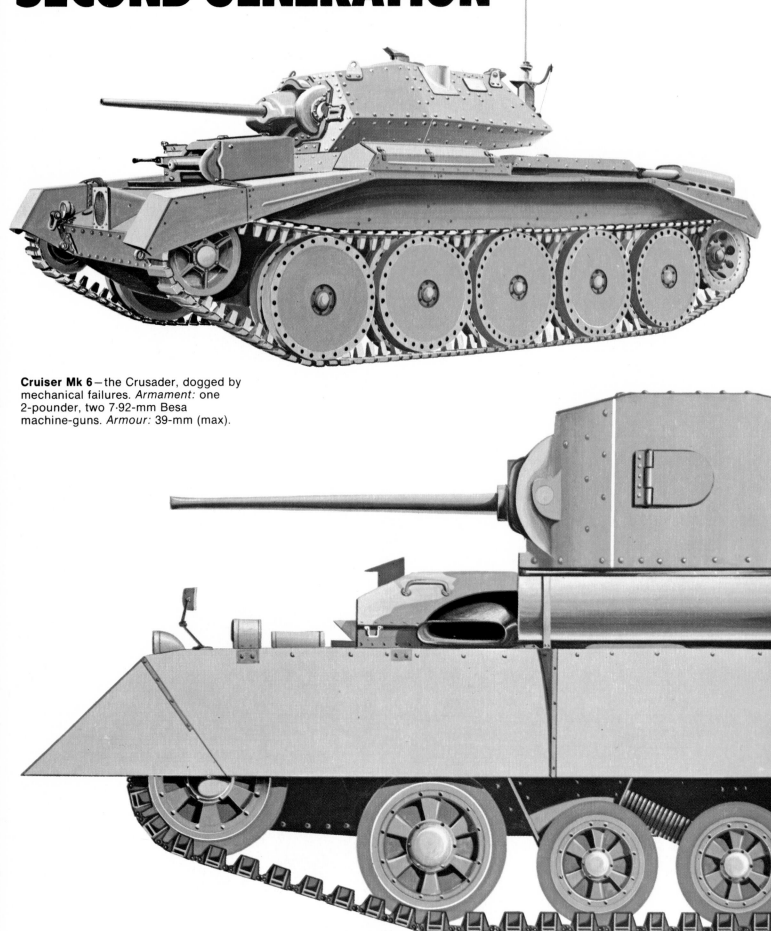

Cruiser Mk 6—the Crusader, dogged by mechanical failures. *Armament:* one 2-pounder, two 7·92-mm Besa machine-guns. *Armour:* 39-mm (max).

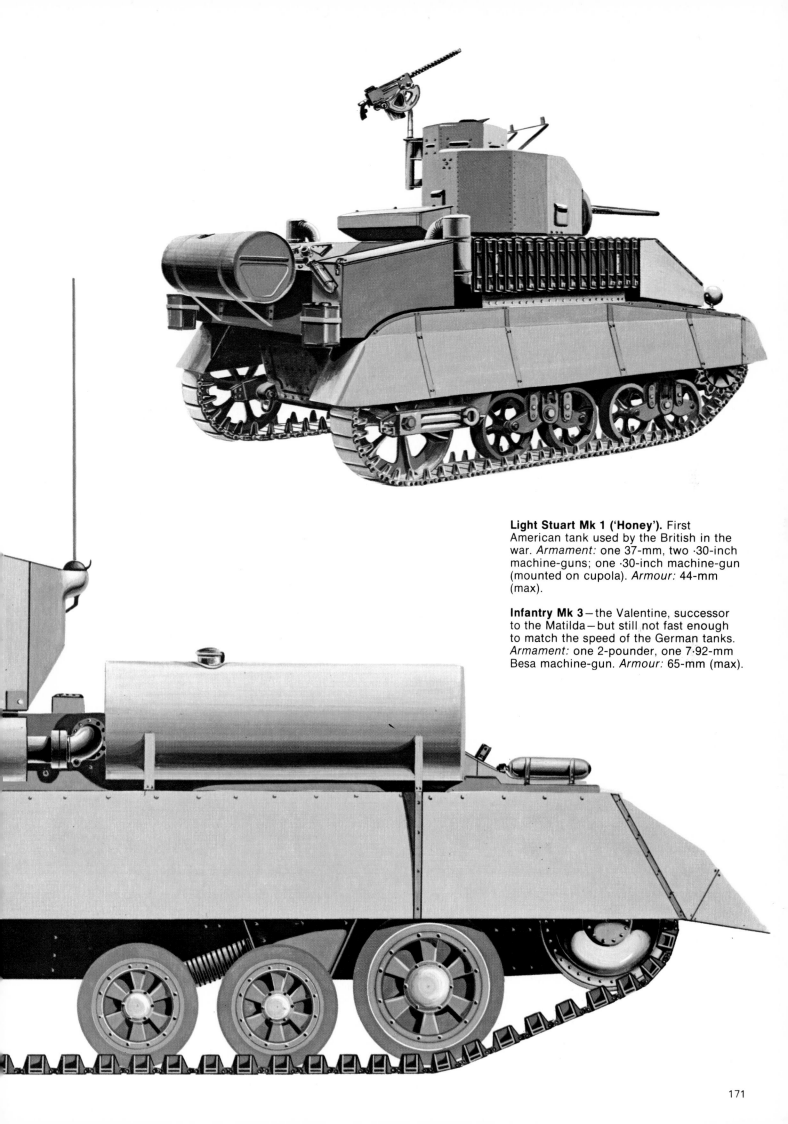

Light Stuart Mk 1 ('Honey'). First American tank used by the British in the war. *Armament:* one 37-mm, two ·30-inch machine-guns; one ·30-inch machine-gun (mounted on cupola). *Armour:* 44-mm (max).

Infantry Mk 3 — the Valentine, successor to the Matilda — but still not fast enough to match the speed of the German tanks. *Armament:* one 2-pounder, one 7·92-mm Besa machine-gun. *Armour:* 65-mm (max).

Italian 75/18 Semovente (self-propelled gun): although much Italian
equipment during the early years of the war was obsolete and ill-suited
to desert warfare, by 1942 they had begun to produce somewhat improved
weapons. The 75/18 Semovente first saw action with the Ariete
Division early in 1942. **Weight:** 12 tons. **Speed:** 20·5 mph maximum.
Crew: Four. **Armament:** One 75-mm gun, and one 6·5-mm machine-gun.
The main armament had a maximum range of 10,280 yards, and a
maximum rate of fire of four rounds a minute. It had an elevation of
22½ degrees and depression of 11 degrees, with a traverse of 17
degrees left, and 20 degrees right

Panzer Mark III Special: by mid-1942 the Afrika Korps had begun to
receive a new version of the Mark III. It was equipped with the long-
barrelled 5-cm gun, similar to the formidable Pak 38, and was also designed
with 'spaced armour' – an extra frontal plate separated from the basic
armour by an air space of 4 inches, and intended to break up the
armour-piercing cap of an anti-tank shell and thus reduce its power to
penetrate the plate behind. **Weight:** 22 tons. **Armour:** 57-mm maximum,
with a 20-mm spaced plate. **Speed:** 25 mph road speed. **Radius:** 100
miles maximum. **Crew:** Five. **Armament:** One 5-cm long-barrelled gun,
and two 7·9-mm machine-guns

AND THE ALLIES

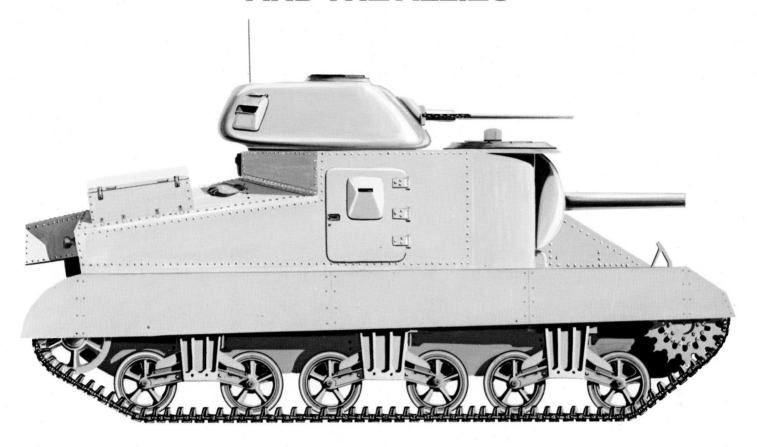

M3 General Grant: The first American medium tank received by the British forces. Its arrival was greeted with enthusiasm, for the 8th Army now had a tank with a gun capable of engaging German tanks and anti-tank crews on equal terms—and this could be done from behind the heavier armour of a reasonably fast and very reliable tank. Its major weakness was that the vital 75-mm gun was mounted in one side of the hull and thus had a very restricted arc of fire. **Weight:** 28·5 tons. **Armour:** 57-mm max. **Speed:** 28 mph maximum on roads. **Radius:** 108 miles maximum. **Crew:** Six. **Armament:** One 75-mm (hull) and one 37-mm (turret) gun, and four ·30-inch machine-guns

Six-pounder Anti-Tank Gun. The development of a larger gun to replace the 2-pounder had begun in 1938, but the stress of general rearmament had meant that the gun was not ready for trials for two years. Its delivery was further delayed by the fact that it was decided to use the tried 2-pounder to re-equip the army after Dunkirk. As a result the 8th Army had only 112 of the new guns by mid-1942. **Crew:** Five. **Weight in action:** 2,560 lb. **Range:** Up to 5,000 yards. Could fire either armour-piercing shot or high-explosive shell—but the latter was in limited supply

Seen below in action, the American M3 General Grant tank – supplied to British forces in the Western Desert – superseded the unreliable Crusader, and in early 1942 became the only Allied tank able to offer a serious threat to Rommel's Panzers

A Sherman tank of the 1st Army: neatness was their hallmark

Two typically tatty 8th Army Shermans muster in reserve

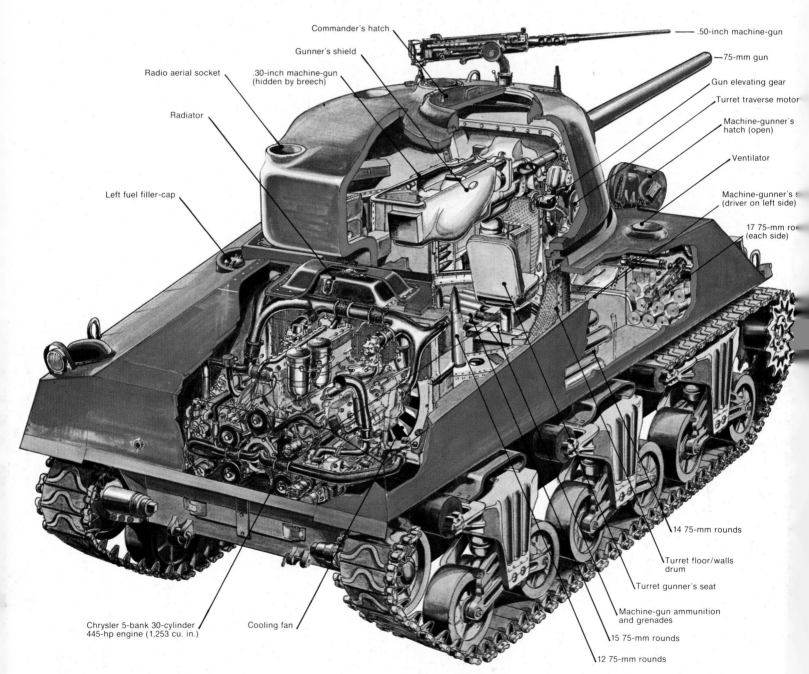

Commander's hatch

Gunner's shield

.30-inch machine-gun
(hidden by breech)

Radio aerial socket

Radiator

Left fuel filler-cap

.50-inch machine-gun

75-mm gun

Gun elevating gear

Turret traverse motor

Machine-gunner's
hatch (open)

Ventilator

Machine-gunner's s
(driver on left side)

17 75-mm ro
(each side)

14 75-mm rounds

Turret floor/walls
drum

Turret gunner's seat

Machine-gun ammunition
and grenades

15 75-mm rounds

12 75-mm rounds

Chrysler 5-bank 30-cylinder
445-hp engine (1,253 cu. in.)

Cooling fan

The Allied Juggernaut

After the earlier designs of the Grant and Lee tanks—which had themselves performed invaluable services with 8th Army in early 1942 —the main American and Allied battle tank came to be the Sherman. Its mass delivery to the Allied armies in North Africa and southern Europe was the result of an un-precedented feat of production. In 1941, American factories turned out 14,000 Shermans; in 1943, this rose to 21,000. And these numbers alone, matched by the virtues of mechanical reliability, gave the Sherman a very significant counter to the German gun and armour superiority. Solidly armoured, formidably armed, this model's most extraordinary feature was its Chrysler engine, built up from five 25-hp truck engines. *Max speed:* 23 mph. *Range:* 80 miles in average conditions. *Crew:* five. *Weight:* 71,900 lb. *Engine:* Chrysler model A57 (30-cylinder, 460-BHP). *Armament:* one 75-mm M3 gun, one ·50-inch machine-gun in hull, one ·30-inch machine-gu on flexible mounting

THE SHERMAN

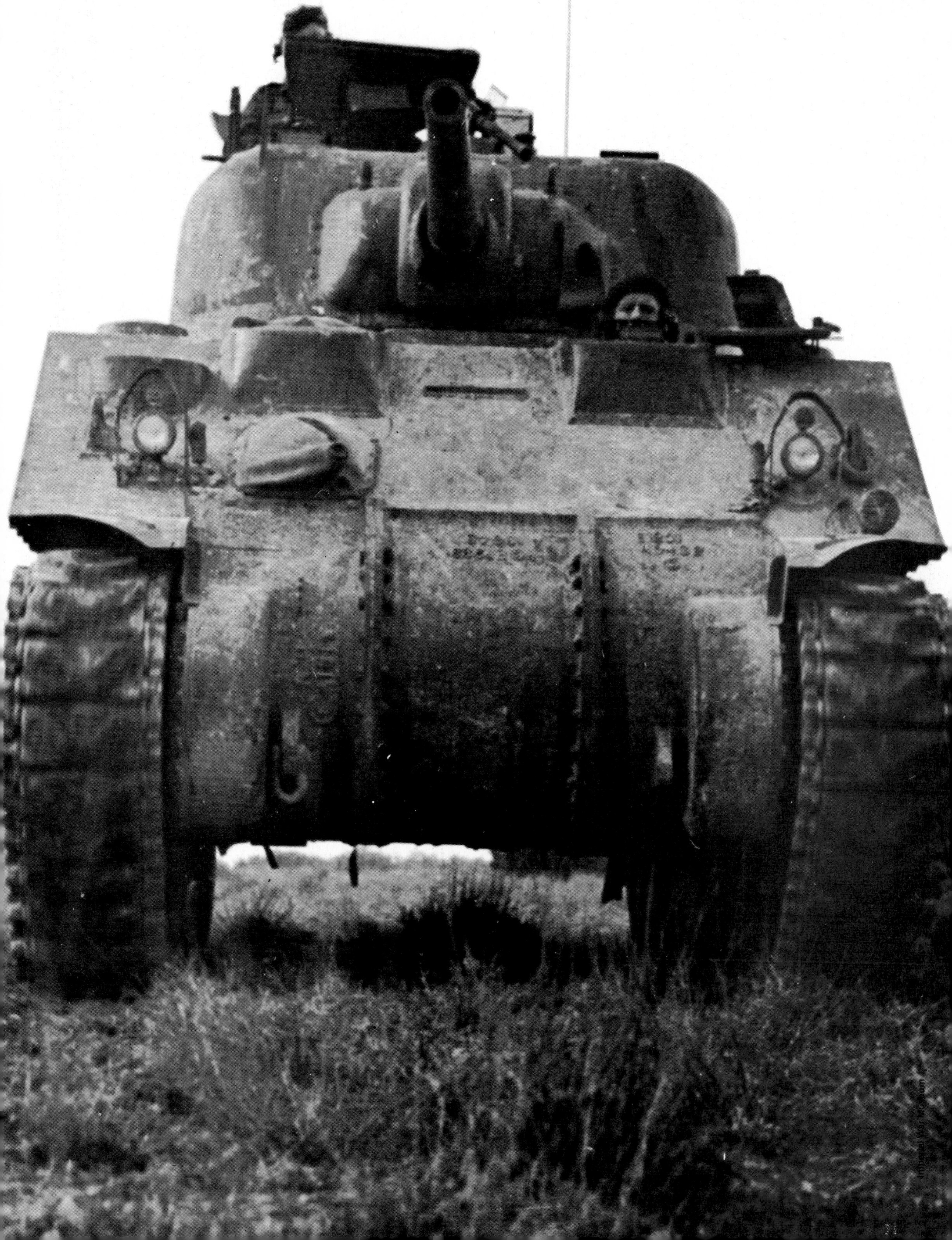

Imperial War Museum

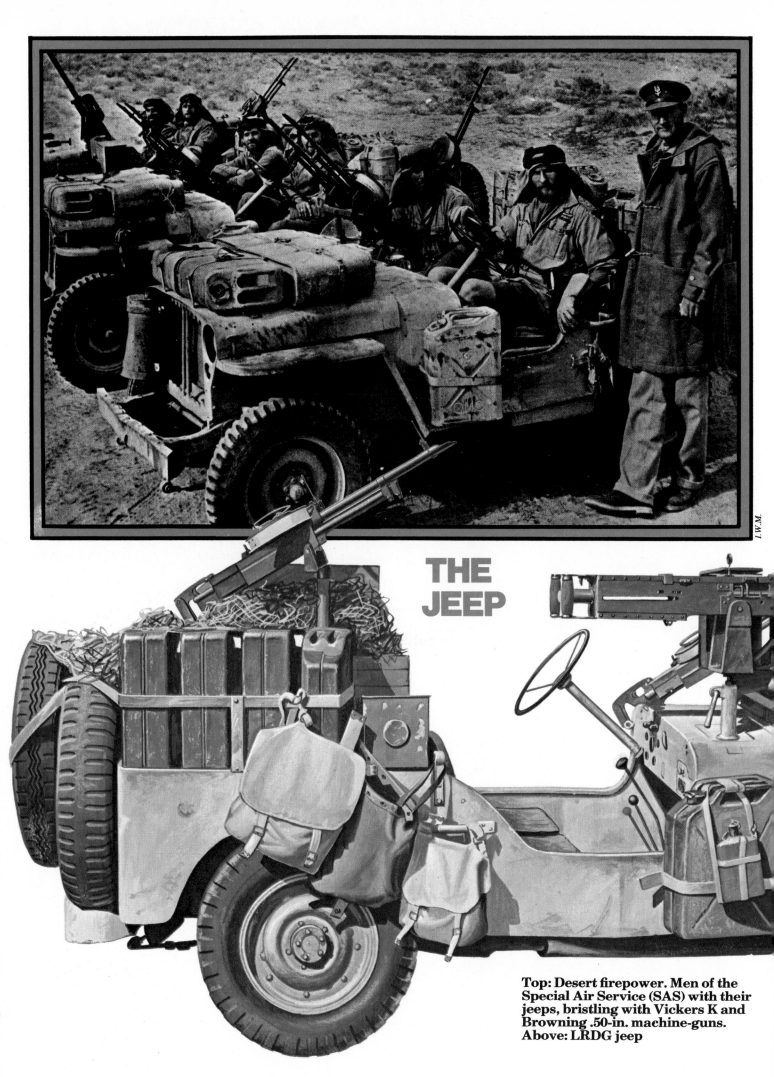

THE JEEP

Top: Desert firepower. Men of the Special Air Service (SAS) with their jeeps, bristling with Vickers K and Browning .50-in. machine-guns. Above: LRDG jeep

Bantam version (model BRC) of the jeep, the first in British army service, equipped with bren on folding anti-aircraft mount

Ford GPW (General Purpose Willys), Ford-built MB

The Jeep was developed by the Willys-Overland Motor Company in 1940 in response to a US Army demand for a 4 × 4 truck which could carry 600 lbs and yet weigh no more than 1300 lb. Willys didn't think much of this specification, claiming that the light weight prevented the vehicle from being made strong enough or powerful enough . . . so they designed their own version. As things turned out, this made sense to the Army as well, and after some modifications to meet a revised weight limit of 2150 lbs, the vehicle was accepted for service in 1941. Manufactured by both Willys-Overland and the Ford Motor Company, the Willys version was the Model MA, and the Ford version the Model GP,

from which the nickname 'Jeep' derived.

Jeeps were turned out by the hundreds of thousands to become the best-loved and most readily recognised of all combat vehicles. Originally intended as a 'Command and Reconnaissance Car' it soon became a combat vehicle in its own right when the Long Range Desert Group festooned their vehicles with machine guns and used them for fast and deep raids into German-held territory in North Africa. The small size of the Jeep allowed it to be loaded into gliders, so that airborne troops were provided with transport and gun-towing vehicles. There was even an amphibious version which proved to be extremely useful in river crossings and for moving troops in Holland.

ALLIED GUNS TO CLINCH THE DESERT WAR

The first British attempts to produce efficient self-propelled guns were not encouraging. The Bishop (below) was weak in design and construction, slow, uncomfortable, and usually more trouble than it was worth; the Sexton (right) was better, being constructed from more reliable components. But in the 5·5-inch and 3·7-inch guns the British artillery had two splendid weapons, which were equal to any of their Axis counterparts; and although the 3·7 was never allowed to give of its best in the anti-tank role, the 5·5 served with distinction, proving invaluable in the interminable bombardments among the Tunisian hills

Bishop Self-Propelled Gun
No two variants were ever exactly alike, but the type basically consisted of a 25-pounder mounted in a Valentine hull. It was not a happy combination, as the two components were usually battle-weary from past campaigns. *Weight:* 18 tons. *Crew:* four. *Max armour thickness:* 51-mm

5·5-inch Field Gun
The 5·5 was one of the best guns ever used by the British army. It began to reach the troops in 1941 and by the end of 1942 was serving on both fronts of the desert war; by the end of the Second World War it had served in every major battle area with both Commonwealth and British forces. *Crew:* nine. *Max range* (with 82-lb HE shell) 18,200 yards

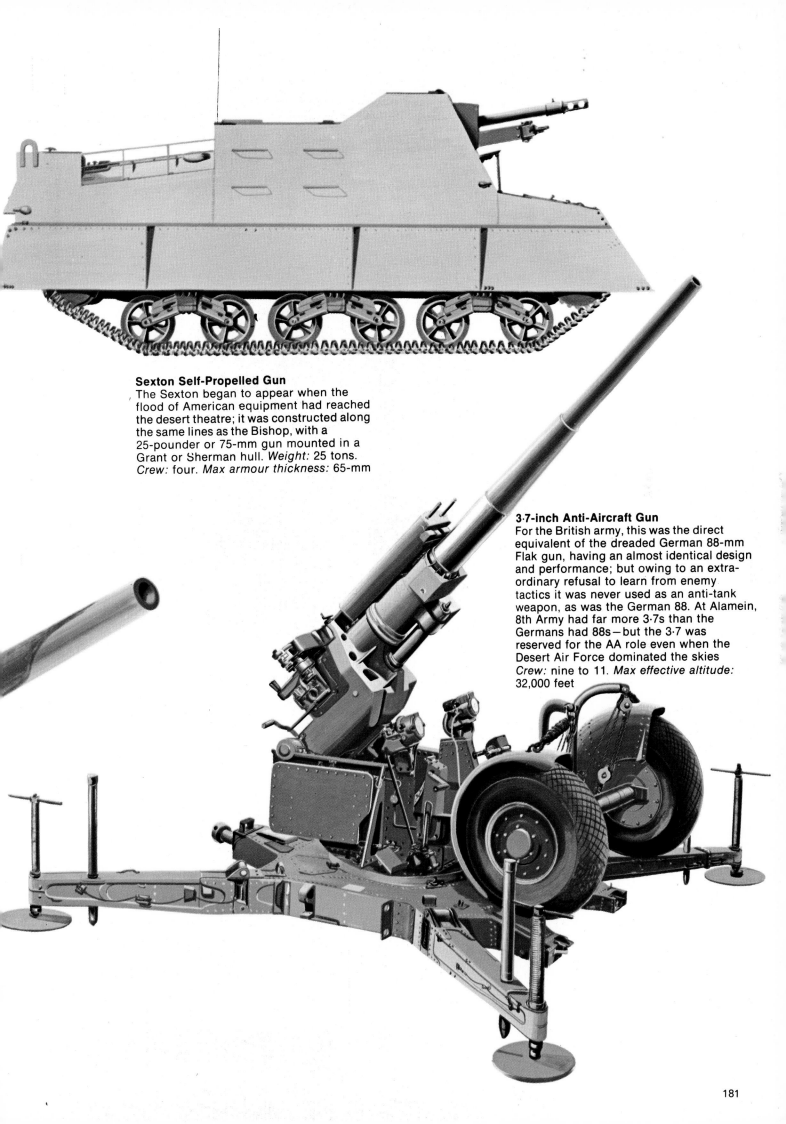

Sexton Self-Propelled Gun
The Sexton began to appear when the
flood of American equipment had reached
the desert theatre; it was constructed along
the same lines as the Bishop, with a
25-pounder or 75-mm gun mounted in a
Grant or Sherman hull. *Weight:* 25 tons.
Crew: four. *Max armour thickness:* 65-mm

3·7-inch Anti-Aircraft Gun
For the British army, this was the direct
equivalent of the dreaded German 88-mm
Flak gun, having an almost identical design
and performance; but owing to an extraordinary refusal to learn from enemy
tactics it was never used as an anti-tank
weapon, as was the German 88. At Alamein,
8th Army had far more 3·7s than the
Germans had 88s—but the 3·7 was
reserved for the AA role even when the
Desert Air Force dominated the skies
Crew: nine to 11. *Max effective altitude:*
32,000 feet

DESERT TRANSPORT

Desert supply lines are particularly vulnerable, as all petrol and ammunition, essential requirements for the battle, must pass along them. Hence one should protect one's own by all possible means and seek to confuse, or better still to cut the enemy's. Operations in the opposing supply area will cause the enemy to break off the battle, since *supplies are the basis of the battle, and must be given priority of protection. [Rommel]*

△ **Fordson (¾ ton)**

▽ **Bedford (3 tons)**

Ultimately, the victor in the desert war was the side which got the most and best supplies in the shortest time. In the summer of 1942 the 8th Army's supply line was very strong: the front line was only 70 miles from the chief depot at Alexandria (see map). But Rommel's army was at the opposite extreme: it had to haul its supplies all the way from Tripoli (1,420 miles), Benghazi (660 miles), and Tobruk (370 miles). The underlying law of supply in the Western Desert was again at work; the farther a victor advanced, the weaker he became—but a beaten army which fell back on its base became stronger in proportion. Rommel stood at the gates of Alexandria, shackled by this law. All his supplies sent by sea were in double danger, from both RAF and Royal Naval attacks. And the Axis transports, struggling eastwards up to the front, were plagued by the roving bands of the Long Range Desert Group and the raids of the Desert Air Force. Meanwhile, the 8th Army's supplies flowed ceaselessly from the rear depots to the front line, bringing reinforcements which blunted all Rommel's attempts to break through—and preparing for 8th Army's resumption of the offensive against Rommel

△ **Leyland (3 tons)**

▽ **Isotta-Fraschini (3 tons)**

△ **Opel (3 tons)**

▽ **Büssing-NAG (4½ tons)**

WEAPONS OF THE EASTERN FRONT

RUSSIA –
THE ULTIMATE
PROVING GROUND

When the German Army invaded Russia in June 1941, it advanced with some 3350 tanks to take on an enemy with a total tank strength approaching 20,000. As with the advance into France in 1940, though, the Panzers again had the advantages of surprise and concentration. On the Russian side, not only was the defence spread thinly over a long frontier, but there was the additional disadvantage that much of the Red Army, particularly the armoured force, was just then in the throes of reorganisation. As a result of wrongly reading the lessons of the Spanish Civil War, the Red Army's armoured divisions had been broken up in 1938–39 and the tanks dispersed in penny packets throughout the infantry formations. After seeing the results achieved by the Panzers in Poland and France, however, the Soviets had second thoughts and began rebuilding the armoured formations. Hence the German attack hit them before this reorganisation was half completed. Because of all these factors the Panzers rapidly speared deep into Russia, destroying about 17,000 tanks for the loss of 2700 of their own, and capturing thousands of guns.

The Russians, however, had two excellent tank designs which were just beginning to come from the production lines: the T-34 medium tank and the KV-1 heavy tank, both of which mounted powerful 76 mm guns, and both of which could make mincemeat of the Panzer IIIs and IVs which formed the principal strength of the German force. The Panzers were saved only by the fact that the were so few of these new tanks available, the were spread thinly, and their crews were f below the standard of training of the Germa crews. Nevertheless, the appearance of thes new Russian tanks shook the Germans to th core. There were no firm plans to replace th Panzer IV since it had been a match for all th opposition so far encountered, but now orde were hurriedly given for a design of 30-to medium tank to deal with the T-34. Indee some Germans suggested that the easiest an quickest answer was simply to copy the T-3 as it stood . . . and they might not have bee far wrong in that estimate if industrial capaci had not been so limited.

Below: A Russian T-34 blazes in the snow in 1941. Right: German armour advances towards Moscow in the winter of 1941

RUSSIAN ARMOUR

T-34. Probably the outstanding tank of the war, the T-34 completely outclassed the German Panzer IIIs and IVs with its speed, sloped armour, heavy armament and superb cross-country performance. **Weight:** 26.3 tons **Speed:** 32 mph **Crew:** 4 **Armour:** 75 mm max **Armament:** 76.2-mm gun; 2 mg

BT-7 light tanks—faster cross-country than Cossack cavalry—during training

....MORE THAN A MATCH FOR THE PANZERS

The Germans had tended to underestimate Soviet tanks design and production, and they received a rude awakening when the *Wehrmacht* encountered the new T-34s and KVs, whose existence had not even been suspected. Overnight, the German armour designs were rendered obsolete; not only were the new Soviet tanks formidable fighting vehicles, but the simplicity of their design meant that they could be turned out in large numbers, and operated by relatively inexperienced crews. So long as they were few in number, and used in small formations to support the infantry, the superior German tactics enabled the *Wehrmacht* to hold its own—but the Russians were rapidly adding to their tank strength—and to their experience.

KV-1 *(above).* First of the Red Army's new heavy tanks, it was an extremely well-armoured vehicle featuring a rear-firing machine-gun mounted in the turret. **Weight:** 43.5 tons **Speed:** 25 mph **Crew:** 5 **Armour:** 90 mm max **Armament:** 76.2 mm gun; 3 mg

KV-2 *(below).* An assault-gun version of the KV-1, it proved unsuccessful because its excessive overall height and general clumsiness made it a sitting target for enemy guns. **Weight:** 52 tons **Speed:** 12 mph **Crew:** 6 **Armour:** 110 mm max **Armament:** 152-mm gun; 3 mg

A Panzer III on the road to Moscow, 1941

T-34
THE BEST TANK IN THE WORLD

Von Runstedt's words, spoken in awe in 1942, were a fitting description of the Russian T-34 medium tank. Its vital part in the defeat of Germany is undeniable—and no tank since has escaped its influence.

On Midsummer's Day, 1941, Hitler launched his biggest gamble; the most ambitious military venture of all time: Operation *Barbarossa*, the invasion of Russia.

He had predicted that 'Once the front door is kicked open, the whole rotten edifice will come crashing down.' And as the German armoured columns crossed the border and swept across the plains of Russia, trapping and annihilating whole armies in rapid pincer movements, the prophecy seemed to be coming true—except that the front door needed little kicking.

In spite of desperate fighting by the Russians, and occasional tactical setbacks, German progress was spectacular. By September the Russian armies had been pushed back to Leningrad in

A column of T-34s on the move. Submachine-gun armed 'tank grenadiers' on fast, powerful tanks were a lethal combination

the north and Kiev in the south. Two-thirds of the Red Army's strength had been destroyed. And the *Wehrmacht* was poised for the decisive blow: the attack on Moscow itself. It looked as though Russia would be conquered before the onset of winter.

Debut of a Legend

But apart from the apparent ease of their conquest, and the awesome size of the country they had invaded, another surprise was in store for the Panzer commanders. Two new Russian tanks, one heavy, one medium, were encoun-

tered. They did not appear often, but when they did they proved decisively superior to the German armour. Both were armed with long, high-velocity 76-mm. guns which shredded the German vehicles' armour from any normal fighting range. Both seemed almost immune to the Panzers' own shells.

The heavy tank was the Klimenti Voroshilov KV-1. The medium tank was the legendary T-34.

The few tactical successes enjoyed by the Russians during those first desperate months of fighting—in the Ukraine in late June and early July, for example—were largely the work of T-34s. And when the Germans were first fought to a standstill, and then heavily defeated in the Battle of Moscow, the German generals realised that their

armour needed much improvement.

Superiority in tanks, the key to their early victories, was now in the balance. General Guderian, who had helped shape the Panzer Divisions and now commanded II Panzer Army, urged the setting up of a special commission to investigate. When this arrived at the front the German tank commanders were almost unanimous in their recommendations: the best answer to the T-34 was simply to copy it!

Unfortunately for Germany this was just not possible. German engineering technology was not up to it, many of the special alloys used in its construction were not available and the state of the War made the necessary industrial reorganisation out of the question.

Praise Indeed

Nevertheless the desire for a T-34 of their own was understandable. The Russian tanks could outshoot the Panzer IIIs and IVs with almost contemptuous ease. Their sloped armour, the protective steel plates angled to deflect armour-piercing shot, shrugged off the German shells. Powered by a revolutionary diesel engine, their top speed of 32 m.p.h. was distinctly superior to the Panzers' best of 25 m.p.h. And the wider tracks of the T-34 enabled it to keep going in snow and mud that left the German tanks immobile and helpless.

So impressive was the new tank that it provoked lavish praise from the normally tight-lipped men of the *Wehrmacht.* Von Kleist called it the finest in the world, von Runstedt the best tank in the world. To admit that the Slav *Untermensch* of the East could produce a superior weapon was a dangerous move in Nazi Germany, but at the time there was no denying it.

Yet the appearance of a superior tank should not have come as such a surprise. According to Guderian a group of Russian tank specialists visited a German tank factory in the spring of 1941 and, on being shown the new Panzer IIIs and IVs being produced, demanded to see the latest tank. When told they were looking at it, they thought of the T-34, refused to believe that these were the best German tanks, and angrily stormed out.

The suspension system (left) designed by Walter Christie was adopted for the Russian BT series (*Bystrokhodnaya Tankov,* or fast-moving tanks) (right)

Like all major advances, the T-34 had been a long time in the making. The foundations of industrial power that made its production possible had been laid as long ago as 1928, with the start of the first Five Year Plan. After a decade of political struggle and post-revolution chaos, Stalin had taken a firm grip on the reins of power, and a determined attempt was made to put Soviet industry on a stable footing.

Tractor factories, the obvious base of future tank production, were established at Kharkov and Stalingrad. Production of tanks themselves climbed from 740 in 1930 to 3300 in 1932; iron and steel production rose rapidly and industrial expansion on all fronts was stepped up.

A key factor in shaping the development of the Russian armed forces during the 1930s was the appointment of Mikhail Tukachevsky, a veteran army commander of the Civil War, to the post of Inspector of Armaments.

A few years earlier, Tukachevsky had written a remarkable essay on strategy, in which he accurately predicted many of the trends of future warfare. He foresaw that a future war would take place on a vast scale, and would involve the military and industrial mobilisation of the whole nation. He predicted that it would only be won by successful offensives, and that these offensives would have to take place at the speed of vehicles rather than of marching men. Tank power, in other words, would be decisive.

New Theories

Backed by a group of young and imaginative officers, he created Russia's first mechanised brigade, and the first regular parachute force in the world, in 1931. By 1932 a Mechanised Corps and an Academy of Motorisation and Mechanisation had been set up. In 1933 his theories were tested in a series of exercises involving the close cooperation of mechanised forces, cavalry and airborne units, backed up by infantry and artillery. One of the young officers involved was the deputy commander of a cavalry division, Georgi Zhukov, later to become famous as the victorious Commander-in-Chief of Soviet ground forces during World War II.

The thinking behind all these ventures was crystallised in the Red Army Field Regulations of 1936. These

emphasised the importance of offensives, and of cooperation between the different arms. A clearly defined method of attack was laid down. Assault groups would attack the enemy weak points, the biggest breakthrough being exploited by massed artillery barrage. Tanks and tank infantry—seven men riding on each tank—would then follow through, encircle the enemy, and destroy him. The emphasis was on mobility: tanks would be used on a vast scale.

It was clear, however, that new weapons would be needed to apply these theories—particularly tanks, which would carry so much of the responsibility. And in the early 1930s there was much activity in this field.

Never slow to investigate promising ideas from any source, the Russians in 1931 bought two of the American innovator Walter Christie's T-3 light tanks. This represented Christie's idea of a new type of tank, fast and light and able to drive on wheels or tracks —in the case of the T-3 at the remarkable speeds of 70 m.p.h. on wheels and 42 m.p.h. on tracks.

The Russians built their own version, the BT light tank, more or less a direct copy of the American machine. At the same time they were experimenting with big, heavily armed and armoured infantry tanks, often multi-turreted, always slow and intended to support infantry advances.

The ideal, though, seemed to lie somewhere between the two—a medium tank which would combine the three basic requirements of a tank: speed, protection and firepower. An early model of this type was the A-20 of 1938, which closely resembled the T-34 in outline but retained the wheels or tracks system, and was armed with only a 45-mm. gun.

One of the A-20's designers, Mikhail Koshkin, opposed the dual drive, which needed much more complicated machinery for its production. Becoming head of the design bureau working on designs for new tanks with the assistance of Nikolai Kurechenko and Aleksandr Morozov, he began working on a new series of tracks-only tanks, the first of which was the T-32 of 1939.

One problem with building the new medium tanks had been finding a suitable engine. The traditional practice of adapting petrol engines designed for aircraft or other vehicles had several drawbacks. Increasing the power

The BT series (left) which had the sloped armour and Christie suspension of the T-34, and were used to test the brilliant V2 diesel tank engine. They had the wheel and track system dropped on the standardised T-34. Top: BT-7s on parade. Centre: In action against the Japanese at Khalkin Gol, July 1939. Bottom: The T-34/76B almost doubled the track-width of the BT series

meant increasing the fuel consumption, which meant bigger fuel tanks and more fuel, which in turn meant more weight and less performance. Petrol engines, moreover, are a dangerous fire risk, and are rather sensitive to the extreme conditions met by tanks.

The ideal was a lightweight diesel engine—and in 1939 the V2 12-cylinder diesel engine appeared. A light, economical engine, built largely of aluminium alloys, it was rugged and powerful—the ideal tank engine.

Lasting Success

The official Russian explanation of the engine's appearance is that it was the result of a 1932 government directive. More likely, it was developed from a Fiat aeroplane engine, one of many foreign engines studied by the Russians during the early 1930s. Whatever its derivation, however, it was tested on a BT-7 during 1939, proved successful (so successful, indeed, that the Russian T-54 and T-62 tanks of today are powered by only slightly modified versions of it) and entered production.

So Koshkin's design and the V2 engine came together, and with a 76.2-mm. gun previously used on several Russian tanks the T-34 was born. Two prototypes were built and tested in early 1940. Among their trials was an 1800-mile round trip between Kharkov and Moscow in the dead of the Russian winter. They passed with flying colours, and in June 1940 production of the tank began at Leningrad, Kharkov and Stalingrad. It now needed a war.

German troops pass a wrecked T-34, July 1941. At this time the tanks were in too short supply to stem the German advance into Russia

Unfortunately for Russia, the War came all too soon. In 1937 Stalin had started his purge of the Red Army, a year-long bloodbath which saw as many as 35,000 officers sacked, shot or imprisoned. These included Tukachevsky, who was shot in June 1937 after being framed by the NKVD (it is alleged with the cooperation of the Nazi SD) for 'collaboration with foreign powers.' This left the army fear-ridden and deprived of many of its best commanders, and did nothing to help it prepare for the German onslaught of 1941.

On top of this, by 1941 the army was being massively overhauled. Many new weapons were approved but not fully deployed—only 115 T-34s, for example, were produced during 1940—and the old army organisation had been largely dismantled, but not yet replaced by the new system.

Operation *Barbarossa*, therefore, found the Russian army in a transitional state. Hundreds of thousands of troops were still in the border areas awaiting redeployment and re-equipment. So, with relative ease, the *Wehrmacht* spearheads were able to net whole armies and conquer huge tracts of territory.

But if the army was almost helpless, the total mobilisation that Tukachevsky had postulated swung rapidly into action to prepare for the inevitable counter-offensive. Vital industrial concerns were moved far to the east, out of the way of the invaders, and as the army desperately traded space for time, new industrial complexes sprang up beyond the Urals.

One of these was 'Tankograd,' formed when the Kharkov and Leningrad tank factories were merged with the tractor works of Chelyabinsk. It was here that the bulk of the Soviet tanks were produced during the War. And as the workers toiled, round-the-clock production rapidly increased. From 3000 in 1942, the number of T-34s produced rose to an estimated 5000 in 1942, and 10,000 or more in each of the next three years. Probably between 40,000 and 50,000 were produced by the end of the War.

The Tide Turns

As production of all types of munitions accelerated (between June 1941 and June 1942 armaments' share of Russia's gross national product climbed from 18.5% to 76%), the tide of war turned inexorably against Germany. Although the spring of 1942 saw further heavy Russian defeats, the Red Army was finding its feet. Its soldiers were tempered by long and hard fighting, inspired by patriotism, equipped with better weapons and spearheaded by the best tank in the world.

By the time of the great Kursk tank battles of mid-1943 the Red Army was the biggest land force in history. And if the vast mass of its troops was infan-

Above: An NKVD captain signs for newly built T-34s in a factory at Tankograd. Right: A T-34/76A. The poorly finished turret armour is typical—but corner-cutting in the factories could save up to 50% of production time. Below right: T-34/76B. The single large turret hatch was a major fault

try, the pivot of the offensives was the tank armies. The T-34s were organised three to a troop, with three troops to a squadron and two squadrons plus a supply platoon forming a tank battalion. In turn, three battalions formed a brigade, and a tank corps, two of which and a mechanised corps made up a tank army, contained three brigades plus motorised infantry, self-propelled artillery and supporting formations.

In order to enable the infantry to keep up with the tanks, special detachments of tank infantry were formed. Armed with submachine-guns, these would go into action riding on the backs of tanks. As enemy positions were breached, they would leap off, wipe out the opposition, and when the action was over simply hitch a ride on the next tank.

The method was crude and casualties high, but the tactic was certainly effective. A mass of tanks, firing as they came, with groups of shock troops crouching behind their turrets had a devastating effect on any enemy.

The crudity of these tactics was mirrored in many faults in the tanks themselves. The T-34's turret could

All pics: Novosti Press Agency

Left: A troop of three T-34/76s. The T-34's low track pressure often allowed it to keep going in conditions that immobilised the German tanks. **Above:** PPsh submachine armed infantry go into action on T-34s. **Below Left:** T-34/85 introduced in 1943 with the 85-mm. gun and a bigger cast turret

Below: Both during the war and after the excellent T-34 chassis was adapted for a variety of specialised roles. The SU-85 (*Samokhodnaya Ustanovka*), or turretless tank was a highly successful assault gun introduced in 1943. Armed with the same 85-mm. gun as the T-34/85, it had a crew of four

accommodate only two men, forcing the commander to act as gunner as well, an unsatisfactory state of affairs compounded by a lack of power, traverse and elevation for the gun. The single large hatch opened forward—too big for comfort in winter, it also impaired the view forward. Moreover, only company commanders' vehicles were equipped with radio, and hand signals are not a particularly useful means of communication in battle.

Unsophisticated

There was too a lack of mechanical sophistication. The transmission was often unreliable, the gearbox rough, the steering primitive. But these were small faults compared with the vehicle's virtues—the powerful gun, excellent performance and effective protection—and were largely attributable to the pressures of wartime production.

If armour was poorly finished, and crew comfort non-existent, at least the tanks were there—and with an average life in battle of 20 weeks or less, the highest quality of finish was hardly a vital necessity. Nor was comfort something the Soviet soldier expected or needed.

In one respect, however, improvement became vital. In 1942 the F2 model of the Panzer IV was introduced, with a long and more powerful 75-mm. gun that was the equal of the T-34's weapon. To maintain the superiority of the T-34, the Soviet tank was fitted with an 85-mm. gun already used to

'Tank Landing Troops' leap into action from a company of T-34/85s during an attack on a German position near Odessa. Similar tactics, using specialised and sophisticated armoured personnel carriers, are practised by the Soviet Army's infantry divisions of the '70s

up-gun the KV-1, and based on an earlier anti-aircraft gun.

The logical step would have been to mount the new gun in the same turret as the KV's, but the extra weight of this equipment would have reduced the lighter tank's performance. A new type of turret, lighter and less well protected than the KV's, was produced to overcome the difficulty. This had room for three men, freeing the commander of his responsibility as gunner. Electric power was provided for traversing and elevating the gun, visibility improved, and the commander provided with a cupola and radio equipment. The new tank became known as the T-34/85, the earlier model the T-34/76.

The improvements restored the T-34's superiority over German opposition, at least until the introduction of the Tiger, Panther and King Tiger in 1942-44. These new tanks, though, appeared in such small numbers that they could hardly hope to stem the Russian advance. Moreover, they were much heavier and less manoeuvrable, and the Russians were by then introducing their own heavy tanks, the JS-2 and JS-3, as well as a range of heavy

and efficient self-propelled guns.

Many of the new SP guns, in fact, were mounted on the excellent T-34 chassis, among them the SU-85 and SU-100. Other adaptations of the chassis mounted flamethrowers and mine-clearing equipment; it was used as a bridgelayer, and with the turret removed it made an excellent recovery vehicle and command post.

A Long Run

After the War it remained in service, not only in Russia but in many Soviet backed armies, seeing action in Korea and during the uprisings in East Berlin in 1955 and Hungary in 1956. In the Soviet Union it was not superseded until the 1950s, by the T-54, and remained in service until the late 1960s. In some of the many small nations to which it was supplied its career lasted well into the 1970s.

Virtually every fighting vehicle produced anywhere since World War II has been influenced by the T-34. The Russian T-62 of today owes a clear debt to it. Its unique combination of mobility, firepower and protection was not equalled for at least two years after its introduction.

The combination of Russian engineering genius and the best ideas around had produced the finest fighting vehicle of its day. And although it was far from being solely responsible for the Russian defeat of Germany, the lavish praise from men like Guderian underlines its importance.

Spring 1945: T-34/85s occupy Heiligenbeil in East Prussia. By the later stages of the war the Soviet superiority in armour was overwhelming, as tanks poured off the production lines and went to the front in their thousands

TANK FIREPOWER

Much has been written about the increase in tank firepower during the war years, but to the layman calibre sizes usually have little meaning. Some idea of the rapid growth in actual striking potential can be gathered from the two groups of ammunition below. These represent the full range of British and German tank guns that saw service. Generally, size for size, German weapons were ahead of those fitted to the various Allied tanks; it was not until the appearance of the 17-pounder that the Allies had something to fight back with on equal terms with the Panther and

Tiger I. But even the 17-pounder was not in the same league as the powerful long-barrelled 88-mm KwK 43 of the Tiger II and the enormous 128-mm gun of the Jagdtiger. Although the latter was a self-propelled tank destroyer and not a true turreted tank, at least two super-heavy German tanks were under development at the end of the war using the same weapon. The complete round for this gun was too heavy to manhandle as a single fixed item, and so the shells and cartridges were loaded as separate units. The armour-piercing projectile weighed 62½

pounds, which was 42 times the weight of the 37-mm projectiles fired from the early Mk III guns. For close support work, some British tanks were armed with the 3-inch howitzer at first and later a larger 95-mm howitzer. The 77-mm was basically a shortened version of the 17-pounder designed to fit into tanks that could not accommodate the longer breech mechanism. In actual size the British 17-pounder case (23 inches long) is about 2 inches shorter than the case of the German 75-mm KwK 42 gun which was fitted to the Panther tank.

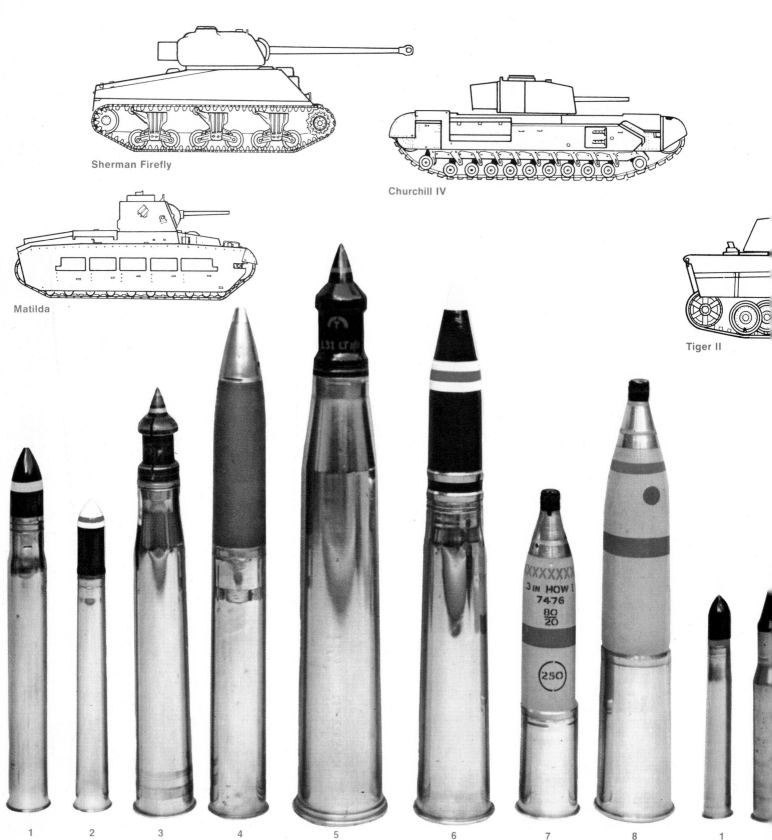

Sherman Firefly

Churchill IV

Matilda

Tiger II

1   2   3   4   5   6   7   8   1

British Tank Ammunition

1 3-pounder Practice. (Cruiser A-9)
2 2-pounder Armour-Piercing. (Tetrarch, Crusader I and II, Matilda)
3 6-pounder Armour-Piercing Discarding Sabot—a light-weight high-velocity projectile with a very hard tungsten carbide core. The outer sabot construction breaks up in the bore, but is held together until clear of the muzzle, when the pieces are spun free of the smaller centre projectile. This then travels to the target at higher than normal velocity. (Cromwell I and III, Centaur I, Valentine VIII and IX)

4 75-mm High-Explosive (Cromwell IV, V, and VII, Centaur III, Churchill IV)
5 17-pounder Armour-Piercing Discarding Sabot. (Challenger, Firefly, 17-pdr Archer)
6 77-mm Armour-Piercing. (Comet)
7 3-inch Howitzer High-Explosive. (Churchill I, III, and IV Close-Support, Crusader CS)
8 95-mm Howitzer High-Explosive. (Cromwell VI and VIII, Centaur IV, Churchill V and VIII)

German Tank Ammunition

1 3·7-cm KwK* Armour-Piercing. (Mk III)
2 5-cm KwK (Short) Armour-Piercing. (Mk III)
3 5-cm KwK 39 (Long) High-Explosive. (Mk III)
4 7·5-cm KwK (Short) High-Explosive. (Mk III and IV)
5 7·5-cm KwK 40 High-Explosive. (Mk IV)
6 7·5-cm KwK 42 Armour-Piercing. (Panther)
7 8·8-cm KwK 36 High-Explosive. (Tiger I)
8 8·8-cm KwK 43 High-Explosive. (Tiger II)
9 12·8-cm PAK 44 Armour-Piercing Projectile and Cartridge. (Jagdtiger)

KwK* = Kampfwagenkanone (Tank Cannon)

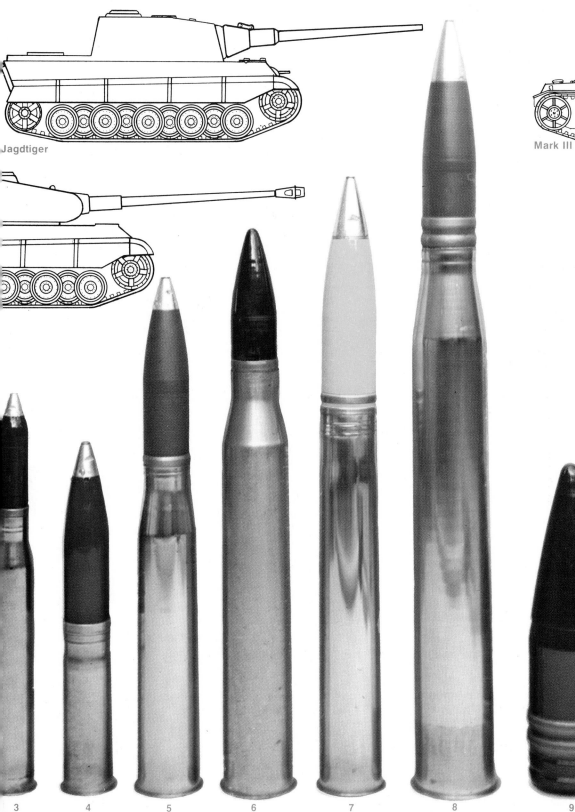

Jagdtiger

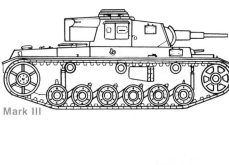

Mark III

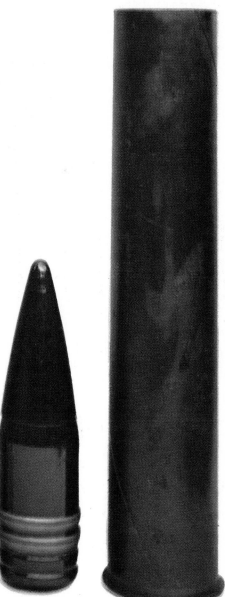

3   4   5   6   7   8   9

THE ARMOURED RACE

With improved armour came the demand for more powerful anti-tank guns for the German infantry. Their 37 mm was now quite useless, and the 50 mm, introduced in 1940, could make little impression on the T-34 or KV at any range. Fortunately the Rheinmettal-Borsig company had been working on a scaled-up version of the 50 mm gun for some time, and this was hurriedly completed and issued as the 75 mm PAK 41 in November 1941. Firing a 15 lb shell it could defeat 116 mm of armour at 1000 yards range, enough to cope with the T-34. Krupp, though, had also produced a 75 mm gun, using a taper-bore barrel to achieve very high velocities which could penetrate 170 mm of

armour at 1000 yards range. However, the special ammunition for this gun demanded a supply of tungsten carbide, and since this was in short supply the gun did not stay in service for long. Krupp's then developed an 88 mm anti-tank gun, the same calibre as the well-known anti-aircraft gun but using more powerful ammunition. This could pierce 160 mm of armour at 2000 yards range and was the master of anything the Soviets could produce; one combat report speaks of knocking out six T-34s, one after the other, at 3500 yards range, while another describes how a T-34 was attacked from behind at a range of 600 yards, blowing the engine block 15 feet from the tank and the turret hatch 50 feet.

The original demand for the 30-ton ta was overtaken by a revised specification l down by Hitler, who demanded a 45-1 tank to carry the 88 mm gun, and the res of this was the Tiger I which actually weigh 56 tons. Over 1350 were built, but, as me tioned elsewhere, its reliability was poor, a after trials at the front a redesign v ordered. This appeared as the Tiger II, a 6 tonner with a more powerful version of 1 88 mm gun.

Two companies, though, continued develop a design to meet the 30-ton or and this eventually appeared as the 45-t Panther, armed with a new and power 75 mm gun. As a result, by 1943, with Tig

Below: A 37 mm PAK 36 anti-tank gun in action during the invasion of Russia in 1941. Right: A Panzer III in Russia, 1941

Hitler postponed the dash for Moscow—the Ukraine was to come first

The Ukraine was the target area of Army Group South, and the wide areas of the steppe offered superb opportunities for the tacticians of Kleist's Panzergruppe to show their paces. In sealing off the Soviet concentrations at Uman and Kiev, the Panzer and infantry forces of Army Group South won the great battle of annihilation, the 'super-Cannae', that Hitler demanded. This victory was not won by smashing the strong Soviet forces in direct assaults. It was the result of a penetration in such depth that the Soviet strategists did not notice the closing trap until it was too late. *(Right)* Soviet shell-fire in the Ukraine. *(Below)* One of Kleist's Panzer regiments driving across the steppe in ideal conditions. *(Left)* German infantrymen at the exhausting task of eliminating their opposite numbers, and *(bottom)* in a lull during the advance, flushed with what seems to be a gigantic repetition of their earlier swift triumphs in Poland and France

and Panthers in some numbers, the Germans were once again able to establish a technical superiority on the Eastern Front. But technical superiority was not to be enough. By sacrificing their armour in the early days of the war the Soviets had bought time, time in which to uproot their tank factories and relocate them behind the Ural Mountains out of reach of the German bombers. In 1941 the Russian tank factories had produced 6590 vehicles; in 1942, after a slow start due to the evacuation and reorganisation, they produced 24,668; in 1943, 24,000; in 1944, 29,000 and in 1945, 25,450; a wartime total of 109,708 tanks and self-propelled guns. By comparison the German production figures for tanks were: 1941, 3256; 1942, 4278; 1943, 5966 and 1944, 9161. These figures tell the whole story: the Germans were driven from Russia not by technology but by sheer weight of numbers; the Soviets could make tanks faster than the Germans could destroy them.

Meanwhile, assault guns were an asset to both sides. The Soviets used the KV chassis to mount 122 mm and 152 mm heavy guns and used them as direct support for infantry in the attack, while the Germans produced a number of 75 mm and 105 mm guns on a variety of chassis, including those of tanks taken from the French. At first sight one of the most formidable German assault guns was the Ferdinand tank destroyer, a self-propelled 88 mm based on a Porsche design which had been a possible starter in the Tiger tank programme. Strongly armoured and with a powerful gun it was a dangerous weapon to the Soviets, but its inability to shoot in any other direction than forward meant that it was relatively easy to attack from the sides or rear. So, once the Red Army got over its initial shock, tank-hunting infantry squads made short work of Ferdinand. Of the 90 built, very few survived their first combat.

Bundesarchiv

THE PANTHER-
HITLER'S ANSWER TO THE T-34

The Panther tank originated with a hurried demand for a 30-ton medium tank capable of meeting the Soviet T-34 and beating it. It was developed by the Maschinenfabrik Augsburg-Nürnberg, incorporating sloped armour and a 75 mm gun twice as long (and thus more powerful) as that of the Panzer IV. First produced in November 1942, the Panther weighed 45 tons, a little heavy for a 'medium' but with its powerful gun, 120 mm of armour and top speed of 27 mph it was nonetheless an excellent design. The hurried development, though, led to some initial teething troubles and of the first 300 made those which survived their first battle had to go back to the factory for extensive modification. After this setback the Panther went on to become probably the best German tank of the war, superior to the Soviet T-34 in every respect. About 5500 were built, a poor figure compared to the production of the T-34 or the Sherman, and one which is indicative of the failure of Germany to mobilise its industry to its full potential.

Sloped armour, a 75-mm high velocity gun, wider tracks and improved suspension gave the Panther a chance against the Russian T-34

PzKpfw V Panther Ausf D

The first production model suffered from a high breakdown rate, a result of hasty development. But the Panther design was a fine balance of protection, speed and hitting power
Engine: 700 hp Maybach HL 230 P30
Weight: 43 tons *Speed:* 25 mph *Crew:* 5
Armour: 120 mm max *Armament:* 75-mm KwK 42 L/70

Russian assault-guns and troops enter Germany from the East

Russian armour crosses the Spree on the outskirts of Berlin

THE SOVIET STEAMROLLER

JSU-152 *(right)*. Based on a JS-1 tank chassis, this Russian medium SP gun was produced in great numbers to spearhead the armoured drive to the West. **Weight:** 46 tons **Speed:** 23 mph **Crew:** 5 **Armour:** 90 mm max **Armament:** 152-mm gun; 1 mg

SU-37 *(below)*. A Russian light tank used extensively for infantry support. What it lacked in firepower it made up for in speed and manoeuvrability. **Weight:** 10.5 tons **Speed:** 32 mph **Crew:** 4 **Armour:** 35 mm max **Armament:** 37-mm gun

SU-100 *(above).* Based on a T-34 chassis, this was the Russian equivalent of the German Jagdpanzer. **Weight:** 32 tons **Speed:** 30 mph **Crew:** 4 **Armour:** 50 mm max **Armament:** 100-mm gun; 1 mg

SU-122 *(bottom).* Also based on a T-34 chassis, this was yet another of the Russian heavy SP guns leading the steamroller of armour from the East. **Weight:** 30.9 tons **Speed:** 34.5 mph **Crew:** 5 **Armour:** 45 mm max **Armament:** 122-mm gun

JS-3 *(below).* Entering service in 1945, this was the successor to the KV-1 of 1941 and a startling improvement on the intermediary JS-1 and JS-2 in the shaping of its armour. **Weight:** 46 tons **Speed:** 24 mph **Crew:** 4 **Armament:** 122-mm gun; 2 mg

Joseph Stalin 2 tanks of a Soviet armoured division roll through the ruins of Berlin during the last days of the war

D-DAY: BALANCE OF ARMOUR

If in no other respect, the British and Americans possessed quantative superiority in armour, and that, in itself, was no mean industrial achievement when it is recalled that, after Dunkirk, Britain had only 200 tanks fit for battle, while the Americans owned hardly a single operational tank worthy of the name.

Whatever British industry could make in 1940 had to be churned out at once, regardless of quality, to rearm the rescued BEF: indeed, Churchill insisted that, for the time being, all research and development should stop in order to concentrate every ounce of energy on production. So, those tanks already in, or about to enter, production—Matilda, Valentine, Cruisers IV, V, VI, and the new heavy Churchill, all armed with the obsolescent 2-pounder gun—rolled forth in growing numbers while the next generation of vehicles waited in abeyance.

To add further to confusion, the British tank supply organisation tottered on rotten foundations. A month before the outbreak of war, what few tank technologists the War Office boasted had been grabbed by the new Ministry of Supply, isolating the War Office from informed tank advice. A purely politically inspired Tank Board had been set up, to head tank affairs in the right direction, but suffered from a surfeit of responsibility, a lack of power—and a flood of resignations and reappointments. It failed in its task. The last in the line of Britain's great tank enthusiasts, Major-General Hobart, had been dismissed from command of 7th Armoured Division in the desert by Generals Wilson and Wavell, because the former had 'no confidence' in Hobart's way of command. When Guderian proved Hobart right in May 1940, the latter was being promoted to Lance-Corporal in the Home Guard; but by autumn of that year he was on his way back to power, having devised a plan in conjunction with General Pile (another tank expert then in command of the

anti-aircraft command) for a new armoured army, governed by a charter strikingly similar to that to be written by Guderian over two years later.

On the insistence of Churchill, Hobart was recalled, ostensibly to raise a new armoured division, but primarily to train all the tank forces. Neither the CIGS, General Dill, nor Commander Home Forces, General Brooke, felt able to accept Hobart's complete plan, so Hobart got his armoured division and General Martel, another of the early tank pioneers, took the watered-down training job, without a charter. For the next two years the tale of British defeat could be linked with mediocre handling of inferior vehicles by officers and men whose courage alone made up for the other deficiencies.

Tank production mounted apace with the aim of filling the establishments of ten armoured divisions each of about 400 tanks. However, the insistence of the pre-war General Staff that a large number of slow, heavily armoured infantry support vehicles would be needed to lead a basically infantry army now led to a short-fall in the number of fast cruisers being built for the armoured divisions: not until later, when US production was tapped, could this deficiency be rectified, so, in the meantime, infantry tanks had to fill spaces in the armoured divisions. In any case, the next generation of cruiser—Mark VII called 'Centaur'—ran into technical troubles, never met its specification or delivery date, and was superseded by a revised Mark VIII 'Cromwell', before the former could be brought into action. And Cromwell, when at last it appeared in 1944, went to battle outgunned and incapable of accepting a larger weapon than the comparatively low-powered 57-mm (6-pounder) or 75-mm gun with which it was provided.

This semi-permanent state of under-gunning stemmed from the earlier, but untested, belief that tank armament could take lower priority after speed and armour, on the assumption that field artillery would supplement the high-explosive dispensing capability the tanks did not possess—a theory which died an instant death in the first major armoured battles when it was discovered that, in a fast-moving encounter, tanks had to be able to provide all sorts of self-support at short notice and that the slower artillery methods often could not compete. Thereafter the delay in making and mounting 57-mm and 75-mm (and later the 17-pounder) guns occurred mainly because of weakness in communication between the War Office and Ministry of Supply—the former not stating their require-

US-built Shermans of a British armoured regiment halted 'somewhere in England' on their journey to the South Coast

ments with sufficient clarity, leading to the army being given whatever the latter thought good for the soldiers. Acrimony ran rife, for instance, when the Ministry of Supply said, in 1942, that it would be impossible to mount the 17-pounder in the Sherman, leaving the War Office to prove it feasible in 1943 and thrust the modification through against protocol barely in time for June 6.

Reorganisation of British armoured forces took place about once a year under the impetus of fresh thought and the demands of front-line soldiers. In 1941 a cry for more armoured divisions to replace infantry ones led to several infantry (including Guards) battalions being converted to armour—an admission that pre-war policy had been wrong, tied to a staunch attempt at retaining old regimental traditions in a changing world. But the disruption in the minds of infantrymen transposed to an entirely new way of thinking and fighting could take at least a year to appease. So when, at last in 1942, the transposition was beginning to make headway, a fresh decision was taken to cut the armoured content of the armoured division by half (and to substitute more lorry-borne infantry) while transferring the redundant armour to independent brigades charged with the task of supporting infantry formations—and this made confusion doubly compounded. Thus British armour multiplied in a state of annual transplantation, the victim of vacillation at the whim of a hierarchy which had never consolidated its concept of future operational procedures.

For the invasion, therefore, the British army, with its large Canadian contingent and the 1st Polish Armoured Division, came to consist of five armoured divisions and eight independent armoured brigades, plus certain specialised armoured formations—of which more later—in all some 3,300 Shermans (barely 1 in 20 with 17-pounders), Churchills (including 100 of the new more heavily armoured Mark VII), and Cromwells—the whole backed by sumptuous material reserves.

America: a New World impulse

The American armour force had not endured the same vicissitudes as the other nations after 1940 because then it hardly existed at all and owned but a few hundred obsolete models, and a small cadre of crews trained in cavalry methods. Its modern battle organisation was of its own devising, but based on a close study of the ideas of the warring nations since, until 1940, American armour had been smothered first by its subservience to the infantry and then the cavalry. The main American battle tank came to be the Sherman armed with either the 75-mm or the slightly superior 76-mm gun. In early 1941 American tank production turned in gestation: in 1942 it gave birth to 14,000 Shermans, followed in 1943 by another 21,000—the rate still rising at the demand of the sort of mass-production urge so characteristic of New World impulse. Numbers alone, matched by the virtue of mechanical reliability, gave the Sherman (and thereby the Allies) their one significant counter to the German gun and armour superiority; while the seething American training organisation churned out a concourse of mass-trained crewmen, full of confidence but still with much to learn, inspired by the drive of that most colourful of armoured generals—the American counterpart of Guderian and Hobart—George S. Patton.

M-4 Sherman
Shermans equipped the bulk of the Allied tank forces that fought for Normandy. Available in massive quantity, they were outclassed by the German opposition. Weight: 33 tons. Engine: 425 hp. Crew: 5. Armour: 81 mm. Speed: 25 mph. Armament: 1 × 75-mm. 2 × mg

In 1943, however, the USA could have had – and should have had – a powerful successor to Sherman: the T-20, mounting a 76-mm gun, which could have seen action in 1944. But a belief that Shermans in large numbers would be good enough to saturate the German defences as well as act with reliability and speed in pursuit, prompted a decision to stop production of the T-20 in order not to disrupt the flood of Shermans coming from the factories. It is the privilege of vast nations to employ big battalions regardless of finesse, and to a considerable extent this was American policy in 1944.

Updating the tank tactics

Every combat army had learned the need to combine infantry and artillery with tank action, although the levels at which co-operation took root differed as did the detailed methods of command. The Germans plumped for mixed battle groups of flexible composition within the division; the British tended to draw a line between armoured and infantry formations, regrouping no lower than brigade level if they could help it; while the Americans followed the German ex-

an infantryman had the new-found ability to penetrate the thickest armour using a recoilless *Panzerfaust* or *Panzerschreck* hollow-charge missile – equivalent of the British PIAT and the US Bazooka.

Of course, the Allies assembled almost as tough a collection of anti-armour weapons in addition to their own assault guns – a US infantry division having both 37-mm and 57-mm anti-tank guns as well as 558 Bazookas; and a British division was no less well equipped and had the well-tried 17-pounder gun. Towed anti-tank guns are strictly a defensive weapon and require time to arrange mutually supporting arcs of fire, to settle in their positions and conceal such protective digging as may be necessary. Hence, anti-tank guns were of more use to the Germans, since they nearly always fought on the defensive from previously established positions. For the same reason, the Germans could make extensive use of mine-fields to shield their positions and to delay penetrations by Allied armour: thereby they gave their mobile reserves more time to shape counteraction at the critical points of rupture. And on the beaches, the mines lay thickest among a cunning arrangement of artificial

ample in the main, but enhanced flexibility by refining control through special Combat Commands (two per armoured division) upon mixed battle groups drawn from a divisional tank strength of 270 (including 83 light Stuarts). This was the latest of several variations on the American theme and was in use by the six US and the French 2nd Armoured Division in mid-1944.

However, unlike the Germans who employed their assault gun units purely in the infantry support role, the American philosophy reached towards the British by setting aside specific GHQ tank battalions to work closely with infantry divisions. This reflected the fundamental difference between Allied and German armour doctrine, for the latter insisted on the merits of armoured divisions being grouped exclusively in armoured corps. Each system had its advantages, depending not a little upon the insight of commanders into the potentialities of armour, but not least upon the restrictive nature of ground and room available for manoeuvre. In Russia the rolling steppes favoured the German armoured corps: in Normandy the intensely close bocage threatened to impose an anti-tank barrier infested by well-supported infantry – a situation which favoured the British system.

The greatest changes in the armoured balance since 1940 had been wrought by advances in the nature of field defences, by improvements in the power of anti-tank weapons, and by the proliferation of mines. Whereas the standard towed German anti-tank gun of 1940 had been the 37-mm, by 1944 it was the long 75-mm Pak 40, supplemented by the big, clumsy 88-mm Kwk 43 – the latter capable of penetrating 168-mm of sloped armour at 1,000 yards. A German infantry division deployed 31 anti-tank guns augmented by towed 88-mm guns from army resources, this formidable array knitting together the main fabric of an anti-tank curtain behind which hid the mobile reserves of armour. And from the close range of 100 yards,

obstacles linked with the natural sea defences and deep inundations.

Every defensive feature favoured the Germans and pulled the balance of armour towards their side of the scales. However, the more powerful weapons are almost inevitably bigger, clumsier, and demanding of increased man- and machine-power resources to move them about the battlefield, culminating in a multiplication of difficulties when seeking satisfactory emplacements. Moreover, the faster a high-velocity shot flies, the greater the difficulty of seeing by what distance it has missed its target (since it gets there before the smoke and dust of discharge have subsided), and so correction of fire is repeatedly made haphazard by this sort of obscuration with a consequent degradation in hit probability. These difficulties all tell against big fieldpieces, the positions of which are compromised once the flash and smoke of discharge appear: ironically they helped restore some of the advantage in favour of armour in 1944.

The German static defences erected along the coastline, set in belts inland and drawn close around vital points – such as the radar station at Douvres in Normandy – raised far more serious hazards to the assault than anything of the sort met so far in the Second World War: they were the products of four years' thought and labour, galvanised by a few months of Rommel's dynamic enthusiasm and his belief in the importance of holding the beaches as a hard crust. Indeed, the Americans seem to have come apathetically to accept these obstacles as a deterrent to the use of massed armour in the lead of the assault: but to the British, recalling their bitter experience at Dieppe, the obstacles acted as a spur to finding ways of destroying them by unconventional methods.

Wholesale slaughter at the water's edge was unthinkable to the British – and the emotions of Churchill ran riot at the nightmare

Cromwell IV
Reliable, fast, the Cromwell was in the forefront of British tank design, but already hopelessly outclassed by the new generation of German tanks and barely a match for the old. Weight: 28 tons. Engine: 600 hp. Crew: 5. Armour: 76 mm max. Speed: 38 mph. Armament: 1 × 75-mm, 2 × mg

Churchill AVRE with fascine
Where the British fell down in battle tank design, they made up in specialised armour. The 'Armoured Vehicle Royal Engineers' doubled as a mobile demolition and construction team, able to bridge a trench or blast a hole in a concrete sea-wall. Weight: 39 tons. Engine: 350 hp. Crew: 5. Armour: 88 mm. Speed: 15 mph. Armament: Petard mortar, 1 × mg

that, once again as at Gallipoli, British infantry might be mown down in heaps at his behest. At Dieppe the Canadians had already suffered something like this fate as, when the tanks came ashore, they were prevented from breaking through the shore obstacles and left the infantry unsupported beyond: while, as the engineers tried to clear pathways for the tanks, the vicious circle drew tight and they were shot down because the unsupported infantry could not subdue the German machine-gun nests.

Special devices
In March 1943 the CIGS, General Brooke, decided to create special armoured units whose purpose would be to land in the van of the assault, open gaps on their own even before the first waves of infantry got ashore, and then dominate the defences without exposing more than a few unarmoured men to direct fire. Teams of specialised armour were visualised as progressively smothering the German defences with aimed fire, detonating the beach minefields, breaking down the artificial barriers, demolishing or bridging the next row of sea walls, concrete blocks, or deep ditches, then disposing of more minefields, while subjugating the remaining pill-boxes, before accompanying the next wave of assault infantry and armour deep inland. Speed came first in these complex operations, particularly in the British sectors, where the nature of the ground aided German armoured counterattack, since the need quickly to gain depth and space inland, to fight a mobile battle, took precedence over almost every other requirement once a lodgement had been made.

Before 1943, most of the essential kinds of special device needed had reached some form or another of experiment or development – indeed, the ideas for most of them originated from the First World War. Primitive flails had been employed in Africa to detonate mines; an Armoured Vehicle Royal Engineer (AVRE), carrying demolition teams and a variegated selection of bridges or fascines for crossing walls and ditches, had been invented (appropriately by a Canadian, named Donovan) after Dieppe and mounted on the Churchill tank; early efforts to help tanks swim had hardened into a simple arrangement whereby a canvas screen, temporarily erected round the vehicles, displaced the tank's weight while its engine drove two propellers – this was Nicholas Strausler's invention, the Duplex Drive tank (DD); another type of Churchill tank had been fitted with flame-throwing equipment, with pressurised fuel carried in an armoured trailer, the whole device called Crocodile; there were also tanks mounting a powerful searchlight called a Canal Defence Light (CDL). Later a host of other inventions came up for trial, to be rejected or accepted, improved, put into production in quantity, the crews trained and methods found to combine them in teams taught to act in the elimination of every possible obstacle combination.

General Percy Hobart, the armoured innovator of the 'thirties, with his brother-in-law Montgomery, who grasped the vitally important role of the 79th Armoured Division's weapons

Sherman Duplex-Drive DD
In the very spearhead of the attack came Sherman battle tanks able to wade out of the sea by the combination of propellers and a collapsible canvas flotation screen displacing the tank's weight. Many foundered, but many more got through to the beaches

Churchill AVRE with SBG Bridge
The AVRE's Petard mortar could throw a 25-lb charge called a 'flying dustbin', specially designed to demolish beach obstacles, a distance of 120 yards. For the crossing of trenches the 'Small Box Girder' Bridge could be quickly manoeuvred into position

Sherman Crab
Designed to flail a path through beach minefields, the Crab mounted a flail drum driven from the main engine. A thick cloud of dust was thrown up and a maximum speed of only 1½ mph could be reached, nor could the main armament be used, hence other gun tanks escorted them on the beaches

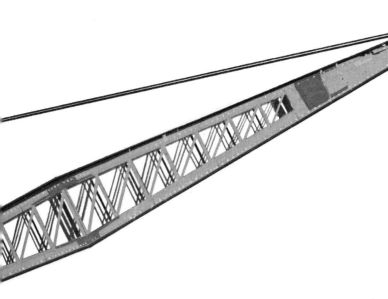

Churchill Crocodile Flame-Thrower
The Crocodile kept the Churchill's main gun armament, but substituted a flame-thrower for the hull machine-gun. Towing 400 gallons of fuel in an armoured trailer, the Crocodile assaulted pillboxes and bunkers, squirting a jet of flame through loop-holes to exhaust the oxygen

This was to be the Twentieth-Century equivalent of a medieval siege train, constructed to substitute machines for manpower and restore mobile, armoured dominance at every stage in an assault, even where the defences were strongest. With only 14 months to spare, Brooke searched for a man to spring a miracle—pitching his choice on Hobart who, at 58 years of age, still looked the only one with deep enough experience of armour in all its aspects, joined with ruthless energy capable of accomplishing so enormous a task in such a short time. But cutting a hole through the Atlantic Wall was but the last stage of Hobart's task: first he had to persuade and bulldoze the military and industrial machines to improve and construct the necessary equipment to his specifications at his speed: above all he demanded that each special vehicle should retain the ability to fight on its own should it be necessary, and then he had to drill ordinary tank crews in the spirit of dauntless improvisation which recognised no insuperable defence. Against all sorts of frustration Hobart succeeded in his task and was ready, early in 1944, to show a wide range of armoured hardware to General Eisenhower, and to his own brother-in-law, General Montgomery, when they came home to take charge of the invasion forces.

There was a brigade each of DD Shermans and Crab Flail Shermans, and another of Churchill AVREs armed with the Petard demolition projectile, a regiment of Crocodiles and a brigade of Grant CDLs, the latter never, in the event, put to use in their intended role of illuminating the battlefield in order to continue an advance in the dark. Other devices with animal names— 'Hobo's Menagerie' or 'The Funnies' as they came to be known—followed in the months to come, but the combination of DD, Flail, and AVRE were the basic elements of the beach assault team which worked ahead of the infantry on June 6.

Montgomery grasped the purpose and significance of specialised armour at once, calling for the necessity of armour to spearhead the assault. Simultaneously, he insisted that the Americans should be offered a half share of everything the British had made, getting Hobart to demonstrate each device to his allies. But, while Eisenhower fell heavily for the DDs, and demanded a brigade's worth, he left the choice of the other items to General Bradley, and he passed it to his staff who, for various reasons, mostly thin, rejected the devices. The terrible outcome of this omission will appear later.

Specialised armour promised to restore balance to Allied armour on the beaches against mines and obstacles. In so doing it might open the way for conventional vehicles to press quickly inland and engage their greater numbers in open battle with the technically superior German armour and anti-tank guns. There was nothing to choose between the determination and gallantry of the men of either side —there never had been—so it remained to be seen if the heavier losses inflicted by a qualitatively superior foe on a numerically superior one might eventually undermine the élan of the latter. Here dwelt a deadly but imponderable threat, hidden behind the soaring morale of the confident British and Americans. In the end a single Tiger which had destroyed a squadron of Allied tanks might be overwhelmed, but would the survivors of that sort of Pyrrhic victory be so ready to stalk the next Tiger when it appeared? And could they go on doing so until the last Tiger had been shot—that is, when no more could reach the battle-front down ramshackle roads and railways from the German interior?

Indeed, the likelihood of the Germans being able to sustain the routes carrying reinforcements and, above all, the fuel and ammunition to nurture a mobile battle, hung in doubt. Here was the crux of the battle—since half replenished fuel stocks in mechanical war can be almost as crippling as no stocks at all, for planning gets clogged by imponderables. In the ability of the Allied air forces to disrupt fuel supplies resided an indirect threat infinitely more potent than their erratic claims to be able to knock out armour with unstable rockets and bombs.

In 1940 the balance of armour could be reduced to comparatively simple terms and almost in splendid isolation, with the other combat elements playing walking-on parts after the tank heroes had trodden the centre of the stage. Now, in 1944, armour still filled a vital role but merged tightly with every other fighting asset of each army. Yet both sides came to grips again acutely aware that aerial supremacy tipped the scales most profoundly, but not irrevocably, while destruction or neutralisation of armour most certainly would be decisive in the final analysis.

THE PANZERS: FRONT LINE OR MOBILE RESERVE?

Panzerjäger IV

A tank hunter built on the Pzkpfw IV chassis, the Panzerjäger IV proved its worth in the close fighting behind the beachhead.
Weight: 25 tons. Speed: 23 mph. Crew: 5. Armour: 80 mm.
Armament: 75-mm gun, 2 × mg

Jagdpanther

A marriage of the Panther suspension and the 88-mm gun in a low silhouette hull produced this potent 'hunting' anti-tank vehicle.
Weight: 46 tons. Speed: 35 mph. Crew: 5. Armour: 80 mm max.
Armament: 88-mm gun, 2 × 7.92-mm mg

Field-Marshal Gerd von Rundstedt, C-in-C West, held a poor opinion of Rommel as a strategist, though he shared his distrust of the Atlantic Wall's capabilities. He believed that the attack would come in the Pas de Calais and that the Panzers should deliver a counterstroke *after* the Allies broke through the outer crust

Panzerkampfwagen V Panther Ausf D

Based on experience gained in Russia, the Panther design was a fine balance of speed, armour and firepower and completely dominated Allied opposition. Weight: 43 tons. Armour: 120 mm max. Speed: 30 mph. Crew: 5. Armament: 75-mm gun, 2 × 7.92-mm mg

Panzerkampfwagen VI Tiger

Massively armoured and heavily armed, one Tiger could hold up a squadron of Shermans. But its size and immobility stranded the mighty Tigers far from the battlefront under the hammer of Allied air attack pounding at all road and rail communications. Weight: 55 tons. Armour 110 mm max. Speed: 25 mph. Crew: 5. Armament: 88-mm gun, 2 × 7.92-mm mg

Ullstein

Rommel looks out over the Channel and its defences

The German tank forces had shown in 1940 that a continuous line of defence is as strong as its weakest point. In the spaces of Russia the panzer crews had learnt offensive and defensive mobile warfare on a massive scale. Now the tank commanders in the West were ordered to buttress a static defensive crust 2,000 miles long—the Atlantic Wall. Both Field-Marshals von Rundstedt, C-in-C West, and Rommel, Commander of Army Group B covering the Channel, agreed that the final outcome of the battle would be decided in mobile battle by tanks, however ingenious the static defence or intense the intervention by aircraft. Where they disagreed was how and where the Panzers should be used.

Rommel, touring the miles of ferro-concrete and barbed wire, could see the cracks in the vaunted Atlantic Wall. In using tanks as a bludgeon behind the sagging rampart, he was aware of a dual problem. The Allies were lavishly provided in equipment, backed by a colossal war-machine—their attack must be smashed on the beaches themselves. Experience in North Africa left him the haunting memory of how air power could cripple the movement of a central armoured reserve. From his command bunker at St Germain-en-Laye, Rundstedt saw the air argument differently. Air power could trap armour grouped close to the beaches, far from the scene of the main assault. The old Field-Marshal, like Geyr von Schweppenburg, commander of the Armoured Reserve, was used to the tactics of the Russian steppe, when intervention from the air was minimal. The 'Russian School' believed in grouping the Panzers in a central region prior to moving it for a blow against the main Allied effort—when it had been identified.

Front line defence or mobile reserve? This was the agonising strategic dilemma which compromise could only further aggravate. By June 1944 the German armoured force in the West could muster 10 Panzer Divisions, a Panzer Grenadier Division, and several Assault Gun Battalions. These units were of varying complements and strength, but they were equipped with fighting vehicles superior to anything that would wade out of the Channel.

German tank design and organisation had profited from the bloody school of the Russian Front, where the lightning thrusts of the *blitzkrieg* era had turned into a titanic armoured slugging match. The formidable combination of General Heinz Guderian, Inspector General of Armoured Troops, and Armament Minister Albert Speer had begun the rationalisation of fighting vehicle production and training with a dual aim—to produce quantity by building up-gunned and up-armoured versions of the old Pzkpfw IV in large numbers, and quality in the formidable new breed of Tigers and Panthers. The *Panzerkampfwagen* V Panther, with its sloped armour, excellent ballistic qualities and 'long' 75-mm gun, was a fine balance of speed, armour, and hitting power. Pzkpfw VI Tiger, with its lavish armour and formidable 88-mm gun, had shown its ability to decimate Allied armour. Both Tiger and Panther suffered from reliability problems and Tiger particularly from lack of mobility, but in battle only numbers could overwhelm them. Backing them up were a wide range of assault guns (*Sturmgeschütz*) and tank-destroyers (*Jagdpanzer*), an armoured anti-tank force to provide defensive hard shoulders round which the battle tanks could manoeuvre.

Rommel's problem was not only how and where to deploy this force, but in securing new equipment from other theatres. On this depended the erratic but absolute dictates of Adolf Hitler.

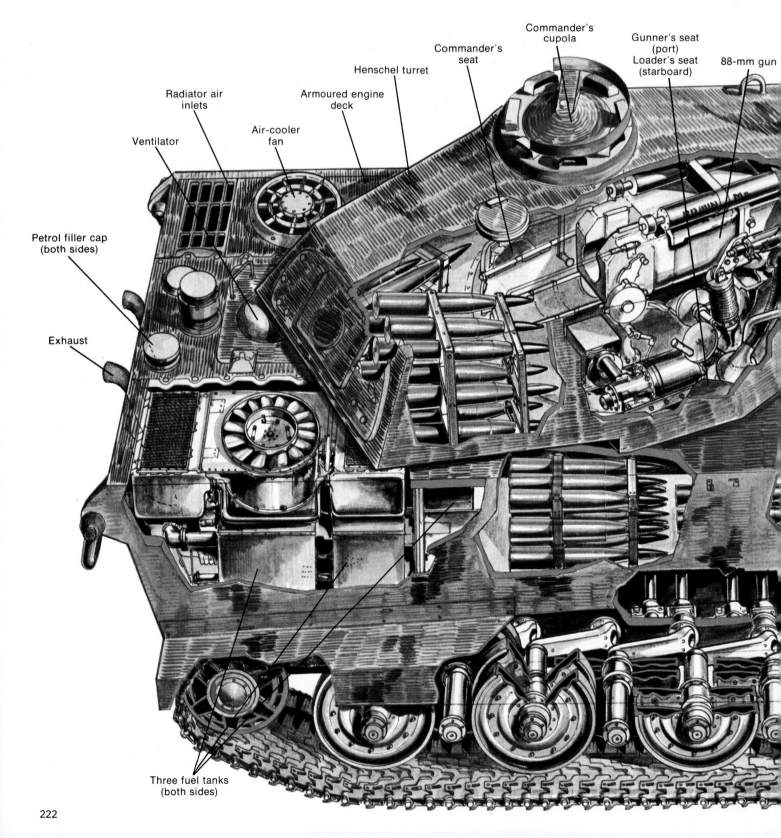

Commander's cupola

Gunner's seat (port)

Loader's seat (starboard)

88-mm gun

Commander's seat

Henschel turret

Armoured engine deck

Radiator air inlets

Air-cooler fan

Ventilator

Petrol filler cap (both sides)

Exhaust

Three fuel tanks (both sides)

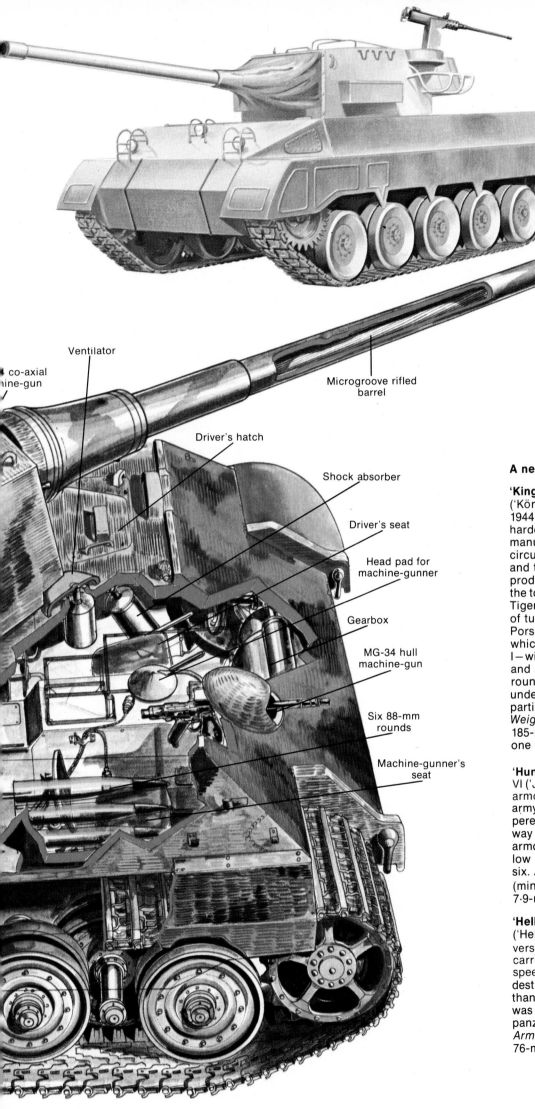

Ventilator

co-axial
ine-gun

Microgroove rifled
barrel

Driver's hatch

Shock absorber

Driver's seat

Head pad for
machine-gunner

Gearbox

MG-34 hull
machine-gun

Six 88-mm
rounds

Machine-gunner's
seat

A new breed of tiger

'King Tiger' *(left).* The Pzkw Mk VI Tiger II
('Königstiger') entered service in mid-
1944—and was one of the best protected,
hardest-hitting tanks of the war. It was
manufactured under the most difficult
circumstances: Allied bombing of factories
and the sources of essential materials
produced a series of delays which limited
the total production figure to 485 machines.
Tiger II appeared with two different types
of turret, Henschel (shown here), and
Porsche. Both were used in a machine
which was a vast improvement over Tiger
I—with a longer gun, well-sloped armour,
and a larger engine giving better all-
round performance. Even so, Tiger II was
underpowered and difficult to manoeuvre,
particularly when crossing bridges.
Weight: 68 tons. *Crew:* five. *Armour:*
185-mm (max), 40-mm (min). *Armament:*
one 88-mm gun, two 7·9-mm MGs

'Hunting Tiger' *(top left).* The Jagdpanzer
VI ('Jagdtiger') was the heaviest
armoured vehicle in use with the German
army—but its manoeuvrability was ham-
pered by excessive weight, and was in no
way compensated by its immensely thick
armour—or by its 128-mm gun, with its
low rate of fire. *Weight:* 70 tons. *Crew:*
six. *Armour:* 250-mm (max), 30-mm
(min). *Armament:* one 128-mm gun, one
7·9-mm MG

'Hellcat' *(top right).* The American M-18
('Hellcat') was a lighter, high-powered
version of the M-10 3-inch-gun motor
carriage (see p. 133). With a top
speed of 55 mph, this fast, elusive tank-
destroyer was used to hit and run rather
than to stand and fight it out; and so it
was the antithesis of the German Jagdpanzer. *Weight:* 20 tons. *Crew:* five.
Armour: 25-mm (max). *Armament:* one
76-mm gun, two ·50-inch MGs

BACKING UP THE ALLIED ADVANCE

In war, mobility is vital: both at the front, and behind it for redeployment and to ensure that supplies and reinforcements keep coming forward. In the Italian campaign—where the terrain with its many steep hills, rivers, gullies, and other obstacles gave the defence a very great advantage—the problems of movement were multiplied. For the Allies, every obstacle had to be cleared under fire and so special vehicles were developed which could withstand considerable punishment while blazing a trail for the troops

▽ **Churchill Ark:** A turretless Churchill Mk III chassis fitted with a ramp over the tracks with extensions 11 feet 9 inches long at front and rear. An Ark could scale a 12-foot wall and span a 30-foot ditch. For vertical obstacles the Ark dropped its ramps on the obstacle and on the ground. Other vehicles drove over it and used fascines if necessary to reduce the drop on the other side. *Weight:* 38·1 tons. *Speed:* 16·4 mph. *Range:* 123 miles. *Crew:* 2. *Armament:* One 7·92-mm MG

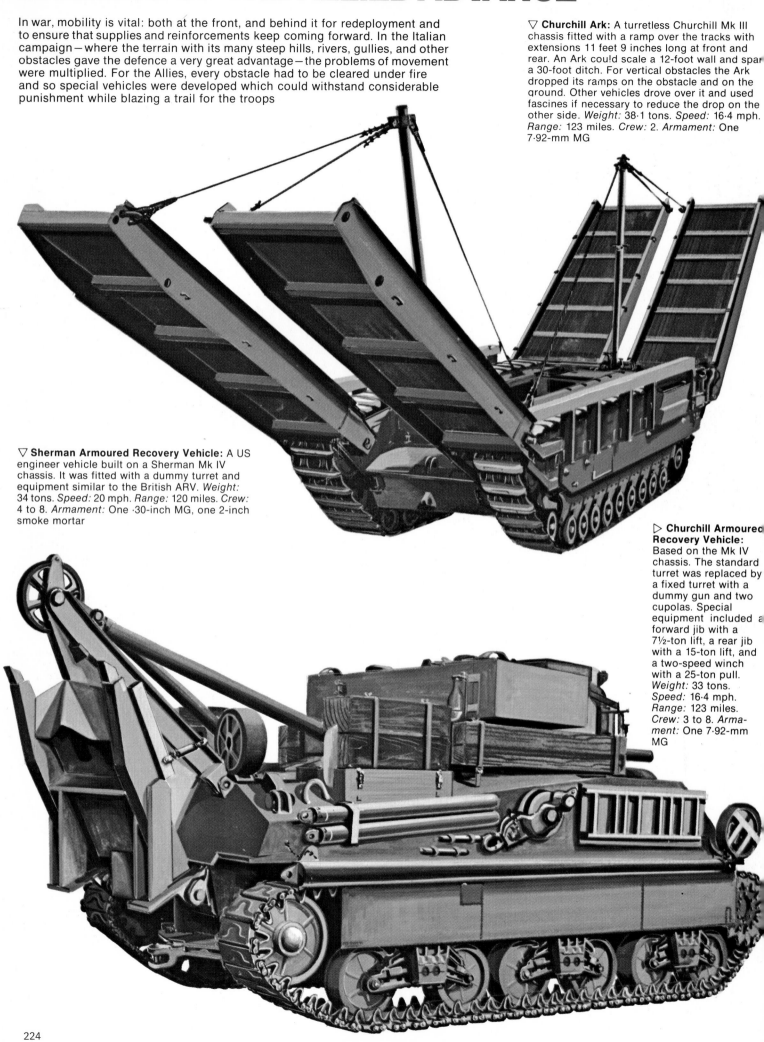

▽ **Sherman Armoured Recovery Vehicle:** A US engineer vehicle built on a Sherman Mk IV chassis. It was fitted with a dummy turret and equipment similar to the British ARV. *Weight:* 34 tons. *Speed:* 20 mph. *Range:* 120 miles. *Crew:* 4 to 8. *Armament:* One ·30-inch MG, one 2-inch smoke mortar

▷ **Churchill Armoured Recovery Vehicle:** Based on the Mk IV chassis. The standard turret was replaced by a fixed turret with a dummy gun and two cupolas. Special equipment included a forward jib with a 7½-ton lift, a rear jib with a 15-ton lift, and a two-speed winch with a 25-ton pull. *Weight:* 33 tons. *Speed:* 16·4 mph. *Range:* 123 miles. *Crew:* 3 to 8. *Armament:* One 7·92-mm MG

A common sight behind the lines in Italy *(top left)*, the British Bailey Bridge was the most versatile military bridge of the Second World War. It was a heavy fixed bridge in which the decking was laid on two main trusses built of 10-foot panels pinned together with horizontal cross members *(see model top right)*. These basic elements—placed in position by hand and machinery often under fire *(above)*—could be reinforced to carry loads up to 100 tons over spans up to 220 feet wide. The Bailey could also be used as a pontoon bridge laid on 60-foot pontoons. It was also employed by the US Army engineers

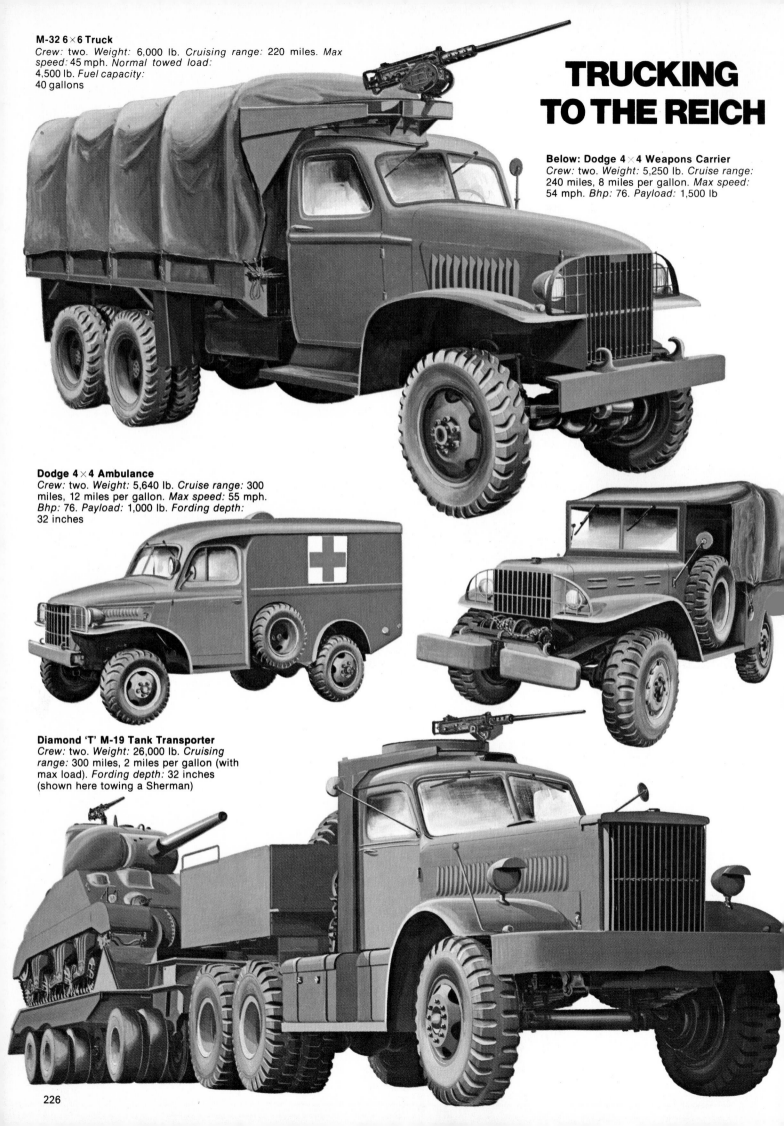

M-32 6×6 Truck
Crew: two. *Weight:* 6,000 lb. *Cruising range:* 220 miles. *Max speed:* 45 mph. *Normal towed load:* 4,500 lb. *Fuel capacity:* 40 gallons

TRUCKING TO THE REICH

Below: Dodge 4×4 Weapons Carrier
Crew: two. *Weight:* 5,250 lb. *Cruise range:* 240 miles, 8 miles per gallon. *Max speed:* 54 mph. *Bhp:* 76. *Payload:* 1,500 lb

Dodge 4×4 Ambulance
Crew: two. *Weight:* 5,640 lb. *Cruise range:* 300 miles, 12 miles per gallon. *Max speed:* 55 mph. *Bhp:* 76. *Payload:* 1,000 lb. *Fording depth:* 32 inches

Diamond 'T' M-19 Tank Transporter
Crew: two. *Weight:* 26,000 lb. *Cruising range:* 300 miles, 2 miles per gallon (with max load). *Fording depth:* 32 inches (shown here towing a Sherman)

UPDATING THE ARMOUR

The Pershing T-25 E1. The best and most 'modern' American tank of the war, the Pershing had a low silhouette and armour well angled for maximum deflection. One Pershing survived 13 consecutive hits from a German 75-mm tank gun at 1,200 yards without one complete penetration. Moreover, its 90-mm gun enabled it to outshoot its main rival, the German Tiger Mark VI. *Crew:* Five. *Length:* 20 feet, 9 inches. *Weight:* 34·7 tons. *Range:* 75 miles. *Top speed:* 20 mph. *Armament:* One 90-mm gun, one ·50-inch and one ·30-inch machine-gun. *Armour:* 89-mm

Below: The Joseph Stalin 3, an improved version of the JS series with a redesigned turret and glacis plate for better shot deflection, was first seen in 1945. It had the same main armament as its predecessors, a 122-mm gun, but heavier armour

Bottom: The Maus, the last German leviathan, appeared in early 1945. Only two prototypes were produced. Maus had a giant 128-mm gun with a co-axially mounted 75-mm gun, but its weight and length-width ratio made it slow and hard to handle

Below: The Pershing (details given above) was developed to replace the M6, whose weight posed grave transport problems: the Americans found it easier to ship two medium tanks of 35 tons each than one heavy tank of 65 tons

Bottom: The Tortoise, a British heavy tank produced at the end of the war, was developed only as an experimental prototype. Like the German Maus, it never saw action and only five models were ever built

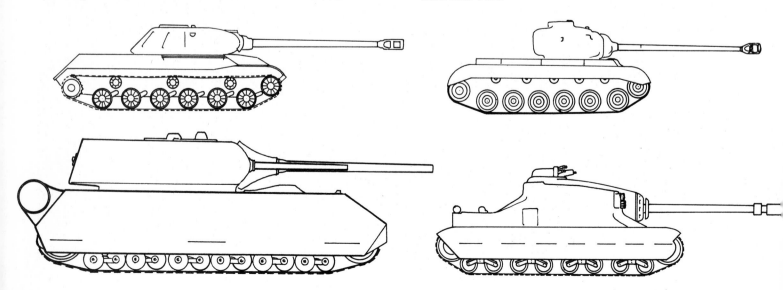

HALF-TRACKS ACROSS EUROPE

In their mechanisation experiments of the 1930s Germany and the U.S. turned to half-tracks. The White Auto Company's M2 was ready when America went to war and still soldiers on with armies around the world.

In every theatre of large-scale land operations in which the United States served in World War II, the ever-present half-tracks played their part —or rather their many parts. To the Allied troops who fought alongside them from 1942 onwards, it seemed that wherever there were Americans there were always half-tracks.

These vehicles, with tracks at the back and conventional wheels in front, could be driven along roads as easily as wheeled trucks. Across country their performance was comparable to that of tanks, and they were faster. Their

armoured hulls gave their crews ample protection against small-arms fire and fragmentation from shells.

They were employed in many different ways, and were accepted as an essential part of the U.S. Army's battle-field equipment. They also did valuable work with the Allies, to whom they were supplied in quantity.

Among the Americans—gunners,

Winston Churchill reviews the Sherman-equipped Guards Armoured Division prior to D-Day from an M5 half-track

infantrymen and others—who rode and fought in these half-tracks, they came to be regarded almost with affection. Travel in them was far from a luxurious experience. But men who, for example, had served in them from the Normandy beachhead to the heart of Germany, could not help forming some attachment for the sturdy 'tracks,' as the GIs called them.

The half-tracks were designed originally for three main roles: as artillery tractors, as personnel carriers for mobile infantry and as reconnaissance vehicles. However, all were equipped to

229

**Above: General de Gaulle reviews a
French motorised infantry
regiment, Paris, 1944. Third vehicle
from front (M3A1) mounts a
captured bust of Hitler. Below: Gun
Motor Carriage T19 of 1941
mounting 105-mm. howitzer**

mount machine-guns, and in practice they were often called upon to operate almost as light-armoured fighting vehicles. Other purposes to which they were adapted were legion.

Of the combatant powers, only the Americans and Germans produced half-tracks in large numbers. In the course of Hitler's rearmament drive in the 1930s, development of vehicles of this kind was rapid. Half-track artillery tractors, towing heavy guns and carrying the gun-crews in transverse seats, were a prominent feature of pre-war Nazi military parades. By the beginning of the war, they had six types in service, varying in weight from 1 to 18 tons.

Russian Ancestry

Though Britain was to use many U.S. half-tracks, she did not produce her own. This put armoured formations at some disadvantage. The infantry elements in armoured divisions often had to rely on vulnerable soft-skin trucks for mobility, or at best on the small Universal Carrier.

The ancestry of the U.S. half-tracks can be traced back to the beginning of the century. A Frenchman, Adolphe Kégresse, was at that time technical

Personnel Carrier M9, with early pattern headlights, built by International and equivalent to the M2A1 but fitted with rear doors. A German MG 42 is mounted in Israeli Army service, 1948

director of the Russian Imperial Garages. The Tsar's Rolls-Royce and Packard limousines, understandably, did not perform satisfactorily on snow and other loose or soft surfaces. To remedy this, Kégresse designed a conversion by which the drive was transmitted to tracks instead of conventional driving wheels—while retaining the front wheels and normal steering.

After the 1917 Revolution in Russia, Kégresse settled in France, where his design was adopted and developed by the Citroën company. During the 1920s, many Citroën-Kégresse half-tracks were produced for agricultural purposes and for service with the French Army. The crossing of the Sahara by some of these vehicles drew world-wide attention.

In 1925 the U.S. Ordnance Department bought two of the French half-tracks for trials as artillery tractors. But it was not until the early 1930s that the Americans really got down to

the development of their own half-track vehicles. For this purpose they acquired a Citroën-Kégresse P17 truck, which they subjected to exhaustive tests.

In general design, and in superficial appearance, the P17 can be recognised as the forerunner of the numerous types of American half-tracks that were to appear.

By December 1932, the first U.S. military half-track vehicle had been produced by James Cunningham of Rochester, New York. Designated the half-track Car T1, it was intended as a reconnaissance car. Modified versions of the T1 quickly followed.

From General Motors there came, in 1933, the slightly larger Half-track Truck T1, from which grew a whole series of models, culminating with the T9. The final version of the latter, built in 1937 by Marmon-Herrington for the Ordnance Department, incorporated front-wheel drive. It was this which was standardised as the Army's Half-track Truck M2.

Converted Scout Car

One of the vehicles issued to the U.S. cavalry units was the White Scout Car. In a development that was to prove most important for the future of the half-tracks, an experimental vehicle was produced by fitting a White Scout Car with tracks, bogies and rear suspension of a type similar to that used in the M2. Further development of this prototype led eventually to standardisation as the Half-track Personnel Carrier M3.

Both M2 and M3 were often loosely referred to as White Half-tracks, and the name came to be used widely—often erroneously—for U.S. half-tracks generally. The White Motor Company was one of the biggest producers of half-tracks; but it was only one of several firms which between them manufactured over 40,000 of these vehicles during World War II.

The Pattern is Set

Many models were to be developed later; but with the standardisation of the M2 and M3 the pattern for U.S. half-track vehicles was set. Delivery of both was well under way by early summer, 1941. In the case of the M2, manufacture was carried out by the White Motor Company, and, on a somewhat smaller scale, by the Autocar Company. The latter was at first the only producer of the M3, but was soon joined by White and the Diamond T Company of Chicago. Both M2 and M3 were powered by the White 160X 6-cylinder petrol engine, which developed 147 b.h.p. at 3000 r.p.m.

The two vehicles were similar, not only in external appearance but in general design. In addition to the engine, many of the principal assemblies and parts were interchangeable. Yet there were differences in the tactical employment for which they were intended.

There were two main functions planned for the M2. One of these was as an artillery tractor, providing also armour-protected transportation for the gun-crews. In this capacity it was used with guns of various calibres, up to the 155-mm. howitzer. Its second main role was as an armoured reconnaissance vehicle. As such, it had better cross-country capabilities than any wheeled armoured car then available.

The main role of the M3, with its slightly greater length and more spacious hull, was as an armoured personnel carrier, and it was employed especially in the motorised infantry and artillery units that formed part of the armoured divisions.

After the entry of the United States into the war in 1941, the planned distinction between the employment of the M2 and M3 tended more and more to be forgotten. Both were adapted for a variety of purposes.

In each case these two half-tracks

M16A1 Multiple Gun Motor Carriage of the postwar French army. Deploying quadmount .5-in. machine-guns, they were known as 'meat-choppers' by the G.I.s

233

had all-round hull armour a quarter-inch in thickness, with a half-inch thick windshield protective plate. There was no overhead armour, but protection from weather was sometimes provided by means of a canvas canopy.

The White engine gave a road speed of 40 m.p.h., and 35 m.p.h. under good cross-country conditions, with a range of 175 miles. Transmission by way of a conventional drive-shaft and rear axle drove sprockets at the forward ends of the tracks. The tracks were made of rubber reinforced with a core of steel cable, and passed under two double bogies on each side, returning by way of an idler wheel at the rear and support rollers at the top.

Cross-Country Work

Four-wheel drive was available for difficult cross-country work, or in snow, mud or slippery conditions. There were eight forward gear ratios, as the four speeds of the gear-box could be duplicated by engaging an auxiliary gear. Steering and controls were normal, and there was a hydraulic braking system operating on the front wheels and the

White Half-Track M3A1 fitted with unditching roller, .5-in. machine-gun and stalk-mounted headlights as standardised for all U.S. AFVs. Length: 24 ft. **Width:** 8 ft. 6 in. **Weight:** 10 tons. **Speed:** 41 m.p.h. **Range:** 212 miles

drive sprockets. In addition, a hand-brake worked by friction on a flange fitted to the drive-shaft. Fuel tanks and ammunition stowage lockers were located within the hull, behind the seats of the crew.

Its hull had space for a crew of 13—commander, driver, and one other in the driving compartment, and ten behind, seated five-a-side facing inwards. The M3 was also distinguished by its rear door and a pedestal mount for a .5-in. machine-gun.

Poor Accommodation

The M2 had accommodation for only ten men. Its other distinctive features included a 'skate rail' running round the interior of the hull. Along this .3-in. or .5-in. machine-guns could be moved on mobile mounts to provide fire in any direction. The M2 was also equipped with a radio mast, not present in the M3.

Progress and experiment were far from over with the acceptance of the M2 and M3 as standard models. There was a confusing succession of designations as new versions were produced. Some of them reached no further than

Left: British M3A1s advance through northern France. The machine-gun pulpit was a standard fitting, mounting a Bren in this case. Below: M3 White Scout Car, from which the half-track hull was derived. 20,918 were built

the experimental stage—like the Half-track Car T16, an M2 with modified suspension and an armoured roof, or the M2E4, which had a Hercules diesel engine.

More important was the series distinguished by the suffix A1. This indicated the addition of a ring mounting for a .5-in. machine-gun over the right-hand seat in the driver's compartment, and three fixed socket mounts for .3-in. machine-guns at the sides and rear of the hull. The M2A1 was the first production model to be so equipped, the skate rail being removed. There followed the M3A1, and others.

By 1942, with both the United States and their allies—especially the Russians—clamouring for supplies of the invaluable armoured half-tracks, it was clear that production had to be increased. The International Harvester Company, large-scale manufacturers of agricultural tractors, were now called upon to contribute. They were invited to produce prototypes based on the M2 and M3, but embodying their own components and improvements.

Twin Machine-guns

The IHC models were standardised as the Half-track Personnel Carrier M5, Half-track Car M9A1 (basically similar respectively to the M3 and the M2A1), and the M14, which was armed with twin-mounted .5-in. machine-guns in the body of the hull.

Though not differing widely from the M3 and M2A1, the M5 and M9A1 could be distinguished in certain noteworthy respects. Their all-round armour was not only one-eighth of an inch thicker, but it was made of homogeneous steel armour-plate—whereas the armour on the M3 and M2 was of milder steel, face-hardened. Also the rear corners of the hull superstructure were rounded, as compared with the squared-off corners on the earlier models. The IHC half-tracks were slightly wider than the M3 and M2, but this made little difference to crew or stowage capacity.

The other major difference was in the power unit. The IHC used the International Red 450B 6-cylinder engine, developing 143 b.h.p. It gave a speed approximately the same as that of the M3 and M2, but the operational range was some 50 miles less.

The M14, and its successors, M15 and M16, were used as towing vehicles in artillery units. In armoured anti-aircraft artillery battalions, the crews could use either the twin heavy machine-guns mounted in the half-track, or the 40-mm. cannon which were towed, according to needs.

With such a variety of similar half-tracks being supplied to the U.S. Army, it was natural that efforts should be made to establish a single basic model,

The vibrations from a pedestal-mounted .5-in. machine-gun shake off the dust of French roads from a U.S. M3

adaptable for all roles. By July 1943, a new model, originally designated Half-track Car T29, was developed by the International Harvester Company as an all-purpose half-track vehicle.

This T29 combined the basic features of the M2 and M3, and was standardised as the M3A2. It had movable stowage lockers, and its ring gun mounting could readily be discarded. Crew accommodation could be varied from 5 to 12, according to its role. Mechanically, and in appearance and dimensions, it did not differ significantly from the M3.

In addition, IHC produced the M5A2, representing an attempt to substitute a single model for their M5 and M9. Despite such efforts to avoid duplication, the pressures of war-time requirements made it necessary to continue the manufacture of different types.

Full-tracks Win Out

By the middle of 1943, a decision was made to reduce production of half-tracks. This was followed by still further restriction by the end of the year. It was now felt that advances in the design of fully-tracked vehicles had rendered half-tracks obsolescent, and after 1943, no new models were put into production. Building of some original types, however, continued until the end of the War.

The Americans used half-tracks in their greatest numbers as armoured personnel carriers for motorised infantry, and in mobile artillery units. But they were adapted for many specialised uses: as armoured command vehicles, mobile artillery O.P.s, as carriages for self-propelled guns, as radio trucks —and even as ambulances. Some were fitted with flails for mine-clearance.

As infantry personnel carriers, half-tracks were a vital asset to U.S. armoured formations. The three infantry battalions in each armoured division were fully equipped with them, as were the armoured artillery units.

It had been the Germans who had been the first to grasp the importance of having mobile infantry capable of close cooperation with the tanks in their Panzer divisions. But shortcomings in the productive capacity of their armaments industry limited the number of half-track personnel carriers available. Only about one in four of their *Panzergrenadier* battalions was equipped with them.

Half-tracks were also employed in the reconnaissance regiments of U.S. infantry divisions. In each of these one assault troop was carried in half-tracks. Light anti-aircraft artillery battalions, equipped with M15 and M16 half-tracks, operated with great success in cooperation with U.S. armoured formations—especially in the break-out from Normandy in 1944, and the subsequent drive across north-west Europe. They effectively used their 40-mm. guns and their twin .5-in. machine-guns against all targets.

The British Army was supplied with large numbers of U.S. half-tracks. These were mainly used in specialist roles. They did not in general replace the fully-tracked Universal Carrier. However, the British and Canadian Armies, in the campaign of 1944-45 in Europe, each held a pool of 200 half-track armoured personnel carriers for use as required for the rapid movement of infantry formations. The 200 vehicles could lift two infantry battalions at a time.

At the end of the War, development was being concentrated upon fully-tracked vehicles; or, where appropriate, on multi-wheeled trucks fitted with low-pressure, broad-dimension tyres. The latter can cope with conditions which would have immobilised wheeled vehicles using tyres of the kind previously available.

Though production of half-tracks ceased after 1945, thousands remained for disposal as war surplus. In many countries they were converted for civilian purposes, and in some they were employed with the armed forces. The Israeli Army, for example, has made considerable use of U.S. half-tracks.

Above: The end of the road. Sten-gun armed British soldiers shelter behind International Harvester built M5 half-track, in the yard of a north German town's Hitler Youth headquarters. Right: Half-tracks come to Europe, wading ashore on D-Day with the DUKWs and specialised armour of the first assault wave

The half-track served a vital need as a vehicle providing both mobility and a significant degree of protection to troops operating in close support of armoured forces, as well as in reconnaissance roles. Although some critics held that it combined the defects of wheeled and tracked vehicles, it could equally be claimed that it had some of the advantages of both.

Strictly a hybrid, it represented a compromise. The fact that it met so successfully the tactical needs that prompted its design was a triumph of American engineering expertise.

THE ROCKET RACE

From the Chinese official Wan Hu, who incinerated himself during the first recorded attempt at manned rocket flight in 1520, to the equally inventive and more successful Wernher von Braun, rocketry has played an increasingly important part in man's attempts to propel his weapons, and himself, through the air. It was not until World War II, however, that the full potential of rockets became apparent. Every major belligerent power made some advances in this field, but it was the Germans who made the greatest progress.

Ancestor of the *Katyusha* and *Nebelwerfer*: a Mongolian rocket battery of the late 13th Century, developed by the Chinese

A British Z-Battery in action. These rockets were intended to supplement the anti-aircraft barrage

The war was in many ways responsible for a dramatic change in rocket technology. In the 1930s the subject was, if not ignored, certainly widely misunderstood and underestimated by the majority of informed opinion; developments took place in irregular, unco-ordinated leaps and the whole subject was more the province of the eccentric inventor than the serious scientific investigator. Today of course the scene is very different indeed. The rocket is part (in some senses a mainstay) of our civilisation, and the technology of rocket development and design has become one of the foremost branches of scientific advance.

It is easy to imagine that progress would have been inevitable even without the stimulus of the wartime effort—but there is evidence to the contrary. In the first place, rockets were first used in war many centuries ago (they were well documented in the 13th Century—and rockets for less warlike purposes date back certainly well over 1,000 years), but without any startling progress in principle being made for literally centuries on end. And secondly it is worth noting that the German A-4 (the V-2 rocket) was still used by the

USA as its most successful space vehicle for research as late as 1952—the American scientists had to use one of their former enemy's weapons for their own research!

So we can see the importance to the history of rocketry of the Second World War. Earlier rockets had been no more than simple 'fire-propelled' charges or flimsy, experimental rigs designed to test an idea. It is believed that the first recorded use of rockets in war was in 1232, when the Chinese fired propelled arrows at invading Mongols. Roger Bacon gave a good formula for the propellant gunpowder in the early part of the 13th Century and the Paduans (1379) and the Venetians (1380) used rockets extensively in war. Indeed it was as long ago as 1520 (or thereabouts) that a Chinese government official named Wan Hu built an apparatus made of kites, fitted with a saddle and with a battery of rockets at the rear—truly the first rocket vehicle. Mr Wan, sadly, was blown to fiery pieces in the attempted launch.

In 1802 a British officer, Colonel William Congreve, began to study the use of rockets in war and a few years later the first Rocket

DOODLEBUGS AND ROCKET BOMBS

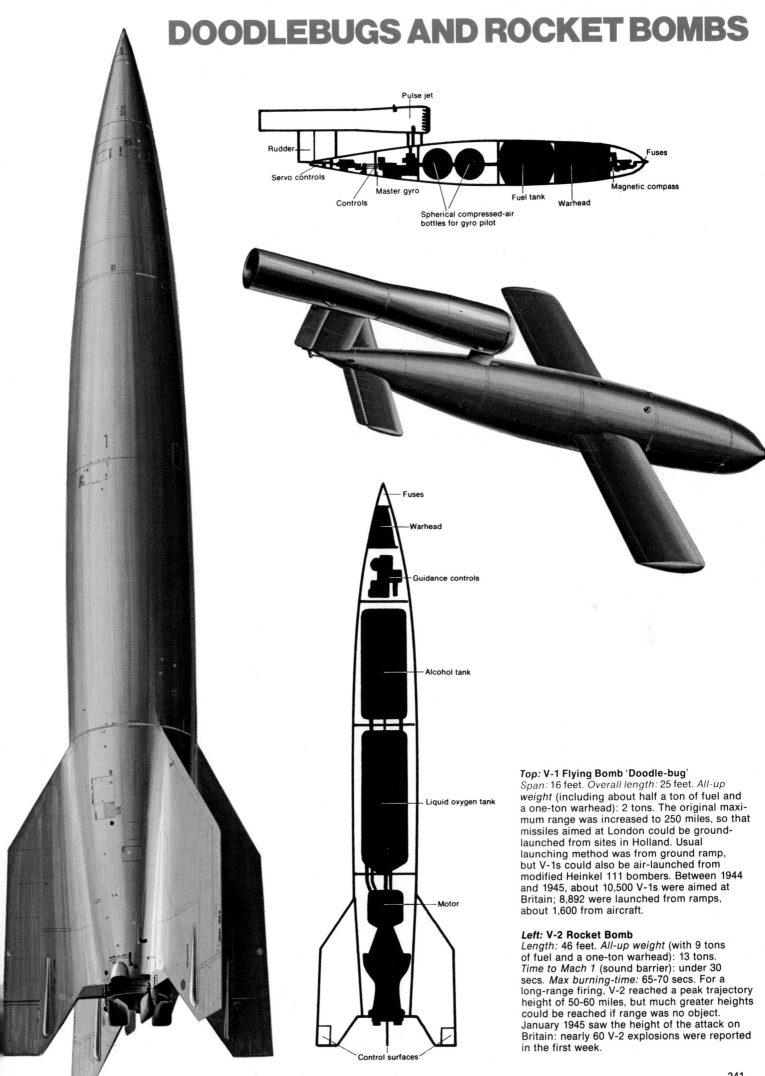

Pulse jet

Rudder

Servo controls

Controls

Master gyro

Spherical compressed-air
bottles for gyro pilot

Fuel tank

Warhead

Fuses

Magnetic compass

Fuses

Warhead

Guidance controls

Alcohol tank

Liquid oxygen tank

Motor

Control surfaces

Top: V-1 Flying Bomb 'Doodle-bug'
Span: 16 feet. *Overall length:* 25 feet. *All-up
weight* (including about half a ton of fuel and
a one-ton warhead): 2 tons. The original maximum range was increased to 250 miles, so that
missiles aimed at London could be ground-
launched from sites in Holland. Usual
launching method was from ground ramp,
but V-1s could also be air-launched from
modified Heinkel 111 bombers. Between 1944
and 1945, about 10,500 V-1s were aimed at
Britain; 8,892 were launched from ramps,
about 1,600 from aircraft.

Left: V-2 Rocket Bomb
Length: 46 feet. *All-up weight* (with 9 tons
of fuel and a one-ton warhead): 13 tons.
Time to Mach 1 (sound barrier): under 30
secs. *Max burning-time:* 65-70 secs. For a
long-range firing, V-2 reached a peak trajectory
height of 50-60 miles, but much greater heights
could be reached if range was no object.
January 1945 saw the height of the attack on
Britain: nearly 60 V-2 explosions were reported
in the first week.

FIGHTING THE FLYING BOMB MENACE

Flying straight and level—as was usually the case when it crossed the coast—V-1 was a small, fast-moving target for the AA guns and the fighters of the RAF. Once contact was made by the latter, there was a choice between tipping the missile over, or blowing it up with gunfire. Both were effective—but there was no possible way of stopping the deadly, invisible plunge of the V-2 rockets

1. Target sighted: the ominous, flying-dagger shape of the V-1
2. Interception: a Spitfire closes in on its target
3. The hard way: a Spitfire tips over a V-1 with its wing-tip
4. Orthodox: camera-gun film shows destruction by gunfire
5. When the auto-pilot failed: a crashing V-1's track
6. But many got through: a V-1 bomb site in London

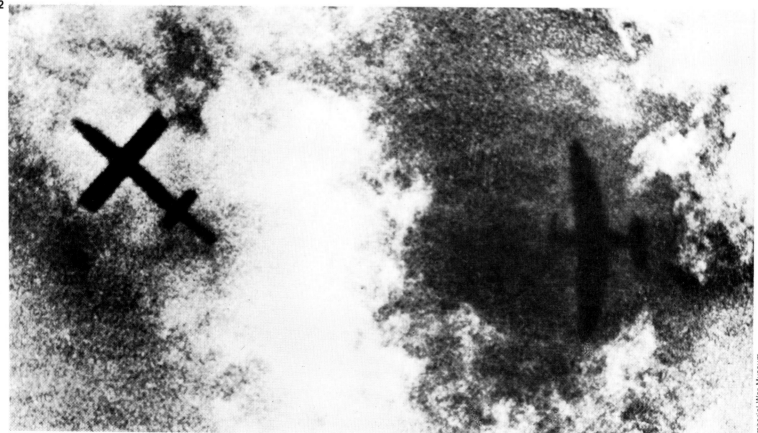

Imperial War Museum

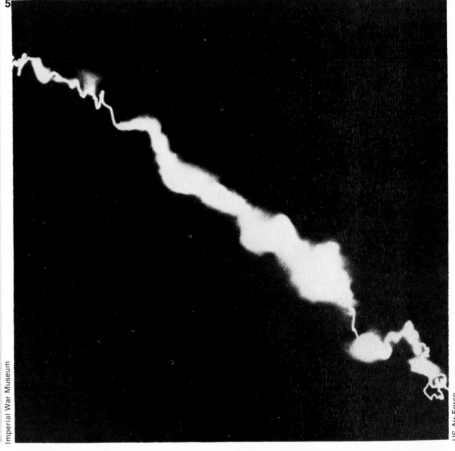

Imperial War Museum

US Air Force

Mirrorpic

243

Troop—175 men in all—was formed. By 1815 the Americans had followed suit with the formation of ten rocket batteries; and later William Congreve was knighted for his enterprise. His book on rocketry published in 1814 was the first work of any detail on this subject. Then, following the use of rockets in ship rescue (they were used to secure a line aboard a stranded vessel) the Frenchman Le Prieur produced a rocket that could be fired from an aircraft—the first air-to-ground missile. The Horace Farman F40P biplane was later fitted with racks of five of these rockets on each side of the fuselage.

The father of the rocket, in its theory at least, was the Russian Tsiolkovsky who—in 1903—had designed a hypothetical liquid-fuelled rocket powered by liquid oxygen and liquid hydrogen. He also expounded the principles of the multi-stage rocket. Later, in America, the physicist Robert H. Goddard made several experimental liquid-fuel rockets, many of which flew in the late 1920s to heights of several hundred feet. By the time he died in 1945, Goddard had done sterling work in the field, but he was still largely unrecognised and had (due to unsympathetic treatment by the US government) been unable to take his ideas past the prototype stage. Not until 1959 was he posthumously honoured by Congress.

Though it is not widely realised, the Russians made similar progress at about the same time. In 1929 a petrol-and-air motor was tested by the Russian designer Tsander, and by 1935 a 10-foot rocket (very like the V-2 in appearance) fuelled by paraffin and nitric acid, had been developed and successfully fired. However, it was the Russian *Katyusha* rocket, a solid fuel device, which came to prominence in the war, rather than their larger missiles. The standard model was 5 inches across, 6 feet in length, and weighed just over 90 pounds—half of that was the warhead. The rocket was feared by the Germans, and it was used with devastating effect during the war years.

Japan: time was too short
The Japanese had carried out piecemeal development, like the West, before the war but not on a significant scale. However, on the stimulus of the war conflict, greater efforts were made in the field. Support arms in the form of short-range rockets were hurriedly produced for limited use. The range was between 100 and 150 yards, and the size of the rockets varied greatly, from 10-pound 3-inchers up to 1,500-pound rockets nearer 18 inches in diameter.

However, the pressure of increased US air attacks was predicted by the Japanese, who then set up a development section at the Naval Technical Research Unit. Solid-fuel rockets were developed for surface-to-air deployment, in the 10- to 55-pound range, and at the same time the first of the *Funryu* missiles was produced, the case being made by the Yokosuka Dockyard, the engines by Mitsubishi. *Funryu* 1 was only experimental. It was designed as a means of attack against warships and had a control guidance system; but the rocket—solid fuelled—was not successful and was abandoned without any flight tests. *Funryu* 2 was more successful. It was produced with modifications learned from the earlier prototype and became a perfectly practical guided missile.

Time was too short, however, with the war nearing its end, for large-scale production to start. However, a liquid-fuelled *Funryu* 3 was produced (again as an unsuccessful prototype), and like the *Funryu* 2 on which it was based it was theoretically capable of reaching an altitude of about 3 miles. *Funryu* 4, the climax of the series, was more successful than the *Funryu* 2. A liquid-fuelled guided missile, it was capable of reaching altitudes of 20 miles although it was never produced on a large scale.

The Japanese also developed air-to-surface missiles which were, in effect, rocket-powered bombs. The framework of these devices was produced by the Kawakasi Aircraft Company and was made of wood, and a Mitsubishi peroxide motor specially designed for the purpose gave them a range of some 3 miles (increased in later modifications to over 5). The maximum thrust developed was in the region of 550 pounds and the rocket motor fired for 75 seconds to accelerate the rocket along its predetermined trajectory. A Mk 3 version of these weapons was also designed, with an audiosensory system intended to 'home' on the shock waves of Allied gun batteries—but the project was cancelled in the early part of 1945.

It was in the same year that the *Ohka* kamikaze rocket plane (also known as the *Madurai*) appeared. This had been conceived in 1943, and was developed during 1944; it was first used in battle in April 1945. The device was a 2,645-pound bomb (which took up more than half of the entire weight) housed in a wooden winged casing equipped with three rocket motors capable of delivering 1,700 pounds of thrust. The overall length was some 20 feet, with fins being just over 16 feet from tip to tip. The device was carried by a mother plane until within 50 miles of the target. Then, with a pilot securely strapped in position, it would be released and

allowed to glide at less than 250 mph towards the target—it was, because of its speed, an easy target throughout the glide phase. The pilot then ignited the rockets, which burned for 10 seconds, accelerating the device to over 600 mph, as he tried to keep it aimed at the target vessel; it was capable of causing considerable damage. The pilot, who was of course sacrificed in the attempt, gave rise to the two nicknames of the device used by the Allies: the British often referred to it as 'the suicide plane'; the Americans gave it a Japanese word, *'Baka'*. It means, literally, 'fool'.

Britain: advisers to the USA
Work in Britain during the years immediately before the war was far greater than is generally realised—indeed the USA sent specialists to learn British rocketry techniques as part of the American effort later in the war. British research and development first produced a 2-inch rocket propelled by cordite. Both the inner and outer surfaces of the charge burned during firing, which kept the exposed surface area relatively constant and prevented the risk of premature explosion; the warhead itself was protected from the heat by a special compound of sodium silicate and ground aluminium. Tests were highly encouraging, and by late 1940 a large 3-inch version—which could be fired in volleys of up to 128 from a pad known as a 'projector'—was brought into service. But of course there were many problems to overcome and the organisation of such a rocket battery had to be developed experimentally with virtually no previous tactical experience to go on. Accordingly, on May 20, 1940, in the back room of a public house at Aberporth in Wales, a meeting was convened under the command of the Ordnance Director, and it was decided at that discussion that the rockets should, in principle, be used as a routine measure against aircraft. Within weeks the Greenwich firm of G. A. Harbey had been appointed to the task of mass-producing the 'projectors', and by September over 1,000 had been manufactured.

The following month, Duncan Sandys (then a major) took control of the experimental battery and organised a rocket section to defend Cardiff with the 3-inch rocket, and the first German plane was brought down on April 7, 1941. By the end of 1941 there were three such batteries (known as 'Z' batteries) in existence, one at Aberporth for training (where there is still a missile testing range) and the other two in operation around Cardiff. Later, pioneer radar, radio-command, and order-of-battle prediction apparatus was assembled on the nearby Penarth golf course, and the UP-3, as the rocket became known, was intensively studied and modified, eventually emerging as a 6-foot rocket with a lethal radius of nearly 70 feet. Within a year—by December 1942—there were 91 batteries in existence, despite persistent enemy raids which twice razed the factory producing the rocket fuses.

At about this time, the British produced the first of their air-to-surface missiles, a modification of the 3-inch rocket, nearly 6 feet in length and capable of a speed of 1,000 mph. By 1942 they had been developed to operational stage, and although their use was confined to naval warfare (particularly against submarines) they were a very successful development. In 1943 the army, which had been investigating the potential of a 5-inch rocket, 6 feet in length, decided to turn the idea down as impracticable and in the tactical sense superfluous. However, realising that it could be used to back up assaults from amphibious craft, the navy acquired the interest instead and began production of the six-unit 'Mattress' projectors for use at sea. They were used, with devastating effect—particularly on the morale of the enemy forces—in the landings on Sicily and Italy which followed. Further trials at Sennybridge, also in Wales, encouraged the army to change its mind during the following year, and a 'Land Mattress' went into production which was used by the Canadians when they fought for the Rhine and Scheldt rivers.

It was towards the close of the war that the most enterprising rocket was developed: the so-called 'Stooge'. This was designed specifically to attack enemy aircraft, particularly (as it happened) the Japanese suicide squads, and was a 740-pound, 10-foot-long, radio-guided missile with a range of some 8 or 9 miles. It had a top speed of 500 mph and carried a 220-pound warhead.

An English scientist, Dr Lubbock, also did some experimental work on liquid-fuel rockets but it came to nothing in practice; however, the British were left with such a fund of knowledge and so wide an experience of solid-fuel devices that after the Pearl Harbor attack the Americans sent specialists to study British techniques. Subsequently a British pilot plant for production of fuel was sent to the USA to help with American developmental research.

America: one step behind Germany
Quite apart from their co-operation with the British later in the war, the Americans had of course carried out much original development in the earlier years and, although they did not make such

1. Explosive warhead
2. Guidance systems
3. Gyros
4. Helium (to prevent oxygen and alcohol from exploding)
5. Oxygen tank
6. Refrigeration tanks
7. Alcohol tank
8. Oxygen feed pipe
9. Alcohol feed pipe
10. Hydrogen peroxide tank
11. Steam generator
12. Pump (driven by turbine)
13. Steam turbine
14. Steam outlet pipe
15. Fuel injectors
16. Igniter
17. Fuel coolant (alcohol, which is heated and mixed with oxygen)
18. Combustion chamber

BOTH ENDS OF THE SCALE

In the notorious German A-4 'V-2', shown in cutaway at left, the rocket war reached its technical zenith; but at the other end of the scale were rocket weapons which either saw longer service or which were equally important in the fields for which they were designed. Some of these are shown below

The Russian *Katyusha* missile was invariably used in mass. The full salvo did have an unavoidable 'scatter', and a considerable part of its effect was on the morale of both Soviet and enemy troops; but *Katyusha* salvoes amounted to a vast concentration of firepower

The British developed the 2-inch AA rocket to supplement their anti-aircraft gun barrage, and the rockets were intended for use against low-flying bombers. Like the *Katyushas,* the British 2-inchers were fired from batteries known as 'projectors'

Developed as an air-to-surface weapon, the US 4·5-inch missile was soon pressed into service as a ground-to-ground missile, fired from tanks, trucks, jeeps; and it was also used by the US Navy in pre-landing softening-up bombardments

The British 3-inch followed the 2-inch into service, and by the end of 1940 3-inch batteries were being used alongside the heavy gun defences in the UK. The rockets were fired from batteries of twin-barrelled launchers in salvoes of 128

The US 'Mousetrap' was introduced late in 1942 after the US Navy had asked for an anti-submarine bomb similar to the British 'Hedgehog'. For this sub-chaser role they were grouped in batteries of four, and scored many kills against both Japanese and German submarines

The British 'Stooge' rocket was a winged missile introduced to combat the Kamikaze menace. It had a power plant of four rockets, was guided by radio control, and had a range of 8 miles

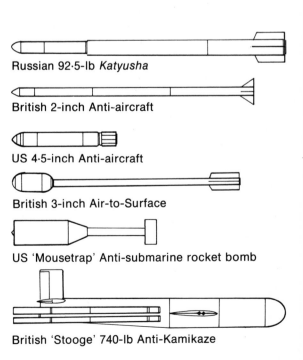

Russian 92·5-lb *Katyusha*

British 2-inch Anti-aircraft

US 4·5-inch Anti-aircraft

British 3-inch Air-to-Surface

US 'Mousetrap' Anti-submarine rocket bomb

British 'Stooge' 740-lb Anti-Kamikaze

Camera Press

impressive practical strides as the German rocketry teams, they did much work in a greater range of devices than is generally realised. For instance, it is perhaps surprising to realise that by the end of the war the US Navy alone had over 1,200 factories engaged in rocket production in different ways.

Almost certainly the first really successful American missile was one of the smallest: the bazooka. It was in December 1940 that development began, largely to find an answer to the insurmountable problem of recoil when an armour-piercing shell was fired from a portable gun; so fierce was the equal-and-opposite recoil that it seemed impossible to design an anti-tank weapon which could be used by the individual soldier on the battlefield. But of course a rocket-propelled missile would overcome all these problems, since the motive force is generated during flight and is not due to the massive reaction of an exploding cartridge. As a result the 3½-pound, 1-foot, 9-inch rocket was developed and this, fired from a 7-inch tube, was capable of being carried by a soldier and fired from shoulder-height in battle. It is said, incidentally, that the device derived its title from a sardonic description applied by an unimpressed major who witnessed the first demonstrations of the prototype. 'Recoilless gun?' he is reputed to have said. 'It looks more like Bob Burns' Bazooka to me!'—so the name was born and it has stuck ever since.

The bazooka in war was a formidable weapon: it could knock out a tank at over 200 yards and was effective against stationary targets (emplacements, etc) at up to 750 yards.

Subsequently (and after a period of Air Corps opposition which was only overcome by witnessing the results of British experi-

ence in the field) similar but slightly enlarged rockets were developed for use in aircraft. One of the most popular was a series of devices 4½ inches in diameter, some of them with a range of several miles, and a slightly smaller rocket (3¼ inches in diameter) was also developed as a test vehicle for proximity-fuse experiments. Later a larger version—$7\frac{1}{5}$ inches in diameter—was used for heavy bombardment on land. Then 20-tube 'Whizz-Bang' launchers, and 24-tube 'Grand Slam' launchers were fitted to tanks, and later a 120-tube launcher—the 'Woofus'—was fitted to landing craft. These missiles had a range of only a few hundred yards and a speed less than 125 mph but they did prove effective for their specialised purposes.

Two other Air Corps developments in 1943 were less successful. The first of these was a 'hydrobomb', a kind of rocket torpedo which would propel itself through the air and then through water to its target by means of conventional rockets—but this idea was soon abandoned as impracticable. Another plan was for a rocket-assisted bomb which—because of the boost in speed it received in flight—would penetrate heavy armour. This idea, too, was dropped; however, the experience gained in its development was used in a navy project. At the time too many enemy submarines were escaping because the pilot overshot his target: by the time the attacking aircraft had sighted the submarine and released its bombs, they were usually too late to land, and so overshot the submarine harmlessly. The navy therefore decided to develop a retrorocket which would slow a bomb and allow it to fall straight down on to the target—this was, in many ways, the same principle the Air Corps had already developed, and after modifications the idea became

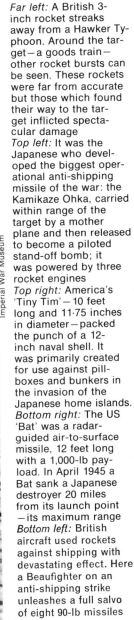

Far left: A British 3-inch rocket streaks away from a Hawker Typhoon. Around the target—a goods train—other rocket bursts can be seen. These rockets were far from accurate but those which found their way to the target inflicted spectacular damage
Top left: It was the Japanese who developed the biggest operational anti-shipping missile of the war: the Kamikaze Ohka, carried within range of the target by a mother plane and then released to become a piloted stand-off bomb; it was powered by three rocket engines
Top right: America's 'Tiny Tim'—10 feet long and 11·75 inches in diameter—packed the punch of a 12-inch naval shell. It was primarily created for use against pillboxes and bunkers in the invasion of the Japanese home islands.
Bottom right: The US 'Bat' was a radar-guided air-to-surface missile, 12 feet long with a 1,000-lb payload. In April 1945 a Bat sank a Japanese destroyer 20 miles from its launch point—its maximum range
Bottom left: British aircraft used rockets against shipping with devastating effect. Here a Beaufighter on an anti-shipping strike unleashes a full salvo of eight 90-lb missiles

reality. The last submarine to be sunk in the war, on April 30, 1945, in the Bay of Biscay, was destroyed by one of these weapons.

The USA also developed, during the later years of the war, what proved to be the largest airborne rocket (fired from an aircraft in flight) used in battle. This weapon—as is often the case—was incongruously dubbed 'Tiny Tim' and was a 10-foot missile carrying 150 pounds of TNT, and designed for attacks on bunkers. It was fired by a length of cord which triggered the ignition sequence when the rocket had fallen a few yards below the aircraft that released it. It was a crude method of firing: too crude in some ways, as the first test—in 1944—resulted in the rocket demolishing the mother-plane entirely. The crew was killed.

Air-to-surface missiles also made an appearance in the American war effort; one, the 'Gargoyle', was developed from a glide-bomb and was fitted with liquid-fuel motors when it went into production in 1944; but it missed the war, and ended up as a postwar test vehicle. The 'Bat' was a long-range radar-guided weapon nearly 12 feet in length and capable of speeds of 3,000 mph. It had a range of 20 miles, but also arrived too late to make any significant impact on the progress of the war.

It is not generally known that the French, during the period of occupation, also made some small progress in rocketry by the development of liquid-fuel prototype rockets at a secret base in Lyons. This was given the title of *Service Central des Marchés et de Surveillance des Approvisionnements* (literally: Central Service for Markets and the Control of Supplies) and developed a perfectly workable LOX (liquid-oxygen) petrol-ether motor which was fired experimentally in 1941. During the tests one of the rockets disappeared and was never found; it apparently flew some 20 miles from Le Renardiere and landed—but the occupying troops do not seem to have made any record of finding it. It was probably just as well.

Germany: supreme in the field

There can be no doubt, however, that the major advances in rocketry were made in Germany. The German scientists and technicians were supreme in their field, and set the pattern that postwar missile development—including the modern drama of space exploration—has followed. And yet much of the German effort in the field was prewar; it was anticipatory—unlike the other developments we have considered—and was designed to fit the nation for its envisaged rôle: as a leading world power, with force to back its arguments.

We must not interpret this widely-held view too literally, however. The gist of it is accurate, certainly, but Germany did have a heritage of rocket development in the early 1930s which was carried out for its own sake by earnest and well-intentioned pioneers, and it is arguable that this in itself engendered the right climate of opinion which in turn gave impetus to the later development of rockets as machines of aggression. Early in 1931 the first of the modern era of liquid-fuel rockets was launched from a base near Dessau. It had been made by an enthusiast, Herr J. Winkler, with financial support from Herr H. Huckel; and the so-called Huckel-Winkler 1 flew, on March 14, 1931, to an altitude of perhaps 1,000 feet.

In May of the same year the first Repulsor rockets were fired to heights of several thousand feet, and simpler solid-fuel rockets

Rheinmetall Rheinbote ('Rhine Messenger')
A four-stage ground-to-ground missile, based on experience gained with the two-stage *Rheintochter*. The first and second stages separated from the missile 6 miles after launch, while the third and fourth stages remained attached to the warhead. Tests were so successful that at least 220 *Rheinbote* missiles were fired against Antwerp in November 1944; but the missile's chief weakness was its very light warhead.
Range: 136 miles.
Warhead: 88 lbs

A4 ('V-2')
First test flights in the summer of 1942 were failures, but in October of that year came the first successful flight. Once full-scale production had been ordered, the completion-time was cut down from 19,000 man-hours in 1943 to 4,000 man-hours in early 1945. This was all the more notable as each A4 contained some 30,000 parts—and the bulk of the workers at the Nordhausen production plant were semi-skilled slave workers: Poles, Czechs, and Russians. The first operational firing of an A4 came on September 8, 1944, and by the end of the war some 5,000 had been fired. Of these, 1,115 came down over England, and 2,050 over Brussels, Antwerp, and Liége. In addition to the normal land-based rôle, there was a project to use A4s against America. Type XXI U-boats were to tow three containers apiece to within range of the US seaboard, each container carrying an A4; but the project came to nothing.

Henschel Hs 117 *Schmetterling* ('Butterfly')
Developed from the Hs 293 glider bomb, the *Schmetterling* was a subsonic AA missile with swept-back wings and a cruciform tail. When first submitted in 1941, the design was rejected, only to be resurrected in 1943 too late to attain full-scale service. It was the most advanced German missile of the war, radio-controlled, with the altitude range to combat high-flying bomber formations.
Range: 3,300 feet.
Warhead: 50 lbs

Konrad *Enzian*
Designed in 1944 by Dr Konrad of Messerschmitts, the *Enzian* was basically an unmanned development of the Me-163 *Komet* rocket fighter, intended for an AA rôle. Some 60 *Enzians* were completed, of which 38 were flight-tested. Although series production began in late 1944, none of these highly powerful missiles ever saw service.
Warhead: 600 lbs (with proximity fuse)

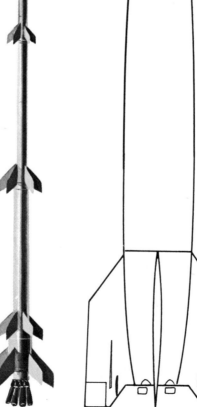

A4-B (Below)
It was practically impossible to enlarge the A4, or to use more powerful fuels to extend its range; and so the Peenemünde team decided to perfect a winged A4, which would use the speed of the missile after power cut-off for a prolonged glide. The result was the A4-B, which had reached test-flight stage by January 1945

A9/A10 (Left)
As a result of the A4-B tests, the two-stage A9/A10 — a projected rocket to bombard the USA from Germany — was rushed ahead: too late to reach prototype stage. The A10 booster was to separate at 110 miles; it was to be recoverable, and special parachutes had to be designed to cope with the thin air of the stratosphere. The A9 second stage, a streamlined winged version of the A4, would then continue under its own power to an altitude of some 217 miles. It would then descend to 28 miles, where the air would be dense enough for the wing controls to guide it on the final glide-path to the target. Range was estimated at about 3,000 miles; the warhead was the standard A4 weight of 2,145 lbs

FROM THE REICH'S ROCKET ARMOURY

C-2 *Wasserfall* ('Waterfall')
Very similar in basic design to the A-4 (V-2) rocket, *Wasserfall* was shorter, with four stub wings. Like *Schmetterling,* it was intended as an AA missile to break up the high-flying US day bomber formations; but only 45 firings had been made by the end of the war, of which only 12 were successful. *Range:* 31 miles. *Warhead:* 550 lbs

Rheintochter R1 ('Rhine Daughter')
A two-stage flak rocket launched from an inclined ramp, *Rheintochter* was designed for use with the *Rheinland* system: two radar plots, one following the target and the other guiding the missile, both of them correlated by a ground controller. The booster unit separated from the main missile just over 1 mile from the launch point. *Altitude:* 20,000 feet. *Warhead:* 250 lbs (with proximity fuse)

were carrying mail on an experimental basis in the same year. Indeed in 1933 a largely unsuccessful rocket was built in Magdeburg as an experimental forerunner of a manned projectile! But in Germany, as in other parts of the world, the slump of the following years put a brake on progress in the field.

However, by the beginning of the war there had been several new developments—and these were directly orientated towards weaponry. The first of the 'A' series (which culminated in the V-2 rocket) was developed about 1933; the A-2 flew to 6,500 feet at the end of 1934, and by 1937 the A-3, a large rocket of 1,650 pounds and standing 21 feet tall, had been flown. Its LOX/ethanol motor was virtually the experimental prototype for the A-4—the V-2 rocket as it came to be called.

Subsequently an A-5 was built, a smaller version of the A-3 and with a much improved guidance system, and by 1939 it had been successfully flown in test flights over the Baltic. Many of the rockets were recovered by parachute and flown again. Most of this work was carried out at Peenemünde, under the direction of Germany's two leading rocket scientists, a Captain Dornberger and Wernher von Braun (who later commanded America's side of the 'space race'). There were, however, other workers in the field: Hellmut Walter had set up his own Kommanditgesellschaft, a firm to produce rockets for assisted take-offs in aircraft, and the Bavarian Bayrische Motoren Werke was engaged in rocket development work in Munich.

As we can see, then, Germany had something of a national heritage of rocket expertise before the declaration of war in 1939, and further developments were clearly possible. One of the first devices to materialise was the V-1, a winged missile propelled by a petrol-fuel pulse-jet developed in the late 1930s by Argus Motoren Gesellschaft from an idea by the Munich engineer Paul Schmidt. It was a principle of almost captivating simplicity. The motor was, in essence, a tube several feet long, closed at its front end by a series of hinged flaps which could only open inwards. In the middle of the tube was a series of perforated fuel-delivery tubes.

As the motor moved at high speed through the air the power was produced in a series of pulses: the shutters at the front end, forced open by the slipstream, admitted a column of air to the combustion chamber, drawing with it a spray of fuel. The mixture was ignited by an electrically heated filament and it burned rapidly, the back-pressure forcing the shutters closed and so propelling the machine forward by the jet of exhaust gases leaving the rear of the motor. Then, because of lack of air, the burning gases were temporarily extinguished and the slipstream was once again sufficient to open the one-way shutters and so another blast of air was admitted to continue the cycle.

This motor is extremely simple to manufacture, almost foolproof to run, and cheap to produce on a large scale—indeed it has only one practical disadvantage, and that is of course that the device needs to be rapidly moving forward before the motor will start at all. A spontaneous takeoff is therefore impossible, and the Germans had to launch the machine at speed from specially designed ramps or from aircraft. The ramps that were built were visible to aerial reconnaissance, however, and many were destroyed by Allied bombing.

As we have seen, the V-1 had much to commend it. But it also had many disadvantages, and these prevented it from becoming the serious threat to the Allies which Hitler had envisaged. For one thing, it was too slow and could be shot down by anti-aircraft gun emplacements or ignominiously tipped over in flight by a judicious nudge from a fighter aircraft and sent to a premature end in the English Channel. The guidance system, too, was unreliable, and of the 5,000-odd V-1s fired at Antwerp only 211 ever detonated on the target. Moreover, less than one-fifth of the V-1s fired at the British Isles are believed to have actually exploded anywhere in the target area.

A little known four-stage rocket was developed in 1944 and tested in Poland. This was the Rheinbote, of which little was ever heard in the West; it was a solid-fuel unguided missile, merely aimed at the target. It was not a success: some 60 Rheinbote missiles were fired at Antwerp in January 1945, but virtually no damage of any kind resulted.

The only rocket offensive

The A4 rocket—or the V-2, as we shall call it—was first given a completely successful test flight on October 3, 1942, and after several delays production of the missile went ahead near Peenemünde. After heavy Allied bombing in August 1943, the assembly line was moved to Nordhausen in the Harz Mountains and towards the end of the war 900 missiles per month were being produced. The V-2 offensive started on September 6, 1944, when two were fired towards Paris. They both failed in flight. Two days later the assault against southern England started but here too there were many problems: the payload was too small, the development time had not been sufficient to eliminate all the teething troubles of the rocket's many mechanisms, the control system sometimes failed suddenly or—because of design weaknesses—the missile would occasionally explode violently on the pad or during its descent. Roughly 4,000 were fired against England in the seven-month offensive, but less than 1,500 reached England at all. Even so they caused much damage and claimed 2,500 lives—although the great speed of the rocket at impact (it landed at over 3,500 mph five minutes after the launch) meant that it dug itself in before detonation and it expended most of its energy on producing no more than a deep hole.

Though the V-1 and—more particularly—the V-2 were giant examples of ground-to-ground missiles, there were also smaller versions in existence. A smoke-rocket, designed to produce cover for advancing assault troops in 1941, proved so accurate that it was modified for bombardment a little later, and the Germans also developed a copy of the American bazooka after its effectiveness had been demonstrated in battle. Later a two-stage anti-tank rocket 2½ feet long was developed; it was guided by impulses sent along wires which unspooled from the wingtips as the missile flew. Underwater missiles were launched with complete success in the latter part of 1943, but (because of fears about the impairment of submarine manoeuvrability that might result) this enterprising idea never became a production-line reality.

A range of surface-to-air and air-to-surface missiles was also developed in Germany during the war years. The Feuerlilie F-25, which first flew in 1943, and the F-55, which followed a year later, were both surface-to-air missiles using sophisticated gyro-control and servomechanisms for direction and stability. The latter missile flew faster than the speed of sound, and both were about 16 feet long. The unsuccessful Enzian, developed at about the same time, was a solid-fuel plastic wood device but it was cancelled when only 25 of the rockets had been produced. The aircraft-like Hecht, a peroxide-powered rocket only 8 feet long, was only developed to the prototype stage, and 80 Rheintochters—of which only 18 were successful—were produced experimentally too. These were 3,500-pound rockets over 16 feet in length and capable of near-sonic speeds. The Schmetterling Hs-117 was 12 feet long and took the form of a midwing monoplane. It was fired from a pad with some success, and began to be known as the V-3, but it never entered large-scale production. The 6-foot Taifun barrage rocket which could reach over 2,000 mph was still in trial stage at the end of the war, although both liquid- and solid-fuel motors for it were in production by 1945. Last in this category was the Wasserfall missile, virtually a smaller model of the V-2, which was intended to have an infra-red homing device for the final 'kill'. Over a dozen of them were successfully fired.

Rockets designed for firing from aircraft were just as varied. The BV series were unsuccessful attempts to make an anti-ship missile that would drop to within 10 feet above the sea and then level off and fly to the target. But the task was too difficult in practice and the idea was abandoned. Several Hs rockets were also designed: winged missiles between 12 and 20 feet long with a range varying between 4 and 10 miles. They were liquid-fuelled, but not a success in practice and many modifications throughout the series were carried out. The X-4 was a 6⅔-foot-long rocket guided by signals sent along a wire unspooled from the wing-tips (rather like the X-7 anti-tank rocket, which was intended for land use) and said to be in an advanced state of production at the war's end; these were descended from the so-called X-1, the SD-1400, a 15-foot rocket with four wings and a tail unit containing automatic guidance apparatus.

However, despite the variety and the undoubted technical skill embodied in all these devices, the war was already moving to its inexorable end. Early in 1945 contradictory directives from different authorities were arriving at Peenemünde and the aura of the chaos inevitable in defeat led to the halting of research and development. Within weeks Braun and his colleagues had moved south, to the Harz Mountains, in an effort to make contact with the advancing American troops. This they succeeded in doing, early in May 1945, when in the town of Reutte they finally surrendered to a counter-Intelligence officer, Charles L. Stewart. It is interesting, with the benefit of hindsight, to recall the difficulty that Stewart had in convincing the authorities that these rocket technicians were of any importance at all, and indeed Dornberger, who was turned over to the British, spent two years in a POW camp in England before being released and joining the others in the USA. In fact, as we can now see, these scientists have probably done more than any other wartime team to alter the face of modern civilisation.

Bibliothek für Zeitgeschichte

V-1 could be carried to the launching ramp on a simple trolley due to its convenient size (for scale see man)

Imperial War Museum

But V-2 was a far bigger affair: a special vehicle, the *Meillerwagen,* was devised to carry it to the launching pad

Imperial War Museum

Here the *Meillerwagen* has erected a V-2 halfway to its launching position

THE GUIDED WEAPONS

The first guided-missile attack in history was launched in 1943, when Dornier aircraft attacked Royal Navy ships with powered bombs. The effect was hardly spectacular, but had these German guided missiles been ready a little earlier – say in time for the Malta convoy actions – they might well have influenced the course of the war.

From the beginning of the war the Germans had concerned themselves with the problem of increasing the effectiveness of their aircraft against armoured warships; and at first there were only two air-launched weapons which could be used: the bomb and the torpedo.

If released from an aircraft flying horizontally, bombs needed to be dropped from an altitude of at least 10,000 feet. Otherwise they would not reach a sufficiently high speed to punch their way through the heavy layer of deck armour on a modern battleship. But a bomb released from such an altitude took about 25 seconds to reach the surface, during which time a warship speeding at 30 knots in open water covered 425 yards. Since ships under air attack almost invariably weaved all over the place, the chance of a hit with a

bomb dropped from high level was slim indeed. One answer to this problem was the dive attack, in which the bomber dived towards the target at an angle of 60 degrees and a speed of 400 mph, and let go of the bomb when at an altitude of 3,000 feet. In this way the bombs were given a good start, and took five seconds to reach the surface, during which time a 30-knot battleship moved only one-third of its own length. But the dive-bombing aircraft were most vulnerable to AA fire during the time of the pull-out. Moreover, the diving attack could not be performed by the heaviest aircraft, and these were the only ones with the range necessary for long oversea flights.

The air-launched torpedo was also a very difficult weapon to use against ships manoeuvring at sea. It had to be released at exactly the right speed and altitude,

otherwise there was a likelihood of the weapon suffering damage upon impact. This was also a danger if there was a sea running. Moreover the dropping aircraft could not help but fly very close to the target ship, and was vulnerable to AA fire from both it and its escorts. Once it had been released and was running true, the 40-knot torpedo was only marginally faster than the 30-knot warship, hence the favourite naval tactic of 'combing' the torpedoes—that is to say, turning away and trying to outrun them. Even when one of the relatively small aerial torpedoes did hit a modern battleship it usually caused little more than local damage, so unless there was a number of hits the ship was unlikely to sink.

The long-term answer to the problem lay in an air-launched weapon that could be

◁ Fritz-X was used against heavily armoured targets such as warships   △ Hs-293 was the world's first guided missile, with a 1,100-pound warhead

Alfred Price

controlled from the parent aircraft during its flight to the target. In this way the aircraft could stay out of range of the AA fire, but still counter the ship's evasive weave. Technically the problem of radio controlling such a weapon was not great, and two German firms—the Henschel and Ruhrstahl companies—each produced a guided anti-shipping weapon.

The Henschel Hs-293 glider bomb was in fact a miniature aircraft, with a wing span of 10 feet. In the nose was fitted a 1,100-pound warhead, and after release the rocket motor under the fuselage accelerated the weapon to a speed of 370 mph in twelve seconds. Then the motor cut, leaving the missile to coast on in a shallow dive to the target. At the rear of the weapon was a bright flare, to enable the bomb aimer in the parent aircraft to follow its progress in flight. The man operated a small 'joy-stick' controller, the movement of which fed the appropriate up-down/left-right impulses to a radio transmitter which in turn radiated them to the missile. Thus the bomb aimer had merely to superimpose the missile's tracking flare on the target, and hold it there until it impacted. The warhead had little penetrating capability, and the glider bomb was intended mainly for use against freighters and the more lightly armoured warships.

In July 1943, even as the British specialist 617 Squadron was re-forming after its attack on the Ruhr dams, the Luftwaffe was forming two special units of its own to use the new guided weapons in action. The units were the II and III Gruppen of *Kampfgeschwader* 100, both equipped with the Dornier Do-217 medium bomber; the former unit was to use the Hs-293 glider bomb, the latter the Fritz-X. The Dorniers would carry two Hs-293s, one under each outer wing panel, or else a single Fritz-X

on the wing between the starboard motor and the fuselage.

By August 1943 the missile-carrying units were trained and ready, and now they moved from their training airfields in Germany to the south of France. In command was Major Bernhard Jope, who had earlier led a successful career flying anti-shipping strikes with Condor four-engined bombers over the Atlantic.

The first guided-missile attack in history was launched on August 25, 1943. That afternoon twelve Dornier 217s of II Gruppe attacked Royal Navy escort vessels off the north-western tip of Spain with glider bombs. Many of the missiles failed to function properly, and only superficial damage was caused to one of the corvettes. In a more successful attack three days later the corvette *Egret* was sunk and the destroyer *Athabaskan* was damaged.

The second of the German anti-shipping weapons, the Ruhrstahl Fritz-X guided bomb, was intended for use against heavily armoured targets. In appearance it looked like an ordinary bomb, except for the four stabilising wings mounted half way along its body. Like the glider bomb, the Fritz-X was radio-controlled by means of a 'joy-stick' controller in the parent aircraft, and also it carried a bright tracking flare in the tail. The 3,300-pound bomb had no power unit; released from altitudes between 16,000 and 20,000 feet, it accelerated under the force of gravity to reach a speed close to that of sound. Fritz-X was aimed using the normal aircraft bombsight, and during the latter part of the flight the bomb aimer corrected the weapon so as to hold the tracking flare over the target.

Some idea of the power of the Fritz-X may be gained from the damage suffered by *Warspite* when she was hit by a salvo of three of these weapons. One bomb

scored a direct hit which penetrated six decks to explode on, and blow a hole through, the ship's double bottom; the other two bombs gashed the side compartments. One boiler room was demolished, and four of her other five were flooded. Fortunately there was no fire, or the consequences could well have been disastrous. As it was all steam was lost, the ship would not steer, and her radar and armament ceased to function.

By the early part of 1944 the Allies had taken the technical, as well as the operational, measure of the German guided missiles. The radio control system fitted to the weapons was a simple one, and easily jammed. Two types of radio-countermeasures transmitter were built. One blotted out the parent aircraft's transmissions altogether; the other, more subtly, radiated a full up, down, left, or right signal on the German control frequency—to produce an effect similar to that of swinging the steering wheel of a car hard over while travelling at speed along a straight road.

When the Allies landed at Normandy in June 1944 the German guided-missile-equipped units smashed themselves bravely but in vain against the almost impenetrable barrier of covering fighters. On the rare occasions when the German bombers did get through, the ship's own radio jammers effectively shielded them from the weapons.

If the German guided missiles could have been ready a little earlier—say in time for the Malta convoy actions—or if the Luftwaffe could have achieved even a temporary air superiority over one of the Allied invasion fleets after Salerno, these weapons might well have had an important effect upon the course of the war. But as it was, the long-term effect of the world's first guided missiles was negligible.

INDEX

Index compiled by Stuart Craik
Page references in *italics* indicate illustrations